general editor John M. MacKenzie

When the 'Studies in Imperialism' series was founded more than twenty years ago, emphasis was laid upon the conviction that 'imperialism as a cultural phenomenon had as significant an effect on the dominant as on the subordinate societies'. With more than fifty books published, this remains the prime concern of the series. Cross-disciplinary work has indeed appeared covering the full spectrum of cultural phenomena, as well as examining aspects of gender and sex, frontiers and law, science and the environment, language and literature, migration and patriotic societies, and much else. Moreover, the series has always wished to present comparative work on European and American imperialism, and particularly welcomes the submission of books in these areas. The fascination with imperialism, in all its aspects, shows no sign of abating, and this series will continue to lead the way in encouraging the widest possible range of studies in the field. 'Studies in Imperialism' is fully organic in its development, always seeking to be at the cutting edge, responding to the latest interests of scholars and the needs of this ever-expanding area of scholarship.

Flagships of imperialism

Manchester University Press

AVAILABLE IN THE SERIES

CULTURAL IDENTITIES AND THE AESTHETICS OF BRITISHNESS ed. Dana Arnold

BRITAIN IN CHINA
Community, culture and colonialism, 1900–1949 Robert Bickers

NEW FRONTIERS
Imperialism's new communities in East Asia, 1842–1952
eds Robert Bickers and Christian Henriot

THE ARCTIC IN THE BRITISH IMAGINATION, 1818–1914
Robert G. David

IMPERIAL CITIES Landscape, display and identity
eds Felix Driver and David Gilbert

SCIENCE AND SOCIETY IN SOUTHERN AFRICA ed. Saul Dubow

EQUAL SUBJECTS, UNEQUAL RIGHTS
Indigenous peoples in British settler colonies, 1830s–1910
Julie Evans, Patricia Grimshaw, David Phillips and Shurlee Swain

SCOTLAND, THE CARIBBEAN AND THE ATLANTIC WORLD, 1750–1820
Douglas J. Hamilton

EMIGRANT HOMECOMINGS
The return movement of emigrants, 1600–2000 Marjory Harper

EMPIRE AND SEXUALITY
The British experience Ronald Hyam

REPORTING THE RAJ
The British press and India, c. 1880–1922 Chandrika Kaul

SILK AND EMPIRE Brenda M. King

LAW, HISTORY, COLONIALISM
The reach of empire eds Diane Kirkby and Catherine Coleborne

COLONIAL CONNECTIONS, 1815–45
Patronage, the information revolution and colonial government Zoë Laidlaw

THE SOUTH AFRICAN WAR REAPPRAISED ed. Donal Lowry

PROPAGANDA AND EMPIRE
The manipulation of British public opinion, 1880–1960 John M. MacKenzie

THE OTHER EMPIRE
Metropolis, India and progress in the colonial imagination John Marriott

GUARDIANS OF EMPIRE
The armed forces of the colonial powers, c. 1700–1964
eds David Omissi and David Killingray

FEMALE IMPERIALISM AND NATIONAL IDENTITY
Imperial Order Daughters of the Empire Katie Pickles

SEX, POLITICS AND EMPIRE
A postcolonial geography Richard Phillips

MARRIED TO THE EMPIRE
Gender, politics and imperialism in India, 1883–1947 Mary A. Procida

IMPERIAL PERSUADERS
Images of Africa and Asia in British advertising Anandi Ramamurthy

IMPERIALISM AND MUSIC Britain, 1876–1953 Jeffrey Richards

THE HAREM, SLAVERY AND BRITISH IMPERIAL CULTURE
Anglo-Muslim relations, 1870–1900 Diane Robinson-Dunn

COLONIAL FRONTIERS
Indigenous–European encounters in settler societies ed. Lynette Russell

WEST INDIAN INTELLECTUALS IN BRITAIN ed. Bill Schwarz

MIGRANT RACES
Empire, identity and K. S. Ranjitsinhji Satadru Sen

THE VICTORIAN SOLDIER IN AFRICA Edward M. Spiers

MARTIAL RACES AND MASCULINITY IN THE BRITISH ARMY, 1857–1914 Heather Streets

THE FRENCH EMPIRE BETWEEN THE WARS
Imperialism, politics and society Martin Thomas

BRITISH CULTURE AND THE END OF EMPIRE ed. Stuart Ward

Flagships of imperialism

THE P&O COMPANY AND THE POLITICS OF EMPIRE FROM ITS ORIGINS TO 1867

Freda Harcourt

MANCHESTER UNIVERSITY PRESS
Manchester and New York

distributed exclusively in the USA by PALGRAVE

Published by MANCHESTER UNIVERSITY PRESS
OXFORD ROAD, MANCHESTER M13 9NR, UK
and ROOM 400, 175 FIFTH AVENUE, NEW YORK, NY 10010, USA
www.manchesteruniversitypress.co.uk

Distributed exclusively in the USA by
PALGRAVE, 175 FIFTH AVENUE, NEW YORK, NY 10010, USA

Distributed exclusively in Canada by
UBC PRESS, UNIVERSITY OF BRITISH COLUMBIA,
2029 WEST MALL, VANCOUVER, BC, CANADA V6T 1Z2

British Library Cataloguing-in-Publication Data
A catalogue record for this book is available from the British Library

Library of Congress Cataloging-in-Publication Data applied for

ISBN 0 7190 7393 6 *hardback*
EAN 978 0 7190 7393 9

First published 2006

15 14 13 12 11 10 09 08 07 06 10 9 8 7 6 5 4 3 2 1

Typeset in Trump Mediaeval
by Graphicraft Limited, Hong Kong
Printed in Great Britain
by CPI, Bath

CONTENTS

TABLES

PREFACE

It was hoped that this work would cover the history of the P&O Company from its origins to 1914. This has not proved possible. However, unpublished draft chapters relating mainly to the post-1867 period have been deposited in the P&O Archive at the National Maritime Museum, London, at the disposal of scholars, and it is intended that a further chapter relating to P&O and the Suez Canal, and originally written as a link between the pre- and post-1867 periods of P&O's history, will appear shortly as a self-standing paper.

It has also not proved possible, regrettably, to keep track of the many people who deserve acknowledgement for help offered over the long period it has taken for this work – whose own origins go back to the early 1980s – to reach publication. Those whom it has not been possible to mention by name, however, should not take amiss the singling out for thanks of the following: the P&O Company itself, for generous financial support; Huw Arthur, for research assistance; and Professor Sarah Palmer of the University of Greenwich and Mr Stephen Rabson, P&O Historian and Archivist at the National Maritime Museum, London, for their invaluable help and criticism over many years, both quite unforgettable.

GENERAL EDITOR'S INTRODUCTION

All studies of empire confront the gap between image and reality, between the propagandist mask and the often fraught face beneath. The very name P&O bears resonances of power, efficiency and regularity, the images of its ships conveying a sense of style and authority, as well as reflecting a more mundane transportation system. Through its own propaganda – in its advertisements, paintings, engravings, and, later, postcards and films – the company has been inseparably bound up with the British empire in the East and in Australia. Even the modern company's cruise ships (now American-owned) were until recently universally decorated with these reassuring and evocative images of the past. The phrase 'flagships of imperialism' neatly conveys this symbiotic relationship between mercantile shipping and empire. But in this book more attention is paid to the fraught face than to the mask. Despite the ebullience and aggressive tactics of its founders, the company was seldom wholly free of internal strife, political controversy or financial problems. Freda Harcourt charts the often difficult origins of this imperial company with an acute sense of political and imperial contexts, as well as with a sharp eye for the interplay of policy and personality.

The personalities are indeed worth studying. One of the striking characteristics of British imperialism is the extent to which so many significant developments came from the periphery rather than from the centre. Harcourt charts the manner in which the origins of P&O lie in the shipping traditions of Ireland, its mercantile entrepreneurs, bankers, and investors. Moreover, many of the leading figures in the history of the company were Scots. In some respects P&O has affinities with other firms founded by Scots: Sir William Mackinnon's involvement in the creation of the British India Steam Navigation Company and other imperial enterprises, for instance; Sir Donald Currie's dominance in shipping to South Africa through his Castle line; the Henderson brothers' roles in shipping to Burma and New Zealand; and the formation of many other companies like the Clan, Ben, Anchor, and Donaldson. The mighty Cunard line owed its origins to Canadian enterprise, and some other local lines – such as Burns Philp, the Irrawaddy Flotilla, and the Straits Steamship companies – were created at the periphery, often with strong Scots' involvement.[1] If the British empire was directed from the metropolis, much of the energy and business acumen came from its fringes.

As Sarah Palmer points out in her 'Afterword', this book will take its place among the works of the 'Liverpool School' of maritime history as well as the studies of Andrew Porter, J. Forbes Munro and others. While P&O has been well served in its company histories, often emphasizing the propagandist mask, it has never before been subject to the penetrating analysis, based on private and public archival sources, offered by Freda Harcourt. The chapters here take the P&O story up to the time of the opening of the Suez Canal.

Draft chapters which carry aspects of the research through to 1914 are available in the P&O Archive. It is to be hoped that other maritime and business historians, stimulated by Harcourt's work, will continue to research the company's copious and significant history.

Manchester University Press and the 'Studies in Imperialism' series are very grateful to Edward Harcourt for doing so much to bring this book to publication.

Note

1 For more on these, see John M. MacKenzie, 'Lakes, Rivers and Oceans: Technology, Ethnicity and the Shipping of Empire in the Late Nineteenth Century', in David Killingray, Margarette Lincoln and Nigel Rigby (eds), *Maritime Empires: British Imperial Maritime Trade in the Nineteenth Century* (Woodbridge, Suffolk: Boydell & Brewer, 2004), pp. 111–27.

INTRODUCTION: FLAGSHIPS OF IMPERIALISM[1]

Once long-distance steam navigation became a technological possibility, in the second quarter of the nineteenth century, there was widespread pressure to develop it: from merchants who wanted it to open up new markets, for example, and from soldiers and civil servants eager for release from their virtual exile in India. But steam was too expensive to be viable as a private commercial proposition, and the industry was able to develop thanks only to government support. This was nowhere more so than in the case of the P&O Company, and its dependence on government finance had a decisive impact on its history in the nineteenth century. This was true in a narrow sense, in that P&O's commercial successes and failures stemmed from the special burdens and privileges of work under contract to the Government; but also more broadly, in that P&O's status as a mail contractor implicated it, as no purely private concern could have been, in some of the major political issues of the day, from the question of how to assess value for money in a public service to the question of Britain's standing as a world power. As a result, in the words of Arthur Anderson, one of the most powerful figures in the company's history, P&O 'attained to a magnitude and public importance unprecedented in the annals of private maritime enterprize';[2] indeed, as the title of this book implies, P&O's ships came to be flagships of imperialism. It is because the history of P&O to 1867 is not merely a self-contained company history but a point of intersection of company history and imperial politics that this study lays claim to the reader's attention.

Burdens and privileges of the mail contractor

The ambitions of the P&O company, its strategy for fulfilling them and some of its business practices incorporated and extended those of its two most important founders, Richard Bourne and Charles Wye Williams, who had worked or aspired to work as mail contractors prior to the foundation of P&O. The company's ambitions were to occupy the main trunk routes to the East, from the Iberian Peninsula through the Mediterranean, to India, China and, ultimately, to the Antipodes. Its strategy was, first, to occupy a line, ideally only where a government contract was available, and, second, to aim for monopoly. Since government contracts, where obtainable, led naturally to monopoly, these two aims went hand in hand. Of course there were limits to the extent to which this strategy could in practice be carried out: the Government was not willing to grant a contract for every line on which P&O had set its sights. But the company was prepared to occupy non-contract lines either as feeders to its main routes or simply to pre-empt competition.

Though P&O's expansion would have been unthinkable without government contracts, work as a mail contractor had its distinctive drawbacks, and these had an impact – at one point a near-fatal impact – on the company's profitability. Mail contracts were awarded typically for a term of several years, so P&O's revenues from government could remain fixed, while costs, such as coal and repairs, rose unpredictably. Contracts came with stipulations as to the types of vessel employed, which were costly. And contract obligations meant that potential profits from passengers and cargo had to be foregone: mail and cut-rate government personnel took up space on board ship, and the unbreakable shackles of a mail contractor's timetable, not to mention the fact that P&O's ships had to be ready to serve as troopships, led to a shortage of tonnage available for purely commercial purposes.

Despite the problems with which P&O had to wrestle as a government contractor, the monopolistic character of its business exposed the company to intense public and political scrutiny. This was stirred in part by the envy of competitors, who accused P&O of inhibiting the development of trade by restricting its volume to precisely as much as its own ships, hamstrung by contract obligations, had the capacity to carry. But the scrutiny also reflected a persistent concern within government that a system of carrying mail with a built-in bias against open competition could not provide value for money. This concern, seized on by aspiring competitors, was an obstacle P&O had to negotiate again and again, especially when its contracts were about to come up for renewal, as in 1847, 1852, 1860–61, and in 1866–67.

Criticism of P&O from outside was matched by internal criticism from stockholders and some ordinary directors of the way in which the company was managed. In the period to 1867, this criticism was targeted chiefly at the most forceful of the company's original three managing directors, Arthur Anderson, who was accused variously of autocracy, secrecy, mismanagement and pursuing commercially irrelevant political connections.

So, was the company well managed from its foundation to 1867, the period of Anderson's ascendancy? In broad terms, after the dynamism of the company's first decade or so of existence, it probably was not. Certainly, the company's financial position was increasingly shaky from 1853 onwards. Burdens imposed by the mail contracts were partly to blame, but there is no doubt that Anderson was increasingly absent and left the company without adequate management structures to make up for it. Anderson's strength was that he was a master at negotiating with government and, relatedly, that he kept an unswerving eye on the importance to the company of cultivating political influence, inspired by his belief that P&O was an undertaking of national, and not merely commercial, significance. But if in his later years this was the only card Anderson held, it proved to be a trump card. Already in 1840, directors of the company had described P&O – with what justification it is not clear – as a 'great national undertaking',[3] and the company's self-presentation – and indeed self-conception – as existing not merely for the good of its shareholders but for the good of the nation was successfully appealed to over and over again in the course of the following decades to answer critics in government when purely economic defences of the company's operations seemed uncertain. This was at no time more spectacularly so than in 1867 when the belief in P&O's importance for the nation – the belief, that is, in its flagship status – was taken up in the relevant departments of government and the company thereby rescued from the brink of financial ruin.

P&O: origins to foundation

Though P&O was always based in London, its origins lay in Ireland where P&O's two most important founders, Charles Wye Williams and Richard Bourne, both had steam shipping companies as early as the 1820s. The proposal in 1834 of a Peninsular Steam Navigation Company, which was to lead indirectly to the formation of P&O, had come apparently not from these men, but from two London shipbrokers who had worked with Bourne, Brodie McGhie Willcox and Arthur Anderson, and who were to become two of the first three managing directors (MDs) of P&O. Though the initial proposal was a flop – Willcox and Anderson had no ships of their own – Bourne saw an opportunity. But, in a way that was prophetic of the future development of long-distance steam shipping in general and of P&O in particular, Bourne saw that a steam connection to the Iberian peninsula could be viable only if a government mail contract was secured to offset the heavy operating costs. Bourne was familiar with the business of bidding for government mail contracts: part of his family's business in Ireland was the carriage of mails by road. Williams, too, at an early stage had seen the need for government contracts to make long-distance steam shipping viable and, urging on the Government the wider benefits to the nation that subsidies would bring, had attempted to secure a contract for the transport of mails across the Irish Channel in the 1820s. His bid was rejected by the Post Office on the grounds that 'a public service of so much importance to the political and commercial interests of the country ought not to be trusted to private individuals'.[4] By the early 1830s, however, opinion had begun to veer towards private mail carriers and in 1837 the Admiralty granted Bourne's Peninsular Steam Navigation Company – quite distinct from Willcox and Anderson's earlier paper company of the same name – a contract to carry mail from London to five Iberian ports, ending at Gibraltar.

Gibraltar, of course, gave access to the Mediterranean, and Bourne's long-range target was a route through the Mediterranean to Egypt, then overland to Suez and thence to India. Demand for regular and speedy communication with India was growing in the early 1830s, especially after the steamer *Hugh Lindsay* brought mail to Bombay from London in the (by the standards of the day) very short time of fifty-nine days. In 1834, Parliament ordered the East India Company to provide a steam link from Bombay to Suez, and Admiralty steam packets began to carry mail through the Mediterranean. However, pressure to put the business into private hands grew from 1835 – warships were unsatisfactory means of transport for passengers and goods – and in 1839 Bourne's Peninsular Steam was asked by the Admiralty to draw up a plan for a commercial service between England and Alexandria, prior to putting the mail contract out to tender. If he was to bid for the contract himself, Bourne needed big ships in a hurry. Williams's fledgling Transatlantic Company was, as it happened, in a position to provide them. The two companies agreed to merge, on condition that a mail contract for the Mediterranean was forthcoming, as indeed it was, to begin in September 1840; and in April 1840 the Peninsular & Oriental Steam Navigation Company was formed.

The first phase of expansion: the Mediterranean and eastwards

P&O's first phase of expansion was into the Mediterranean, followed by its first steps east of Suez. In the Mediterranean P&O had, from 1840, one monthly contract line from Southampton to Alexandria which carried mail on its way to and from Calcutta and China; in 1845, a second Southampton–Alexandria line opened to carry mail on its way to and from Bombay. Because of the space taken up by mail, on these contract lines P&O relied mainly on passengers rather than cargo to generate revenue. But the Mediterranean passenger trade was a problem for the company: revenue was lost through contractual obligations to carry passengers at discount rates, and through the inability, thanks to shortage of tonnage, to adjust to the seasonality of demand. This inflexibility shows the commercial disadvantages of being a mail contractor.

Branch lines were experimented with as a way of trying to make the main Southampton–Alexandria line(s) more profitable. A non-contract branch from Gibraltar to Genoa was opened in the mid-1840s, intended as a cargo route to profit from the silk trade. However, shortage of tonnage, Anderson's overestimation of the potential of silk and political instability in Italy made the line unworkable, and it was abandoned in 1854. There were two further non-contract branches, Malta–Marseilles and Malta–Constantinople. The latter, for which P&O unsuccessfully sought a mail contract, initially proved lucrative as a result of cargo trade. However, to ward off competition, P&O needed to stay ahead of the game on this rapidly developing trade route, but contractual obligations elsewhere meant the company could not find the right ships at the right price to keep the available business to itself. Though the line closed as a result of the Crimean War, the fact that other companies were able to occupy it profitably once the war ended shows that the root cause of the failure was the structure of P&O's business and not the war.

As to matters east of Suez, P&O was committed by its charter of incorporation to begin a contract service to India within two years of its foundation, but the company's dream of a contract for steam communication with India became a reality only in 1844. Though P&O was supported initially by the East India Company in the former's efforts east of Suez, relations between the two turned sour, and P&O's eventual success in securing a mail contract was a sign of the British Government's growing belief in P&O's importance. In 1841 the East India Company granted a 5-year subsidy of £20,000 per annum for a service from Suez to Calcutta, and P&O began to build ships accordingly. But this sum alone was not adequate and the expectation was that a government mail contract would shortly be secured. By 1843, however, P&O's first regular Calcutta–Suez service had started but no government contract had materialized. P&O submitted a proposal in which the main mail line to and from India would be via Bombay, going Bombay–Suez–Alexandria–Marseilles and then overland through France to England, with Calcutta–Suez–Alexandria–Southampton as a subordinate 'heavy mails' line. The East India Company, however, rejected this 'comprehensive' scheme, insisting on keeping to itself the Bombay–Suez mail line for fear that without it the Indian Navy, which carried mail on that line, would become redundant. The Treasury and the Board of Control for India joined the debate on

P&O's behalf, making the long-awaited contract with P&O for the Calcutta–Suez line and driving a bargain over the level of its contribution with the East India Company. Moreover P&O quite reasonably thought that the Indian Navy would be forced to cede Bombay–Suez sooner or later, so the second half of its strategy for trunk routes to India was shelved rather than abandoned.

Expansion to China, and opium

The next stage of P&O's expansion on the great eastern trunk routes with the aid of government subsidies also began with the award of the 1844 contract, which included a subsidy for a connection between Ceylon and China; this service was inaugurated in 1845. But in addition to this contract route, P&O was able to extend itself further in the Far East unaided by mail contracts, thanks to the company's carriage of opium from India to China. A non-contract line from Bombay to Ceylon, which in addition to opium carried mail, began in 1847, enabling P&O to establish itself at Bombay while it waited for a mail contract for the Bombay–Suez route pending the discontinuation of the Indian Navy's service; and further non-contract connections between Calcutta and Hong Kong and Hong Kong and Shanghai were in place in 1851. The viability of P&O's lines from India to China, and indeed the prosperity of the company as a whole, depended so heavily on opium as a cargo that this phase of the company's eastward expansion needs to be set in the context of a more general understanding of the opium trade.

The East India Company, and after 1858 the British Government in India, controlled the sale and in large part also the production of opium in India, almost the world's sole source of the drug. The market for it was China, where, though officially illegal, it was the only foreign import. The opium industry was significant in broader political and economic terms in at least three respects: first, opium exports from India to China covered Britain's trade deficit with China, created mainly by British imports of tea and silk; second, these export revenues made up for the fact that to increase revenue by increasing taxation was a problem for the Indian Government given the poverty of the population; and, third, the export of opium to China represented a longed-for opportunity for foreign merchants to open up China's huge internal market to trade more generally. This process gathered pace after 1833 when the British Government abolished the East India Company's monopoly on trade with China and, especially, after the Treaty of Nanking in 1842, when a military defeat forced China to open up five ports to ships from the West.

Prior to the advent of steam, there had been a thriving opium trade to China by sail, from both Bombay and Calcutta. But sail also had its drawbacks. Opium, because of its low volume and high value, was the ideal cargo for steam, and once regular private steam services were introduced east of Suez by P&O's 1844 contract the impact on the trade, and on the India–China trade more generally, was significant.

There were two sides to the Indian opium industry: Bengal opium, produced by the British Government in India and shipped from Calcutta; and Malwa opium, produced independently but taxed by the British Government, and shipped from Bombay.

A syndicate consisting of Jardines and three other firms dominated the Malwa trade when P&O arrived on the scene in 1847, and the Bombay syndicate thenceforth relied on P&O's vessels to carry opium, rendering sail almost redundant from Bombay. But, familiarly, P&O's contract obligations meant that it was able to provide only limited tonnage. This led to the formation of the Eastern Steam Company to compete with P&O, and to put pressure on the Government to relieve P&O of the mail contract from India to China when it came up for renewal in 1852 on the grounds that P&O was stifling the development of trade. After the failure of Eastern Steam, the Bombay syndicate considered going into steam on its own, but decided against it and, though familiar problems created by P&O's obligations elsewhere did not go away, increased tonnage after 1853 made it acceptable for Bombay shippers to rely on P&O.

By contrast P&O's entry into the Calcutta drug trade was not a success, and the story of its failure illustrates once again how the company was inhibited in its pursuit of purely commercial goals by its contract obligations. The commercial and political uncertainties of 1847–48 prevented P&O from occupying the Calcutta–Hong Kong line as planned. Eventually a steamer was placed on the Calcutta–Hong Kong–Shanghai line in 1851, incurring the hostility of the opium syndicate on the grounds that it would render its own clippers uneconomical. (The difference from the syndicate's reaction to the same development at Bombay is presumably explained by the fact that when steam came to Bombay it could send clippers to be used at Calcutta, but when steam arrived at Calcutta there was nowhere for the locally redundant sailing ships to go.) In response, Jardines ordered its own steamers, and together with the other major local shipper, Apcars, had steamers on the line by 1855. However, the anticipated fierce competition with P&O did not take off. Why? A coal shortage in the East in the run-up to the Crimean War meant that P&O barely had enough coal to meet its contract obligations; the East India Company finally relinquished the Bombay–Suez line, and P&O could not pass up the opportunity to occupy it, adding to pressure on tonnage; and the outbreak of war in the Crimea required P&O to send ships as troop transports, making the tonnage problem still worse. In 1854 P&O's recently established line to Australia was abandoned and in 1855 the Bombay–China service was reduced to monthly calls in order to preserve the service from Calcutta to Shanghai. When peace came in Europe, P&O made a fresh bid for the Bengal opium trade but, after a rate war with Jardines in 1856, the company suddenly withdrew. P&O once more had troopship obligations for the Persian Expedition (1857) and for the Second Opium War, which its competitors did not; the overall financial situation for P&O was worsening and the line was not profitable thanks to a lack of return cargoes; and Jardines was able to sustain its shipping enterprise with profits from its independent agency and commission business, for which no analogue existed in P&O's case.

Australia and new rivals

The early 1850s saw the completion – for the time being at least – of P&O's plan to occupy the great eastern trunk routes with the opening of the first steam mail service to Australia. The period also saw P&O facing its most serious competition yet, both over the route to Australia and in the Mediterranean, from the India and Australia Steam Packet Company (I&A) and from Eastern Steam. This competition demonstrates how much P&O was envied because of their position, at least within the British context, as a monopolist. It also shows the difficulty, despite calls for competition both from commercial rivals and from within government in order to secure better value for money on mail services, of getting genuine competition off the ground. Simply through being the first long-distance steam company on the routes in question, P&O was at a great advantage: would-be competitors did not come to the competition for contracts equipped with their own fleets of ships; and, quite apart from the fact that ships take time to build, investors were unwilling to commit the money for doing so without the certitude – a commodity in short supply in any genuinely open competition – that a contract would be theirs.

As its name suggests, I&A was founded with an eye on a steam connection to Australia, though the company's ambitions were much broader than that. The advent of long-distance steam shipping gave rise to pressure from Australia on P&O and on others to begin a steam connection to the colony. But though a line to Australia was, in the long run, part of P&O's global strategy, the company was initially hesitant: a government mail contract would of course be necessary, the costs and potential profits of the route were hard to gauge, and the company was in any case stretched to its limits – this in 1846 – by its contract and other commitments in the Mediterranean and on routes to India and China. P&O saw, however, that were the Government to tender for a contract to Australia, it would be necessary for it – however reluctantly – to occupy the line, since the route might otherwise give competitors a foothold from which to challenge the company elsewhere.

Thus when P&O was stirred into action over the Australian connection, it was thanks to the perceived threat from I&A, founded in 1847. There were two prongs to I&A's strategy: to challenge P&O in the Mediterranean, by conveying European mails via Trieste (rather than through P&O's preferred Marseilles) in collaboration with Austrian Lloyds; and to win the contract for the Australia–Singapore route and from there to challenge P&O in India and China.

As regards the Mediterranean, I&A was encouraged by the 1847 report of a House of Lords Select Committee into Post Office revenue in which P&O's monopoly was heavily criticized and it was argued that P&O should meet more of its costs from passenger fares than from government subsidies. The report obliged the Treasury and the Admiralty to meet its demands: the Government decided to determine P&O's two contracts to Alexandria in 1848 and tender for them anew, in the expectation of savings. Tenders were received from both P&O and I&A, and negotiations were then pursued privately between each company and the Admiralty. The Treasury awarded the contract to I&A on cost-saving grounds despite an Admiralty report praising P&O and emphasizing the company's huge investment in steam to date. It turned out, however, that I&A had no ships and no infrastructure, and its bid collapsed.

As to Australia, I&A was no more successful there than it had been in the Mediterranean. Once again its plans depended on collaboration with other companies, and I&A pressed P&O to agree to carry their mail, passengers and cargo once they had reached Singapore from Australia, but P&O refused. In P&O's tentative deliberations on the matter, the company came up with its own scheme for an Australian service in 1847, but this was ignored. Tenders for a service from Sydney to Singapore and back were advertised by the Government in 1848. Once again both P&O and I&A tendered, and as the lower bidder I&A was awarded the contract; but, for the same reason as in the Mediterranean – the company was entirely without means – the bid failed and I&A was wound up.

P&O's next challenger, Eastern Steam, was formed from the ruins of I&A, with Robert Wigram Crawford MP – a member of the Bombay opium syndicate – as chairman. It sought a second service on all P&O's lines and a single service to Australia (with a route from Trieste to Alexandria once again to be provided by Austrian Lloyds). P&O meantime devised a new scheme that would renew all its contracts east and west of Suez and add Australia as a low-cost feeder to their India and China lines. Crawford set up a Select Committee on Eastern mail services, including Australia, in 1851, and a race was on to settle who should get the new contract before P&O's existing contracts expired in December 1852. The evidence presented to the Select Committee for and against P&O rehearsed by now familiar considerations such as the injuriousness versus the benefits of competition and the difficulties of making competition happen. Tenders went out in 1852, and P&O's was superior: the company could start sooner – after all P&O already had a fleet of ships, which Eastern Steam did not – and could do the job for less. The contract went to P&O and the service began in 1852 (under contract from 1853), though P&O's Australian connection did not prove a success, and it was discontinued, albeit temporarily, in 1854.

Company constitution and internal divisions

P&O's constitution and the initial distribution of its capital were hammered out in 1840. The composition of the new company's board was to reflect equally the two merged companies, Peninsular Steam and Transatlantic, and shares in it were to be distributed according to the value of the ships which the founders had put in. The constitution also laid down the duties and privileges of the three MDs. This was important, because relations between MDs on the one hand and ordinary directors and shareholders on the other were to become an issue repeatedly over the following 10–12 years: the deed of settlement seemed almost wilfully ambiguous in its description of the MDs' powers in relation to those of the ordinary directors, and in any case the personal clout of two of the MDs, Willcox and Anderson, meant that they did not always adhere to the deed.

Two factors, over time, brought the problem of the MDs' powers into the open. First, provision was made in the deed for a minimum of 10 (and a maximum of 16) board members. This was a tactical decision, taken with a view to leaving the door open for directors from P&O's defunct early rival, East Indian Steam, to come on board. This marked the beginning of a division on the board, albeit never absolute, between its founder members, who might otherwise have been content to run the company relatively informally as a group of friends, and – the label says it all – the 'outsiders', i.e. non-founding board members, some of whom of course had their own views about how things should be done. The second factor was the growing importance of the shareholders: as they grew in number, so they increased in importance as a constituency able to challenge the MDs and call them to account.

As a result, company meetings in the 1840s and early 1850s – both of the board alone and of the board with shareholders – tended to be disputatious. The main dispute to begin with was between Sir John Campbell, an 'outsider', and Anderson, the most forceful of the MDs. The dispute was partly a matter of personality and personal ambition – Campbell, P&O's deputy chairman, coveted the chair, but thanks to Anderson was continually passed over for it – but it also reflected wider issues. One such was the extent to which it was important for P&O to foster political connections through the composition of its board and, especially, through its chairman. Campbell took the purist line that 'no commercial man . . . [would] give one extra passenger or one extra bale of goods' to the company, whoever occupied the chair.[5] Anderson took the opposite view – he and Willcox became MPs in 1847 – and in fact all Campbell's rivals for the chair were MPs; in the light of the importance of government contracts to P&O's business, and consequently the importance of being able to steer opinion within government in the company's favour, Anderson was surely right.

In the course of the decade, disputes within the company broadened to include shareholder opinion, too, and one explanation of Campbell's long innings at P&O, despite his obvious differences with Anderson, was that he gradually became a standard-bearer for an important section of shareholders, and indeed dissident ordinary directors, so Anderson could not have removed him without damaging the company. These shareholders wanted evidence that the MDs were running the company well, and among the themes that divided them and the MDs were the latter's level of remuneration and their secrecy, and underlying these the perennially vexed question of the balance of power between them and the ordinary directors. But though the MDs' – and especially Anderson's – autocratic management style evidently upset some people, the various challenges to his position up to the mid-1850s failed to extract any significant concessions, and the period ended with Anderson's dominance more entrenched than before.

Finance and technology

The expansion of P&O's fleet from 1840 to 1867 represents the point of intersection of the company's financial fortunes and misfortunes, its business strategy and technological developments in steam shipping. Business strategy aside, P&O would have been under constant pressure from the 1840s through to the late 1860s to raise finance for shipbuilding thanks simply to technological changes. These changes meant that ships rapidly went out of date, so any company had to move in order even to stand still; and P&O sometimes did not move quickly enough. But P&O's strategy – expand where possible under government contract, and always seek monopoly – meant that the demands on the fleet, and therefore the need to raise new capital, were greatly intensified. Buying into new technology was necessary in order to stay competitive, but was attractive too as it offered ways to cut costs.

The first wave of the expansion of the fleet came as soon as the 1845 mail contract was secured. This came together with a declaration of intent from the board to pursue a policy of financial rectitude: funds for depreciation, insurance *and* good dividends. But the company's history from then to 1867 shows that these worthy aims could not all be met at once.

There was further expansion around 1846, and the intention was to issue a further £500,000 in shares once the initial £1 million was paid up. However, the first half of 1847 saw a depression, the building programme was cancelled and the £500,000 could not be called on. At this point the MDs realized that it would cost far more than they initially thought to expand eastwards. They thought of a partnership with government to maintain a stable dividend, and though such a plan was in fact enacted some twenty years later at this time it came to nothing.

Meanwhile paddle steamers were being supplanted by vessels with screw propulsion. P&O was slow to jump on this bandwagon, but realized that it needed not only more ships but ships with screw propellers. Hence, at the start of the 1850s, the company ordered the building of more ships and tried to buy some, too, though the economic recovery meant that this had to be on the shipbuilders' terms. By May 1855, the company had 41 ships, of which 21 were screw propelled.

The award of the 1853 mail contract made renewed demands on the company's fleet, as contract mileage increased 50 per cent as compared to 1845. The £500,000 extra share capital granted in 1847 would not be enough for the 14 new ships which the MDs calculated would be necessary. Though only £200,000 of the £500,000 had been issued in October 1852, the MDs decided not to issue the rest; and the option of raiding the insurance fund was also rejected on the basis that it would compromise the dividend (if there were few accidents, returns from the fund were added to the dividend). Hence, given the buoyant state of the money market at the time, the board decided to raise the money through debentures, gaining permission in 1852 for an issue of up to £500,000. These were taken up quickly and the building programme began.

Another downturn in 1853 made the cost of the new mail contract hard to bear for P&O. This made the dividend a problem that year, though 7 per cent was eventually declared. The Crimean War increased the demand on ships, and all the newly built ships were taken up for government use, some of them being sold to the Government. In 1855 a further £1 million of share capital was issued: shares were once again becoming a preferred way of raising money, as the rate of interest on debentures had reached 5 per cent, and indeed the company paid off £220,000 of debentures in that year.

Profits were buoyant as a result of the war, and the company was able to pay more than usual into the depreciation fund in 1857. However, when the war ended profits slumped back once again. P&O needed to increase its tonnage on eastern routes in order to stave off competition, but money was tight and only nine new ships were built in 1857–60, supplemented by some purchases. At the end of 1860, P&O had a total of 52 ships, of which 43 were working for the company.

In 1860, share capital had reached the new permitted limit of £2 million, and at 5 per cent the cost of debentures was still high. However, fuel consumption was the largest item in P&O's running costs, and further building was necessary in order to achieve economies. This led the company to invest in new 'compound' engines, *Mooltan* – the first ship so equippped – coming on stream in 1861. Many more were ordered in the early 1860s, at a cost of nearly £1 million. However, though *Mooltan* achieved savings in fuel consumption, the new technology was still in its infancy and this new generation of ships proved a relative failure.

Commercial principles and the needs of the nation

Anderson declared in 1861 that P&O was 'better organized and performed more efficiently . . . than at any former period of its progress'.[6] But though Anderson won his battles with shareholders and his boardroom rivals in the 1840s–50s, these battles, and the poor state of the company's finances and fleet by 1867, give rise to the question of whether the company really was well managed, especially after 1852. Anderson spent much time out of the country and pursuing other business interests – he was, for example, the chairman of the independent Union Steam Collier Company – but did not make up for this by effective delegation. Several of his new junior appointments were unsuccessful; when Willcox retired as an MD no replacement was made; and power was further concentrated in Anderson's hands by his becoming chairman on Willcox's death in 1862. There is also doubt about the quality of his business decisions at this stage in his career: in 1860, he ordered seven new vessels with a new and experimental type of engine. Since at that point Anderson favoured short-term contractual arrangements with the Government, the point of spending on this scale – the cost was over £800,000 – is not clear, and in the event the technology was not a success either, the ships soon needing replacing. The company was in dire financial straits in the three years from 1853–54 and again in 1866–67 and 1867–68. Costs of the company's mail contract business were becoming unmanageable, and though from 1862, and especially during the American Civil War, the shipment of specie to Egypt, India and China kept things on a more or less even keel, the end of the American war and its effects on business in India and elsewhere brought into the open the company's underlying weaknesses. There were real fears in the management department that the company would have to be wound up, and in 1867, unprecedentedly, no dividend was paid.

At the end of the 1850s, P&O needed to renegotiate its contracts from India to China and Anderson's intention was to seek a single consolidated contract for all the company's lines. Meanwhile responsibility for mail had shifted from the Admiralty to the Post Office, and a Select Committee report had said that all Post Office business with regard to mail contracts should come under the supervision of the Treasury in order to ensure value for money – and this meant, in the Treasury's view, competition. It therefore tried to drive a hard bargain with P&O.

At this point the situation in China became important. Westerners were keen to extend the opening up of China to trade begun by the Treaty of Nanking and found a pretext to do so, sending an expedition to China in 1857. With government business in China increasing as a result, P&O set up a second 'voluntary' (i.e. non-contract) Bombay–Shanghai line in the same year, which carried *inter alia* mail and government personnel. The Government's expedition to Peking was still going on when, in 1860, the Post Office began negotiations with P&O, and the company was able to threaten to withdraw the 'voluntary' service as a bargaining counter. The negotiations over the second China line and over contracts more generally therefore went in P&O's favour, though the Treasury covered the subsidy awarded by increasing postal charges and acknowledged that P&O's power as a monopolist would eventually have to be addressed. The 1860–61 negotiations show how P&O's involvement in government business helped it to win subsidies, and also highlight a continuing argument within government between those with a relatively narrow conception of value for money, who were hostile to P&O – as witness also the 1847 House of Lords Select Committee report on Post Office revenues – and those who supported spending on the company for broader imperial and political ends.

The argument between these two points of view was played out all the more dramatically in 1867, the nadir of P&O's financial fortunes. This was a year in which Anderson was negotiating with the Post Office for better contract terms than those agreed at the beginning of the decade. It was also the year in which the Treasury served notice on P&O that a new contract for the India and China lines would be awarded, by competitive tender, to begin early in 1868. An 1866 Select Committee on contracts for postal services to India, to which P&O gave evidence, lent weight to the second point of view, stating that 'a question of profit or loss, within reasonable bounds, is a consideration entitled to little weight in the case of so important a postal service as that between England and India'.[7] George Ward Hunt, financial secretary to the Treasury in the new Tory ministry that had come to power by the time the Select Committee reported in 1867, on the other hand, was a keen advocate of the first, narrow, point of view. P&O won the first round of the argument. Hunt made the mistake of advertising his (as his critics put it) 'unpatriotic' intention[8] to invite the French steamship company and mail carrier Messageries Impériales to tender for the new contract. Opposition Liberal MPs exploited this fact in Parliament to accuse the minority Government of disregarding the national interest in the narrow pursuit of economies; the shaky condition of P&O's finances and fleet were overlooked and government subsidies to the company held up as money given by the Post Office for the nation.

Britain's great power status was challenged in 1866 by the Prussian victory at Sadowa; in reply, Disraeli launched his new conception of Britain's claim to greatness, greatness through imperial possessions. Public attention was focused on Britain's role as the centre of an empire by visits to London in 1867 by the Sultan of Turkey and the Viceroy of Egypt. And Britain showed off the efficiency of its army without fear of provoking its great power rivals by an expedition to Abyssinia, fêted as adding 'immensely to the strength of the nation';[9] the ships which carried the troops to Abyssinia were P&O's, securing the company's association with the idea of greatness through empire. In the wake of this public relations success for the company, P&O

was awarded a new contract for all lines to India, China and, by this time, Japan, in late 1867. Concurring with the substance of the case which for years P&O had been making on its own behalf, the Post Office official in charge of the negotiations agreed to increase the company's level of subsidy in order to compensate it for the loss of freight and passenger revenues consequent on its role as mail contractor. 'For the sake of keeping up such a communication with the East as the Nation requires [P&O] must set commercial principles at defiance',[10] he said: the interests of the nation had decisively won the argument against the bottom line, and P&O's future was assured.

Summary

The crisis and rescue of 1867 represents the great caesura in P&O's history to 1914. Up to that point, the company's history divides roughly into three periods: first, the period from its London and Irish origins to its foundation in 1840; second, the period of expansion from 1840 to 1853, when under the new arrangements the company had mail contracts for routes all the way from England to Australia; and, third, the financially troubled period from 1853 to 1867. The second two periods correspond, neatly enough, to the time of Anderson's ascendancy in the company.

Chapters 1–4 of the book cover the first two periods roughly chronologically. Chapter 1 concerns the prehistory of the company in the 1820s and 1830s, ending with P&O's foundation in 1840, and the crumbling away of its rivals, and its first steps towards a contract for India in 1841. The next three chapters concern the period of expansion to 1852. Expansion in the Mediterranean and to India is dealt with in chapter 2. Chapter 3 focuses on expansion from India to China, on the opium trade so crucial to that stage of expansion, and on the competition it brought with it; the 1852 cut-off point is overrun for the sake of following the fortunes of the company's opium lines shortly thereafter. Expansion to Australia, and the competition P&O faced on this and other lines up to 1852, is the topic of chapter 4. Chapters 5 and 6 bring the reader back again to 1840, and from distant parts back to P&O's London headquarters. Chapter 5 focuses on boardroom disputes and on the consolidation of Anderson's power from the 1840s to the early 1850s, chapter 6 on the company's finances and fleet to shortly before the crisis of 1867. Finally chapter 7 deals with Anderson's handling of the company from the second half of the 1850s and returns to a more chronological approach, with an account of the contract negotiations of the 1860s and their political context.

Notes

1 Some of the broad themes of this book are broached in F. Harcourt, 'The P&O Company: Flagships of Imperialism', in S. Palmer and G. Williams (eds), *Charted and Uncharted Waters: Proceedings of a Conference on the Study of British Maritime History* (London: National Maritime Museum, 1981); in this preliminary study, the company's history after 1867 is also discussed.

2 *Herapath's Commercial and Railway Journal* (henceforth *Herapath*), 17.6.1854, p. 596.

3 P&O/15/2, 31.3.1841 (archive information is given in the Bibliography).

4 *Parliamentary Papers* (henceforth *PP*), 1828, 11 (501), *Post Office Steam Packets, Steam Communication.*

5 P&O/1/101, 26.11.1847.

6 P&O/1/105, 18.1.1861.

7 *PP*, 1866, 9 (428), *Select Committee on East Indian Communications*, q. 2949, *Report*, p. viii, no. 28; hereafter, in the notes, SC abbreviates Select Committee.

8 *Herapath*, 8.6.1867, p. 573.

9 See F. Harcourt, 'Disraeli's Imperialism, 1866–68: A Question of Timing', *Historical Journal*, 23:1 (1980), pp. 99–104.

10 *PP*, 1867–68, 41 (1), no. 7, enclosure 3, 'Memorandum of Mr Scudamore', para. 20.

CHAPTER ONE

'A large capital and great arrangements': P&O to 1840[1]

In a world in which man has flown to the other side of the globe in hours, been connected instantly to family, friends and anyone else by telephone, even walked on the moon, we should not forget that things were not always so. In the early years of the nineteenth century, people marvelled at the way steam navigation could shrink the sea-crossing between Dublin and Liverpool to not much more than half a day. Once the technology of steam shipping was established, its development was unstoppable. Improvements in the course of the 1830s made shipowners ready to risk navigating further from coasts and channels. Merchants, too, wanted better communication, to open new trading areas or to reach existing ones more rapidly. Technology and commerce went together. The only obstacle was money: no shipowner could sustain unaided the heavy expense of long-distance steam voyages. But under pressure from many different interests, the British Government was led to grant subsidies to companies which could capture the world's great sea routes: the North Atlantic, the South Atlantic and the Eastern seas.

Two outstanding shipowners and businessmen merged their interests in 1840 to create P&O, the shipping company that until 1914 was to be the most successful of all. Richard Bourne had been waiting since 1837 for the Government to decide whether to grant a subsidy for a Mediterranean line that would be the gateway to India. Charles Wye Williams, whose City of Dublin Company was the model shipping concern of the 1820s–30s, had had his eye on the North Atlantic route, and when in 1839 he failed to win that prize, he turned his attention eastwards. Both Bourne and Williams were Irish, and as the histories of the two men show, the contribution of Ireland to the development of ocean steam navigation and to P&O was immense. But there were other contributions, too, not least the London shipbrokerage of Brodie McGhie Willcox and Arthur Anderson.[2] There were also the City magnates, though they chose to put their shipping proposals to the East India Company rather than to the Government, apparently forgetting that the former was a tired concern with little influence and with financial problems. And there were the civil servants and military officers living in India, hitherto in virtual exile, who looked to steam to carry them to and from home. But India had to be reached either by the Cape of Good Hope or by the Isthmus of Suez, and experience showed that the Cape route was simply too far and the shorter route via Egypt needed large expensive vessels, and so government support, to make it viable. The Government therefore came under sustained pressure from this interest group, joined by India and China merchants and their agents in London, and once the East India Company lost its monopoly on trade with China in 1833, the Government was ready to listen.

The Irish dimension[3]

Ireland had a maritime economy. The country was without the coal and iron which made large-scale industrialization possible in England and Scotland in the early 1800s, but from the 1750s up to 1815 Irish entrepreneurs were able to turn what was an overwhelmingly agrarian economy to good account by exploiting the market in the West Indies and the American colonies for salt meat, butter and naval stores. Demand was so heavy that the ports of Cork, Limerick and Galway could scarcely keep up. In this thriving maritime economy, a lively light-industrial sector grew up in and around Dublin: brewing and distilling, coach-building and shipbuilding, wool and cotton textiles, and of course linen manufacture, at that time dispersed rather than concentrated in Belfast as happened later. As prices rose in the last quarter of the century, and especially during the Napoleonic Wars when the peak of prosperity was reached, capital accumulation went on apace.[4] Though dependent to a large extent on the English economy, the importance of the Atlantic trade gave Irish entrepreneurs familiarity with distant markets and incidentally enabled them to make a significant contribution to British expansion in the Atlantic. Dublin's status as the tenth-largest capital city in Europe in 1800, and the largest after London in the British Isles, was proof of the buoyancy of the export-geared Irish economy, the financial power-house of which was Dublin.

Ireland's economic situation was to change dramatically within a few years of the peace of 1815. The Atlantic market contracted sharply, not least because of American competition, and worse was to come in the mid-1820s when relaxation of the Navigation Acts swept away the protection for their products that Irish merchants had enjoyed in the West Indies. New outlets had to be found. Some of the slack might have been taken up if a domestic market could have been developed, but though the undeveloped areas of Ireland were extensive, the prospects for developing them were dim. Land was either profitable or unprofitable, and the country effectively had two economies: the thriving and dynamic regions in the south and east, and the poverty-stricken regions, mainly in the west. So when in the 1820s and 1830s efforts were made to improve inland navigation, the object was to make waterways into more efficient feeders for the export trades, not to develop an internal market in its own right. Almost coincidentally with the slump after 1815, steam shipping became viable on short sea-routes. In 1821 the first regular mail and passenger service began to ply between Holyhead and Howth (for Dublin) in steamships specially built for the English Post Office. For Irish capitalists, this new outlet for investment was the very opportunity they were seeking. Rapid and efficient sea transport would not only enable them to integrate Irish trade more securely with that of Britain but also would open foreign and more distant markets to steam. Especially when steam navigation was in general use, the export trades were entirely concentrated in southern and eastern ports. Cork retained its importance for trade with southern England, but Galway declined rapidly, with Limerick not far behind.

Interest in private steam transport began early. The first of the pioneer Irish steamship owners was George Langtry, the Belfast merchant whose *Waterloo* plied between Dublin and Liverpool in 1820. Two years later the St George Company was established by Joseph Robinson Pim, a Dublin Quaker who was merchant, banker, insurance broker, company director and much else. Hard on his heels, Charles Wye Williams set up the Charles Wye Williams Company. The trigger for much heavier investment in steam shipping was the abolition in 1825 of duties between Britain and Ireland. This action gave a decisive push towards the integration of the British and Irish economies, and was the main factor that encouraged capital to flow into steam shipping, reaping the benefit of the pioneers' efforts. As far as can be ascertained, in 1820–22 there were 7 steamships with a total tonnage of 1,458 plying between Irish ports and the mainland. In 1826 no less than 14 steamers (2,814 tons in total) were registered in Irish ports, 13 of them new vessels (total tonnage of 2,763) built in that year. By 1830 42 steamers (collective tonnage of 8,423) plied between Irish ports and Liverpool, probably only 4 of which (amounting to 624 tons) were not in Irish ownership. These 42 steamers represented an investment of £671,000, of which only £39,500 was not of Irish origin. Though these figures might seem small, they are much higher than the comparable figures for tonnage and investment in London, Liverpool or Scotland.

On the other side of the Irish Channel there were complementary pull factors at work: rising population, rapid urbanization and greater industrial activity. Demand from England for Irish meat, grain and flour, spirits, beer, hops and labour increased steadily, with linen – still competitive in price and quality – the most valuable commodity. By the 1830s, Ireland was exporting a considerable tonnage of bulk cargo. More produce was shipped from Dublin in 1833 than had come from the whole of Ireland in 1800. Scarcely any unfilled space remained in steamships on outward voyages, but the 'back', or return, cargoes were much smaller, if more valuable, consisting chiefly of British manufactures, and these voyages were often made in ballast. Charles Wye Williams declared: 'England is the manufactory for Ireland: Ireland the Granary for England.'[5]

Yet, although the balance of Ireland's trade was in decline, Irish shipowners had gained command of the seaborne trade-routes. This outcome was achieved despite the heavy capital required in steamships, and the risk of losing it in the lag before any profits could accrue. Investment in any business other than retailing and banking was encouraged in Ireland by the Anonymous Persons Act, a legal arrangement denied to entrepreneurs in England. Passed in 1782 by the Irish Parliament, the Act was part of its 'economic nationalism' policy to promote investment in trade and industry.[6] Although steam shipping was not a technical possibility in 1782, the Act was tailor-made for it. A company could have any number of shareholders, all of whom had limited liability; and the amount of capital could be anything between £1,000 and £50,000. Procedure was simple: first, persons who decided to form a company had to appoint one or more of their number to be the 'acting partners', or managers. In that capacity, these men were empowered to carry on the business in the shareholders' names under certain conditions. Then, after all the names of shareholders and managers had been recorded in the Registry of Deeds in Dublin, together with the purpose of the company and a deed setting out the basis on which the company would be run, the rest of the shareholders became 'anonymous persons', or sleeping partners. The formation of paper companies was inhibited because a quarter of the capital had to be paid up either before registration or within 10 days of it; the remainder, in cash, had to be paid within the following 12 months; thereafter, the company had a life of 14 years, unless it was dissolved sooner. Dissolution was as simple as formation: the fact had only to be recorded at the Registry and the capital was returned with interest to the shareholders. The death or bankruptcy of one of the managers (if there was more than one) did not mean the end of the company if the shareholders agreed to appoint a successor. There was no recourse to Parliament, the Board of Trade or any other department either in founding or winding up a company. Only the active manager or managers, not the anonymous persons, were liable under the Bankruptcy Acts. The company could sue and be sued. Through this instrument Irish capitalists enjoyed the security of limited liability, a privilege not afforded British entrepreneurs until 1856. Most shipping companies worked under this Act, but the owners who did not approve of limited liability and operated under the traditional 64ths system – about 30 per cent of them – were not necessarily disadvantaged. Pim's management was very different from that of Williams. Each vessel plying under the St George flag was 'a distinct and separate property', owned by different parties but sharing the same principal shareholders. The Malcolmsons of Waterford and the Richardsons in Dublin, both Quakers, also preferred the 64ths system to limited liability for their companies, each of which consisted of their own families.

It fell to Irish shipowners to bring ocean steam navigation from its infancy in the early 1820s to the maturity it had reached by 1840. Motive force, surplus capital, and unusually complementary markets in Britain created the opportunities to exploit steam transport. It was no accident, then, that the origins of P&O were in Ireland.

P&O's founders: Charles Wye Williams[7]

Charles Wye Williams (1779–1866) was one of the greatest pioneers, perhaps *the* greatest, in the first two decades of ocean steam navigation, yet his significance in the founding of P&O has seldom been mentioned in published histories of the company. His own company, best known as the City of Dublin Steam Packet Company, was a model thanks to the innovations he introduced not only in steam shipping but in finance and management. Born into a well-educated family in comfortable circumstances – his father was the secretary of the Bank of Ireland, his brother Richard a banker – Charles was trained for the law and became a member of the Irish Bar.[8] A passion for machinery and the new technology of steam, however, drew him into practical pursuits.[9] First engaged in building and fitting out a new linen mill in the Belfast area, he introduced powerful machinery that transformed the finishing process of that textile. He also took a keen interest in the inventions of John Oldham, engineer of the Bank of Ireland (and later of the Bank of England), one of which, in 1818, was of critical importance for ocean steam navigation. This was the revolving paddle-wheel. Williams spent over £1,000 so that Oldham could patent it, and, with modifications, it became the standard form of marine steam propulsion until the introduction of the screw.

Fired by the possibilities of steam navigation, he was in 1823 the first promoter to start a steam shipping company under the Anonymous Persons Act, the Charles Wye Williams Company, with a capital of £50,000. Reckoning that a substantial capital would be needed, he had no difficulty in finding 32 shareholders, all of them Irish, to take up the 50 shares of £1,000 each.[10] It was so unusual for a private company to commission two vessels simultaneously, as Williams did, that his shareholders begged him to begin with a single vessel while he felt his way. 'In truth', he wrote long after, 'had not my partners been bound, by deed, not in any way to interfere, under the risk of personal liability', he would have had to concur.[11] In 1824, his vessels were the first to carry cargoes by steam from Dublin to Liverpool.

There were few precedents to guide him, so he created his own. For a healthy business, a sound base was necessary. Competition was ruinous to all parties; on the other hand, monopoly was abhorrent and unlikely to be maintainable. The solution was, where possible, to regulate the trade by agreed standard freight rates, pooling of revenue, demarcation of companies and inducements to shippers. Soon after he launched his company, the Liverpool and Dublin Steam Navigation Company, set up by William Laird and Joseph Robinson Pim in Liverpool and known as the Mersey Company, started to run against Williams and continued to do so for eighteen months, before Williams won the contest.[12] This experience confirmed his view that a company with a large capital and several vessels was better able to withstand competitors; small concerns with 'confined resources' could never do so. Moreover, a well-founded company could afford to lay up vessels for as long as was required for repairs to be thoroughly executed, giving shippers and passengers confidence in the safety and efficiency of steam shipping. Without sufficient resources, small companies were tempted to go in for 'ruinous *overworking*' of the fragile engines and the 'expensive half-trading', trying desperately to make a profit.[13]

Williams set about establishing regulatory practices. First, the competitor had to be done away with or rendered harmless. In the case of the Mersey Company, a take-over, with its vessels, was the best solution. This strengthened Williams's hold on the Dublin–Liverpool line, and he reorganized his company in 1826. With the new name of the City of Dublin Company and capital of £100,000, he gave Laird and Pim seats on its board to make sure that they had a personal interest in the new dispensation. Next, to avoid competition, he laid down a demarcation that confined Pim's St George Company to ports in the south of Ireland and England, with access to Liverpool from Dublin strictly limited.[14] Finally, a fair distribution of earnings began in 1826 by pooling their passenger fares. Two years later Williams also had such an arrangement with George Langtry, now a steamship owner of substance on the Belfast–Liverpool line. Williams made it known that 'the entire trade of Belfast is between Mr Langtree [*sic*] of Belfast and the City of Dublin Company'.[15] However, Williams could not have wanted absolute monopoly, nor did he come anywhere near it. Many other companies working out of other ports on the south and east coasts, like Waterford, Wexford, Cork and Newry, found niches that did not interfere with the Dublin–Liverpool line.

The City of Dublin Company expanded rapidly. Up to 1833, there were 11 vessels with an average of 200 tons; then, to match the improvements in machinery up to 1839, 9 more ships were built, their average being 350 tons. Liverpool built 9 in 1833, average 125 tons, and, in 1839, 9 with an average of 170 tons. Williams lost the cover of the Anonymous Persons Act in 1825 when City of Dublin doubled the capital limit of £50,000, and by 1828 capital had jumped more than twice again to £225,200 with nearly 500 shareholders, most of them residents of Dublin. In this year he sought incorporation for his company, but Parliament rejected both this and two further petitions in 1833 and 1836. It was alleged that prejudice against an Irish company was the reason,[16] because the (English) General Steam Navigation Company had become incorporated in 1834 with a capital of less that £400,000,[17] yet City of Dublin had reached £450,000 by 1836. Each petition, however, was authorized in Acts of Parliament which confirmed the limited liability of the shareholders and the right of the company to sue and be sued.[18]

Improving and extending inland waterways was a matter of great importance to Williams. The Shannon and the canals then in existence were unable to cope with the fast-growing export trades and British imported manufactures. A steamer was placed on the Shannon in 1827 by John Grantham, a civil engineer employed by the Government to survey the river, but competition from another small-scale concern was disastrous for both. Williams bought up both vessels, formed the Inland Steam Navigation Company and began operations in 1829. From being, as Williams put it, 'almost wholly useless as a means of internal intercourse', river boats and barges made the river 'the interchange of commodities between the ten counties through which it runs'.[19]

It was at about this time that Williams began to take an interest in barges. Hulls and engines were usually built separately by different firms, often at some distance apart. When the time came to marry hull to engine, he urged builder and engineer to consult with one another so that they could secure the engines to the ship's framing properly. They refused, so he became his own engineer, devising the best method of fixing the engines himself. This training taught him the 'absolute necessity' of having a competent engineer to attend to engineering problems. In due course the Birkenhead builders William Laird and his son John undertook both the construction of engines and the building of hulls, possibly on Williams's advice.[20] The first iron vessels to be made on the Mersey were commissioned by him. Lairds made an iron barge in 1829 and two more in 1832. Then in 1833–34, the Lairds built the iron steamers *Lady Lansdowne*, which was employed on the Shannon, and *Garryowen*, which was Williams's first regular sea-going iron steamer. Concern about safety at sea led to these two vessels being fitted with iron bulkheads according to Williams's own specification.[21] These were the first steamers to be so constructed; a decade or so later, iron bulkheads became obligatory. He did not patent them because he wanted everyone to use them.[22]

Repairs were expensive: even in the careful City of Dublin Co., £13,000 could be spent on repairs, as it was in 1834. Williams had a 'very large establishment', so repairs could be done 'within any reasonable time' and in the 'efficient way we do them ourselves'; good tradesmen were 'permanently employed' and 'we keep as accurate an account as if we were working for strangers'.[23] He found it more efficient to trade with vessels built for specific cargoes. Some of his vessels were designed to carry cattle, a trade created by the steamship. *Ballinasloe*, built in 1829 and the first purpose-built cattle ship, was fitted with 'a powerful blast cylinder to blow air' to the cattle holds.[24] When fresh butter became a sizeable export, part of a 'different description of vessel' was shut off to provide a 'cool chamber', a kind of prototype for development.[25] Some vessels carried only grain, and others were exclusively for cabin passengers and their servants, horses, dogs, carriages and small parcels.

In the early stages of ocean steam navigation, both Williams and Pim were advocates of state subsidies. Williams argued that the State would gain far more than the price of a mail contract: subsidies would provide a ready-made mercantile fleet that could easily, 'in a single day, become capacious transports for troops, arms and stores [and serve as] valuable aids to the naval force of the country'.[26] In 1827, their proposals were rejected by the Post Office,

> chiefly on the broad principle . . . that a public service of so much importance to the political and commercial interests of the country . . . ought not to be trusted to private individuals. [The Government] would

> scarcely consent to leave the whole communications between Great Britain and Ireland dependent on the mercy of private individuals, whose private and personal interests, from the conveyance of passengers, goods or cattle, would be the first and only objects of pursuit.[27]

Williams and Pim may have wanted to show the Post Office what a private company could do in a competition, for in 1826, having successfully established a mail service by steam between Dublin and Holyhead, the Post Office decided to open another line from Dublin to Liverpool. Government vessels carried mails primarily, but also took cabin passengers. The two Irish owners, now united in their effort to guard their Dublin–Liverpool line and afraid that their revenue from cabin passengers would suffer, began a 'formidable competition' against the Post Office,[28] and before long the Government was obliged to enter a secret ten-year peace treaty that gave City of Dublin Co. the better deal on departure times; and Williams insisted on continuing free passage for all his shareholders and their families.[29] During the 10 years of the agreement, the Post Office lost the fares of more than 11,000 passengers.[30] This got the Post Office into trouble and the 1826 agreement was withdrawn. While the Government considered the wider question of whether to contract the mails, a second fierce rate-war was fought. Again, Williams came out on top, but this time there was a public settlement, the company openly entering into a mail contract with the Government in 1839, for which Williams was paid £9,000 per annum.[31]

Steamships were more regular means of communication than sail. In these early years, it took about 14 hours to cross the Irish Channel by steam against 2–3 weeks by sail. Turn-around time was thus far shorter and insurance costs were greatly reduced. The scale of City of Dublin's operations was large: in 1831, its steamers made 500 round voyages, and 800 in 1839.[32] Constant increase in tonnage on all Irish lines to the mainland prevented absolute monopolies and pushed freight rates steadily downwards, so that by the 1830s there was generally little difference between freight rates in steam and sail. In 1830, according to Williams, a steam vessel in the Channel trade had to make an average of 1.5 departures a week to be profitable, but a sailing vessel made on average only 8 departures a year. Bulk cargoes of labourers, live cattle and grain developed into important export trades, compensation for the low demand for butter and cured meat. Linen and cabin passengers were both staples, with linen the most valuable source of revenue.

Steam shipping was not only much more costly than sail: it was more demanding of its managers. Ownership of sailing ships was often a part-time occupation; most owners (aside from the mariner–owners) were merchants or manufacturers. Williams knew that management of steamships had to be a full-time occupation if they were to be run efficiently. Thus from the start he had no interests other than the management of steamships, save for his endless search for improved engines, safety at sea and experiments with fuel. In 1830 he resisted the call of his Liverpool and Dublin admirers to stand for Parliament, preferring not to meddle in politics and to limit his contacts with government to parliamentary inquiries, where his advice and knowledge was frequently sought and given.[33] 'My politics', he declared, 'are – *trade and commerce*. These are the great pioneers of civilization.'[34] Combative when a competitor loomed, he knew the value of loyalty from his shippers. For the convenience of free passage, he gave them free storage facilities, a reduction in town dues and, most important of all, rebates on the freight of cattle and goods after six months' unbroken support. Usually 5 per cent, rebates were doubled in times of danger to his company. 'Conferences' or 'rings', so common later in the century, added little if anything to Williams's regulatory schemes. An almost unfailing 6 per cent return on capital also pleased the shareholders.[35] Williams preferred to hold this level of dividend, charging another part of the accounts according to circumstances. He kept reserves 'to meet all future wants and emergencies', for such a fund would 'afford the best guarantee to the Shareholders of the stability and perpetuity of the concern'. The dominance he established in Irish Channel trades had much to do with the strict rein he kept on his company's finances by ploughing back profits. The company was its own insurer for sea risk, thus saving on insurance. No more capital was issued for some years after Parliament sanctioned £450,000 in 1836, but during 1830–39 the company was able to distribute £213,941 in dividends, £86,306 in rebates and build 16 vessels.[36] It was a very prosperous concern indeed.

Owners like Williams soon realised that the larger and more powerful the vessel, the more economical it was to run. They also found that longer voyages were more economical and less damaging for the primitive engines of the day and consequently more profitable.[37] So Irish owners took advantage of refinements to the machinery that made it more efficient and capable of reaching more distant ports. In 1827, Williams dispatched *Leeds* (a steamer of more than 400 tons, the engine of which was better than any machinery on the Irish Channel) on a regular summer service from Dublin to Bordeaux, a considerable distance, but a line worth working;[38] and in the early 1830s, Pim was sending his vessels to St Petersburg. Soon it would be possible to go even farther afield.

In both management and organisation, then, the City of Dublin Co. presented a unique model of an efficient mercantile concern run on lines appropriate to the new demands of steam shipping. No individual made so marked a contribution to the development of the business of shipping in all its aspects than Charles Wye Williams. He set the pace, laid down the ground rules and created precedents for others to follow. He was recognised by his contemporaries as representing 'the new class of shipping interests, which is yet [in 1830] so little understood but which is so powerfully influential in advancing the best interests of Ireland'.[39]

Williams had established his company's headquarters in Liverpool in the early 1820s because of its superior dock and harbour facilities, and he lived there in the parish of St James. A few Liverpool businessmen were taken on to City of Dublin's board of directors. Joseph Christopher Ewart (1799–1868), of a family of prominent merchants in London and Liverpool, was one of them.[40] In the late 1830s, to ease the burden of management, Williams promoted Francis Carleton (1800–1848) to the office of joint manager with himself. Carleton, also a Dublin man, had been City of Dublin Co.'s secretary for several years past.[41] Like Williams and Ewart, Carleton was to be a founding director of P&O.

P&O's founders: Richard Bourne

In the tight-knit circle of Dublin's elite entrepreneurs and professionals, Williams was almost certainly acquainted with Richard Bourne. Bourne and his brothers were well known in Dublin and in the more prosperous parts outside because they ran an extensive road-transport business. It included coach-building, the operation of mail coaches, and the laying out and maintenance of roads. From their headquarters at 48 Dawson Street, next to the Hibernian Hotel, a dozen or more roads radiated out in several directions, servicing at least twenty of the more populous towns in southern Ireland.[42]

Their business had its origins in the late eighteenth century. At that time, road transport was unable to provide the communication demanded by the burgeoning Atlantic trade that depended on the Dublin–Limerick–Cork axis. In 1789, as a remedial measure, the Irish Parliament adopted the English mail coach system. In partnership with others, William Hawker Bourne (died *c.* 1837), an older brother, secured a mail contract for the Limerick road in 1790. As the roads were too rough to take mail coaches, private contractors were appointed to lay out, repair and maintain the principal arteries. William Bourne bought into a road contract partnership in 1793 and eventually came to control the Dublin–Limerick–Cork highways. Frederick Bourne, another brother (died 1843), built the Dublin–Ashbourne section of the road to Drogheda, thereby opening a new route to Belfast. Henry Bourne (died *c.* 1820), the eldest of the four, also had a share in the business. Since road contractors often had to put substantial sums of their own capital into road works, they would take the risk only if they had long leases and a monopoly of the tolls. At first, William Bourne negotiated a 33-year lease on his roads but long before it had expired he persuaded the Irish Postmaster-General to extend it to 50 years, bringing the expiry date up to 1848. Frederick also had a long-term monopoly of his road to the north.

The Bourne's transport business was a large, integrated undertaking. At Blackpits in Dublin they built their own mail coaches in partnership with James Hartley (another founder of P&O, died 1857) who later became a small shipowner and set up as an insurance broker in London. Some 800 horses grazed on land owned by the Bournes, and they built hotels and inns along their roads for the refreshment of the passengers who took Bourne's coaches. All these operations involved a great number of people. Better roads meant faster communication to and from Dublin, Limerick and Cork, and to Belfast via Ashbourne. Over the years the brothers grew rich. In Dublin society there was no stigma attached to men of business. The Bournes were 'persons of opulence' and were described as 'some of the most important men in the country'; as wealthy individuals they enjoyed 'consideration in society'.[43]

Fermoy may have been the Bourne family's home territory, for the youngest brother, Richard, was born there, but the family's fortunes appear to have come from a 500-year lease secured by Henry, the eldest brother, on nearly 300 acres of 'profitable land' in Queen's County. In 1787, at the age of 17, Richard joined the Royal Navy and was elevated to Lieutenant 10 years later after he took part in the capture of *La Souris*, a French vessel of 16 guns, thereby fending off the attack of a French flotilla. After some years on half pay, he returned in 1804 to command the twelve-gun schooner *Felix*. In January 1805, he was first to see and convey to Rear Admiral Sir Thomas Graves the intelligence of the escape of a French squadron from Aix Road off Rochefort, and went on to fight 'an action of great gallantry with a privateer of far superior force', but in 1806 he was put on half pay again after being severely wounded in an action off the Spanish coast. In 1840 he was given the rank of retired commander under an Order in Council of 1816,[44] and thereafter adopted the courtesy style of 'Captain Richard Bourne, RN'.

On leaving the Royal Navy in 1806, Richard joined his brothers and began a second career in their road- and mail-contracting business;

he acquired a monopoly of the road to Galway and became a partner in the coach-building factory. In 1816 he made a socially advantageous second marriage to Louisa Helena Blake of the Blakes of Ardry, an ancient Irish clan which owned extensive lands in County Galway; some of them had settled in the West Indies and built up a trade with Ireland in tobacco and other commodities.[45] Her grandfather, Joseph Blake, had represented Galway for many years in the Irish Parliament and was given a peerage, as Lord Wallscourt, after the Act of Union.

In 1825, the year in which tariff barriers between Ireland and England were taken down, William Bourne moved into steam shipping while still having the roads. Conceived as a strategic extension of road transport, the venture was undertaken at a propitious moment. Named the Dublin & London Steam Marine Company (Dublin & London hereafter), the route chosen was tactically prudent since it did not interfere with the City of Dublin Co.'s interests. A serious illness which obliged Richard to give up his Galway road and leave Ireland about that time may explain why he did not initially take a part in this enterprise. The new company offered a passenger-only service in *Thames* and *Shannon*; with a combined tonnage of 656, these steamers were the largest of the 19 new steam vessels to be registered in 1826–27, and powerful enough to ply throughout the year between Dublin and London, calling at Belfast, Falmouth and Plymouth. Cabins were fitted up 'in a style of elegance' suited to the carriage-owning public who were assured that 'accommodation for Horses, Carriages, &c. are of the best description'. Operations began in 1827 and both vessels 'ran successfully all last winter'. The fare for adult cabin passengers was £3.10*s*.[46]

In the following year a competitor arrived with a vessel under Joseph Robinson Pim's control. In 1829, Pim added *William Fawcett*, a new ship owned by him and by William Fawcett, its engine-builder. Pim's ruthless rate-cutting forced Dublin & London to reduce its cabin fares by a third, and in 1830 the Bourne's company was near to collapse. At this point Richard Bourne took charge of the company to save the family name from bankruptcy.[47] He became the main shareowner with 38/64ths of the vessels, the other 26/64ths being divided among his brothers, William and Frederick, and three associates prominent in the business community, James Hartley, William Henry Fortescue and Simeon Boileau. Further funds may have come from other directors, for William Lunell Guinness was listed in 1833 and others came and went during the next few years.[48] Richard Bourne increased the company's tonnage with the purchase of *City of Londonderry* in 1831 and his new *Royal Tar* in 1832, and was not intimidated by Pim's rate-cutting. Pim went as low as £1.10*s* for cabin passengers, but Richard raised his brother's last rate to £2.2*s* because he judged that there were always well-to-do passengers who would pay more for a superior and exclusive service (a policy P&O was to adopt). Fastidious members of the public were assured that they would not be 'exposed to the effluvia' of cattle or pigs, for none would be carried; further refinements were a surgeon on board and a catering service.[49] Richard Bourne's tactic paid off. It was Pim who withdrew at the end of 1832, clearly in some financial embarrassment. *William Fawcett* was sold to Bourne, and Pim turned his attention to the east coast of England and the Baltic trade.[50]

Richard Bourne became a steamship owner in his sixtieth year. 'Being friendly to mechanical improvements' in the coach business, he had no difficulty in mastering the essentials of steam:[51] transport by sea in business terms was not so different from road transport. William Bourne observed that becoming a road contractor in the 1790s had been 'a very desperate speculation', requiring a large capital with little return in the early years. At sea, too, the highest risk was a new route that had to be developed before it could yield a profit, but if well-managed the profits could be high. The Bournes knew that the criteria for success on road or sea were, first, substantial unoccupied areas because these presented the best opportunities for speculation and, second, 'the exclusion of all competition'. Sometimes extreme measures were necessary to keep rivals away. In July 1837, for example, Richard and William agreed to carry mail on the Limerick road without payment from the Post Office 'rather than allow a new contractor to establish himself on the road'; and to keep competitors out it was usual to manipulate bids for contracts.[52] Such practices were easily transferred to the business of steam shipping.

Bourne had won the fight with Pim on the Dublin–London line. He cannot have emerged unscathed, however, because in 1832 all shipowners in the Channel trade had much to grumble about. The huge amount of tonnage that had come into it meant that freight rates were 'reduced to the most ruinous state' and 'the complaint is universal that there is more loss than profit in shipping'. Even City of Dublin ran fewer voyages in that year than in 1828, despite the fact that the volume of produce exported to England was greater than ever. It was obvious, then, that Channel trade had built-in limitations, especially in view of Ireland's increasing dependence on Britain. As Dublin's importance as a financial centre gradually declined, Belfast rose to prominence, but its developments were more industrial than financial.[53] The trend in the 1830s was for merchants to by-pass Dublin and Liverpool and seek direct contacts with London and other towns on the mainland to expand their business. Shipowners for their part found that the coastal trade became less rewarding in inverse ratio to the tonnage exported. After a decade of working steamships on the Irish Channel, owners also learnt that long voyages were more economical than short ones. All these factors pointed to expansion further afield as the rational option. Bourne's contact with London led him to look for more favourable markets for steam, and to find them from a base in London rather Dublin, in foreign ports rather than British.[54]

Other changes likely to influence his thinking were also in train. One was a curtailment in the road business. In 1831 the Irish system of private road management was abolished, to be replaced by a Board of Public Works. The Bournes had no objection to this new order, but they demanded compensation for their road leases up to 1848, the date when they were due to expire. They also insisted that they had a claim against the Post Office for a toll on horses that they had not collected since 1811. There were, of course, two sides to this argument and lawyers grappled with it for years. Post Office opinion was unequivocal: the Bournes had invented the complaint; moreover, 'a more barefaced act of injustice (to afford to it the lightest appellation) was never before contemplated even in the Irish Parliament . . . To compensate Mr [William] Bourne for a loss he had never sustained!!!' But eminent counsel for the Bournes persuaded the Treasury to give way to some extent, for the new road regulations could not be effected until these claims was cleared. So, with the Treasury's misgivings, the brothers were compensated, though they did not get the whole of the £55,000 they asked for.[55] Their coach-building activity was also affected when the Post Office introduced competition in the supply of mail coaches, but these attempts soon faltered because, despite the 'high character' of Richard Bourne, he and a fellow contractor were quite capable of forming 'a combination'.[56]

The advent of the railway age was another reason for change. Rail connections between London and Liverpool or Bristol were bound to have an unfavourable impact on Dublin & London's passenger traffic. If shipping was to become Richard's principal investment, moving out of Irish waters was a necessary step to take. In this strategy, he was one of the many Irish owners who, having established themselves in coastal shipping in the 1820s, were ready to extend their horizons. These ambitious entrepreneurs were responsible for the great surge of investment in Irish steam shipping in 1835–37, targeted on medium- and long-distance navigation.

The problem with operating over longer distances with the inefficient engines then available was the prohibitive cost. Though Williams and Pim had in 1827 tried unsuccessfully to persuade the Government to offer subsidies for mail services, opinion began to veer in favour of private companies in the early 1830s.[57] In 1832, the Post Office invited tenders for the first mail contract by steam for the Rotterdam–Hamburg line, commercially important because of the timber trade. Aiming to trade with the east coast of England and northwest Europe, J.R. Pim put in the lowest bid. Although his price was accepted, his fortunes were damaged by his recent punishing contest with Bourne's Dublin & London, so, whether for 'incompetency or unwillingness', he was not able to perform the contract. Owners of the London-based General Steam Company, already working the line after having failed to win the subsidy, gladly bought from Pim, according to rumour with 'several thousands' but more likely with £2,000 a year.

Shortly afterwards, politics made it expedient to arrange for a faster and more regular mail service to the Iberian peninsula. Imports of sherry and port had established a firm link with that region in the eighteenth century, and during the Napoleonic Wars contacts were strengthened by Britain's strategic interest and military success. Upheavals in Spain and Portugal in the 1820s were watched from a distance by the British Government, but continuing instability in the 1830s brought these two kingdoms to the forefront of public affairs. After first supporting the two newly installed regimes unofficially, Britain stopped being 'so squeamishly neutral' and intervened openly on their side. The reason for this was that Lord Palmerston, British Foreign Secretary, had conceived a two-fold diplomatic plan: one aim was to prevent France from exercising too much influence in the peninsula (Palmerston suffered from Francophobia); the other was to form an alliance in Western Europe to counterbalance the dominance of Austria and Russia in the Near East. Spain and Portugal were easily netted, and in April 1834 France was persuaded to join Britain in the manoeuvre. Palmerston was then able to flaunt the Quadruple Alliance as a 'liberal' bulwark against the machinations of the autocratic Eastern powers.[58]

News of events in the Iberian peninsula that preceded this alliance received wide coverage in the press. Sir Charles Napier who, disguised as a Spanish admiral, commanded a naval force in 1833 to crush opposition to the new government in Portugal, was fêted on his 'brilliant victory'.[59] To finish the job, another expedition was organized a year later by Juan Alvarez y Mendizabal, a statesman in a former Spanish government who, under the new regime, had been appointed Minister in London in 1834. In the intervening years, since his exile from Spain in the 1820s he had lived in London and established himself as a merchant and banker. For his mission he needed steam transport. He was on friendly terms with Richard Bourne who knew something of Spain from his wound in 1806,[60] and Bourne made his *Royal Tar* available for charter to the Spanish Government at Mendizabal's request.

Mendizabal has been credited with persuading Richard Bourne to run a line of steamers to Spain and Portugal.[61] Was this the case? The implication of government policy must surely have caught Bourne's attention: to keep the two shaky Iberian regimes in the Quadruple Alliance, good communication with the peninsula was essential; and, as we have seen, Bourne had good reason to be on the look-out for new shipping opportunities: disturbances in the peninsula had been a hindrance to commerce for the previous six years.[62] If relative calm were to be established, trade would quickly pick up. It is not difficult to see Bourne, who was frequently in London, broaching the subject himself with Mendizabal.

However that may be, *Royal Tar* made four round voyages to the peninsula between May and November 1834 under the agency of Willcox & Anderson, a London shipbroking concern. Of the four other steamers the agency chartered, one was owned by the City of Dublin Co. This seems to have been the first contact made between this agency and Bourne and Williams.[63] It was while Willcox & Anderson was handling *Royal Tar* that a shipping company was mooted by the agents; in August they published a prospectus for a Peninsular Steam Navigation Company to trade with Spain and Portugal, but it did not go further than that. When a company with the same name was eventually formed in 1837, it was an entirely different enterprise and became an essential link in the chain of events that led to the foundation of P&O.

P&O's founders: Willcox and Anderson

Brodie McGhie Willcox (1785–1862) was of English and Belgian parentage, his Scottish names being derived from his maternal uncle Brodie Augustus McGhie, a shipowner and shipbuilder in London. Willcox grew up in Newcastle and moved to London in the early 1800s, presumably to work under his uncle. A contemporary referred to him as 'a young man of no influence and but limited money'. He was acceptable enough in 1812, however, to have married the daughter of a Belgian merchant resident in London and to become a partner in a small shipbroking and insurance concern with a Mr Carreno. Arthur Anderson (1792–1868) was taken on by the partnership as an assistant. This young man, born in Lerwick, Shetland, joined the Royal Navy as a youth and was paid off in 1815 as a captain's clerk. Arrived in London, his 'only capital was a plain but sound education, good moral and Christian training, a clear head and great industry'. His uncle, Peter Ridland, introduced Anderson to Christopher Hill, a Scarborough shipowner, who in turn passed him on to Willcox. Anderson was the junior in this concern until 1822 when Carreno retired. After taking his place as Willcox's partner, Anderson was able to marry Hill's daughter Mary Ann. Willcox & Anderson was said to be 'simply a small shipping commission business, with the addition of the part ownership of a few vessels', and the partners were described as 'plodding and industrious'.[64] Their main commission business was in sailing vessels trading mostly with Portugal and Spain, and occasionally South America. Until the British interventions in the Iberian peninsula in the early 1830s, they appear to have had little or nothing to do with steamships. Their acquaintance with Richard Bourne in the spring of 1834 was the beginning of a long relationship. Working under Bourne's direction over the next few years, they discovered in themselves latent talents that led them to fame and fortune.

The background of these two shipbrokers raises the question of whether the proposal of a steam company to trade with the Iberian peninsula came from them or from Richard Bourne.[65] His experience in steam shipping and as a man of business suggests that an initiative of this kind would have come from him. London's shipping community had not yet taken to ocean navigation on any scale. General Steam was the largest steam shipping company in London, but except for two vessels recently built for the Rotterdam–Hamburg line, all the others were built for rivers or coastal routes until as late as 1836. In Ireland, by contrast, as we have seen, economic circumstances demanded ocean steamships so that new and more distant markets could be found. If the dynamism of Irish owners and investors was set alongside the number of shipping companies they formed and the size of vessel they worked, the project of a shipping company for the peninsula trade was more likely to have emanated from Bourne.[66] And if these factors were added to the sound reasons for Bourne's wishing to move out of the Irish Channel, all the circumstantial evidence points to him as the originator. On the other hand, he was certainly not responsible for the text or the timing of Willcox & Anderson's publication of the prospectus of a paper Peninsular Steam Navigation Company in August 1834, and Bourne's name does not appear anywhere on it. He might have been thinking about extending his interests at that time but there is no evidence of him wanting to throw off his Dublin–London line at once. Bourne was far too shrewd to make a precipitous decision or a public declaration of intent at such a preliminary stage. That would alert rivals and make him vulnerable on two fronts: by attracting a competitor's attention to his Dublin–London line, and by broadcasting his plans for the peninsular coast, if indeed he would have made any plans while *Royal Tar* was on a military expedition. Willcox's assertion that he was the 'father' of P&O was made after Bourne's death and could not be challenged.[67] Whatever the truth of the matter, the 1834 prospectus was a flop. The directorate was made up of merchants in London (including Mendizabal) and the Iberian peninsula but none of them was willing or able to part with his money, and neither Willcox nor Anderson was in a position to act alone.[68]

Spain and Portugal were still effectively virgin territory as far as commercial steam shipping was concerned, the very opportunity for which Bourne was looking. As a businessman he had to be convinced that investment in the area would turn out to be profitable. For this, two conditions were mandatory: the line had to be commercially viable out and home, a question that could only be settled by trial runs; and a mail contract had to be secured to offset the heavy operating costs.

Bourne's intention to experiment on the Iberian line, then, did not involve unsustainable risk, and what was learned from it would provide useful information. His decision-making was both prudent and consistent: he took account of the changes taking place on land and sea in Ireland, and kept the option of pulling out of the peninsular trades if need be. In 1835, he dispatched 3 of his steamers to the Iberian coast – *Royal Tar*, *William Fawcett* and *Liverpool* – which between them made 12 round voyages, calling mainly at the central and southern ports from Oporto to Gibraltar, though a few were dispatched exclusively to northern Spain. As most of the latter group returned in ballast, they were probably employed by the Spanish Government.[69]

Bourne was evidently impressed by Willcox and Anderson's performance as managing agents for these voyages. In Anderson especially, he scented a kindred spirit, relatively youthful and imbued with the enthusiasm, energy and enterprise needed to fulfil Bourne's own ambitious schemes. On his part, Anderson admired what the older man had already achieved and was grateful for the new horizons Bourne opened for him. Satisfied with the results of the experimental voyages in 1835, Bourne encouraged his agents to invest in a vessel of their own, for 'he thought it right that they should have a pecuniary interest in the success of the undertaking'.[70] Accordingly, with support from their Iberian friends, Willcox and Anderson commissioned *Iberia*, their first steamship. *Iberia* embarked on its maiden trip to the peninsula in October 1836.[71] During that year Bourne's own ships made 19 voyages, while vessels he chartered made a further 9. For political reasons (a rebellion in Bilbao had just been subdued) Bourne's steamers reduced their number of calls to the northern ports. This allowed for greater concentration in the south: at least one call a month was made to Lisbon, Cadiz and Gibraltar, the ports that would attract most cargo and which, in the case of Gibraltar, gave access to the Mediterranean. Also in 1836, Bourne ordered three new large steamers: *Braganza* and *Tagus*, both over 700 tons, and *Don Juan*, at over 900 tons, the largest and most powerful steamship yet built.[72] All were ready for sea in 1837. Because of their size, none of them was meant for coastal trade, confirming that Bourne had made his decision to move on. Between January and August 1837, an unofficial mail service was in being. Its regularity and punctuality attracted much favourable comment from merchants and passengers, and Willcox and Anderson gained valuable experience of this new mode of operation.

Commercial prospects, too, were good. Having travelled to Lisbon in 1835, Willcox reported that '*William Fawcett* is actually coining money. In little more than three weeks her earnings amount to nearly £2,000 . . . If we get the mails it will be a fortune but rely upon this, unless we are quick we shall lose all . . . It is much easier to prevent or at least down an opposition than it is to regain a position once lost.'[73] As to the likelihood of a mail contract, there was reason to be optimistic. The Post Office was under scrutiny by Parliament for its inefficiency, and the upshot of various inquiries was that the new policy of subsidising steam navigation was to be administered by the Admiralty from 1837 onwards. Admiralty officers, unversed in mercantile costs and earnings, needed to 'ascertain how many persons were inclined to speculate in steam' on this route.[74] Bourne's plans and proposals were to hand. His calculations were based on the ample means and tonnage he could deploy; and his long familiarity with officialdom as a mail, road and coach contractor in Ireland was a valuable asset. As Bourne expected, his steamers on this new line enticed the British & Foreign Steam Navigation Company, a London concern, to compete with him. Though it fought vigorously with its two vessels for about a year, it had to sell out to the Commercial Steam Packet Company, also London-based, and the latter was the challenger when tenders were invited for the mail contract. However, there was no real competition. In August 1837 the Admiralty granted the contract to Bourne: he was an experienced shipowner, a man of means; he had 'the better class of vessels' and more of them than his rival; in fact, Bourne's tender was 'the most advantageous for the public'. In September 1837, the Peninsular Steam Navigation Company (Peninsular Steam) began to operate with the mail contract and an annual subsidy of £29,600. A weekly mail service was required, calling at five ports, including Lisbon and Gibraltar.[75]

Bourne's aim achieved, he was free to divest himself of Dublin & London. Williams had already set up his British & Irish Steam Packet Company which began a regular Dublin–London service in September 1836 so that he could be sure of occupying the line as soon as Bourne left, but Bourne waited until the Iberian mail contract was signed and sealed before he let go of it. In October 1837 *Thames* and *Shannon* were sold to Williams for £40,000, a sum that included goodwill and premises in London and Dublin. A condition of the deal was an undertaking by all parties not to interfere with one another then or in the future. Thus Bourne promised not to take any part in lines occupied by City of Dublin or British & Irish without mutual consent. Similarly, Williams and his partners agreed to leave the peninsular trade up to the French–Spanish border to Bourne. Of the sale price, £5,000 came to Bourne in shares in the new British & Irish, giving him or his associates the right to serve on the new company's directorate. The appointment of Willcox & Anderson as the London agent for City of Dublin forged another link between Williams and Bourne.[76]

The mail contract was the essential ingredient for Peninsular Steam's long-term success. 'Coining money' in summer and autumn was not difficult, as Willcox had found. There might be a market for Manchester goods (Bourne dispatched *City of Londonderry* and *Manchester* from Liverpool for one and two voyages respectively in 1837), while fresh and dried fruit, nuts, olives, wine, foodstuffs, plants, cork and an occasional consignment of ivory and silk (overland from the East) filled cargo space on return voyages. But winter and spring were lean. Anderson introduced an autumn tourist season for invalids and others who wished to escape the British winter by going to Madeira via Lisbon. The 'large and splendidly fitted-up STEAM VESSELS'[77] which they were offered helped intermittently but could not make up for seasonal losses. Only the certainty of government money, paid quarterly in banker's drafts, could provide the stability that was needed.

Peninsular Steam had little corporate identity. The two groups of owners that constituted the company – Bourne's associates and *Iberia*'s owners – employed the same managing agent, Willcox & Anderson, and had to abide by the terms of the mail contract. In all other respects, however, vessels remained the property of their owners, not of the company. To help administer his expanding business, Bourne appointed James Allan (1811–1876) as his assistant. A young Scot from Aberdeen, Allan had been clerk to Dublin & London in Dublin. Now he looked after Bourne's affairs in London, and was later to go on to an important role in P&O. Willcox and Anderson liked the loose organization of the company. It consisted of 'a few individuals having no separate interests, doing their own work & save [*sic*] all the heavy cogging & expensive machinery of Directors, Salaried Offices &c. Our saving upon this head over other Companys [*sic*] in addition to its working better form a large annual profit.'[78]

Later, when P&O was formed, these 'few individuals' did not find it easy to work with 'outsiders'. *Iberia*'s accounts were made up after each voyage (as required under the 64ths system), and profits shared out at quarterly intervals among her owners. How Bourne dealt with the financial side of his vessels is unknown. The brothers were used to working together with a few close friends like James Hartley; and Richard Bourne was evidently able to raise funds without appealing to investors outside his own circle. There is very little information about the overall profitability of Peninsular Steam. Anderson stated long after the event that the vessels ran 'at a considerable loss' before the mail subsidy was granted, and there is no reason to doubt it. Even with the subsidy 'the undertaking was found to be the reverse of profitable' at first, unsurprisingly since *Don Juan*, Bourne's most expensive vessel, was wrecked on its second homeward voyage and Bourne had to bear part of the loss because the vessel was not fully insured. (Anderson was on board and was quick to defend Captain John Ralph Engledue, the master. Engledue had such a hold over Anderson that one wonders what really happened on that foggy night.[79]) Some indication of how the line fared comes from the scattered records of *Iberia*'s performance.

Profits varied considerably according to season. In June 1838, £1,500 was available for dividends and in September £3,000, the profit on each 64th varying between £23 and £47 per quarter. In 1839 spring voyages yielded £1,500, summer voyages £2,000. The only surviving winter record, January 1840, was £1,000 and this presumably included earnings from the tourist and invalid trade to Madeira.[80] Expenses were high. Reductions in port and customs dues were negotiated for mail ships between the British and Iberian governments,[81] but machinery needed frequent repair and the Admiralty's inspections of mail ships were thorough. A plaintive response on one occasion, that 'no sett [*sic*] of Engines however perfect to appearance even new ones are not exempt from casualties arising from hidden imperfections in the Iron &c', gives a flavour of the exasperation owners felt, as much because of the prying eyes of naval officers as of the unreliability of engines.

The weekly service required by the contract suited the company because it left no niche for competitors. Breakdowns of machinery meant constant chartering that could cost anything between £32 and £40 per ton per day. The subsidy of £29,600 (£570 per week) helped with operating costs, but was regarded by the contractor as less than generous. Anderson asserted that Peninsular Steam performed the service for £5,500 less than the Admiralty vessels which the company replaced. In 1842, when vessels on the Peninsular line were criticized for their slowness, Willcox's retort was: 'we have old-fashioned boats because we are paid an old-fashioned price'. Contractors naturally always tried to get the highest price they could and complained about the parsimony of the Treasury. But it would have been out of character for Bourne to run the line if, in spite of the contract, he judged that it would not eventually produce reasonable returns. Indeed, the company was 'already yielding a fair return' early in 1840 if not before.

Having secured the Peninsular contract, Bourne and his associates were well placed to pursue their strategy. As his agents put it, 'our main object for which we are preparing all our means is to *extend* our line, that is to say to lengthen [it eastwards]'.[82] Their target was to go through the Mediterranean to Egypt, overland to Suez and thence to India.

The Indian connection[83]

A feature of the early steam age was the excitement it stirred up. An officer in the East India Company's army observed that the question of steam communication generated more ideas, more arguments and more committees than any other public question, and its importance grew with the years. The new technology of ocean navigation promised to do away with the long voyage to India by sail round the Cape of Good Hope; a round voyage could take anything up to a year, so that letters were an uncertain way of keeping in touch. Not surprisingly, all manner of benefits were expected from steam communication. Lord William Bentinck, Governor-General of India from 1828 to 1835, saw steam on the high seas 'as the great engine' of 'moral improvement' in the immense spaces of India, 'where the human mind [had] been buried for ages in universal darkness', and the Bishop of Calcutta, 'that enlightened prelate', spoke of 'opening the flood-gates of measureless blessings to mankind'. A more mundane view looked forward to 'a quick interchange of information . . . of the first advantage in commerce and in the conduct of all public business'.[84] Yet while the 'Indians' – both official and mercantile – held a number of aces, they failed to achieve their aims. Some of their proposals were simply unworkable thanks to their obvious lack of experience in running steamships on any scale. But the main reason for their failure was that there were too many divergent interests and no agreed direction. After years of campaigning, it was eventually left to Bourne and Williams to establish steam communication between Britain and the East.

As early as 1822, when only a handful of small vessels plied on short distances, a project to bring India closer to the metropolis by steam was adopted at a public meeting in the City of London.[85] This initiative was welcomed in India, but dissension surfaced as soon as practical matters were considered. Enthusiasts in Calcutta, supported by others in Madras, set up a Bengal Steam Committee and opted for a steamship on the Cape route. Subscriptions from these two Presidencies paid for the steamer *Enterprize* to be built in Britain and dispatched to India. Its size (470 tons) and power (160 nominal horse-power [hp]) were demonstrably inadequate as the vessel struggled to make the long voyage round the Cape in 1825.[86] Zeal could not overcome the technological shortcomings of the time; indeed, voyages by steam on the Cape route did not become economically viable until about forty years later.

A rival group of merchants and officials based in Bombay rejected the Cape route from the first. A few adventurous men – and women – went to and from Bombay by the Red Sea route. Using any available means to reach Suez, they crossed by camel or donkey and took ship at Alexandria for England. The inconvenience of this tortuous route did not stop the determined, for it was significantly shorter than the Cape. To prove the point, the Bombay Government built locally the 410-ton *Hugh Lindsay*, the first vessel to steam from Bombay to Suez. But the four round voyages between 1830 and 1833 made by Captain John Wilson of the Indian Navy showed that vessels would have to be much larger and more powerful to withstand the monsoon seasons.[87] While argument between the Calcutta and Bombay Presidencies about their routes grew more heated, a third scheme was put forward: river navigation up the Euphrates and then by way of Syria to the Mediterranean. Many voices all clamouring for government attention in London could not be ignored, especially after *Hugh Lindsay*, slow and inefficient though it was, brought mail to Bombay from London in what was then the unbelievably short time of fifty-nine days.[88] The Government was pressed to take action that would satisfy the demand for regular communication with India.

As a counterpoint to these demands, British merchants engaged in the China trade were conducting their own campaign for the abolition of the monopoly over the China trade enjoyed by the East India Company. In 1813 its monopoly over Indian trade had been ended after a parliamentary review. Another review was due to take place in 1833, and from 1829 onwards the China lobby was very active in Britain. A country-wide campaign was launched by William Jardine for free access to the China trade. Jardine, who was a partner in the firm of Jardine, Matheson & Company (often referred to as Jardines), the most important of the 'private' China traders, led the promotion. Another prominent advocate was George Gerrard de Hochepied Larpent, partner in Cockerell & Company, a firm engaged extensively in the India and China trades. He was chairman of the influential East India Trade Committee in the 1820s and of the East India and China Association when it was formed in 1836. Parliament duly ended the East India Company's monopoly in 1833.[89]

Success in this campaign served to impress on the public how much Britain's trade balance depended on trade with India and China; and since the East India Company had to remit £4 million each year to Britain by way of tribute, there was no doubt about the importance of their interdependence. These facts strengthened the case for improved communication with the East. In 1834, Parliament ordered the East India Company to provide a line of steamships from Bombay to Suez, the cost to be shared between the two governments. Admiralty steam packets that plied in the Mediterranean between Gibraltar and Malta extended this line to Alexandria so that mail brought through Egypt could be picked up. These arrangements were intended to subdue the discordant steam lobbies while the Government tried to decide which of the proposed schemes would provide a permanent chain of communication.[90]

The scales soon tilted in favour of the Red Sea route, although Calcutta and Madras complained of being deprived of a direct steam route to Suez, and some still wanted the Cape route. However, when in 1835 the route on either side of Suez began to be worked by warships, there was much criticism of the service the two governments were giving the public. Warships were not fitted up for civilian passengers; nor did they have any space for merchandise. Beset by financial troubles, the East India Company was reluctant to spend any more money on the mail service. Such indifference angered the mercantile community, and to satisfy the growing demand for steam transport, one or two small private steamers ran erratically between Bombay and Suez while campaigners pressed for the line to be handed over to a commercial company capable of providing a more appropriate service. In 1836, 'most of the principal houses connected with India in the city of London' proposed to run a line of steamers themselves, though nothing came of it.[91]

Parliament considered the matter again in 1837. Bourne, Willcox and Anderson used this inquiry to promote their own interest by making sure that the efficiency and economy of Peninsular Steam's service was used as an example of what private enterprise under contract could do. More than that, they sent agents to provincial towns 'to get up public petitions against the existing line to Bombay' by the Indian Government's vessels. Lord William Bentinck, one of the most ardent advocates of steam communication who chaired the parliamentary committee on his return from India, was, according to Anderson, 'very urgent' that Peninsular Steam should undertake the short route to India at once. But such a hasty act would have been foolhardy. Just embarked on the Peninsular mail contract, its owners 'were unwilling to grapple with more than they were reasonably able to accomplish'. Besides, a contract to India was not yet on offer. At Bentinck's request, however, they 'furnished him . . . with much detailed information' for his evidence before the parliamentary committee. The outcome of the inquiry was to recommend an extended steam service with government support.[92]

Expectation that a new system of government aid for long-distance steam shipping was about to come into force sparked off intense interest among entrepreneurs and owners.[93] There was general concern about the backwardness of British shipping compared with that of the USA, both in tonnage and design; and this fact, with its strategic implications, led to the decision to stimulate steam shipping by subsidizing the cost of extending steam to the great routes of the world.

The transatlantic connection

Public interest in the North Atlantic mail contract had already been aroused by the time tenders for it were invited in 1839, and shipowners were among those willing to invest in experimental voyages so as to be ready to compete for the prize. The first commercial steamship company specifically formed to build a vessel – *Great Western* – for the North Atlantic was set up in Bristol by the engineer Isambard Kingdom Brunel and his backers. Interest in London was muted. Meanwhile Dr Junius Smith, an American living in London, tried to find supporters for his own British & North American Company but only succeeded at the third attempt, and even then it was 'hard work to prevail upon McGregor Laird and others to join him'. However, J.R. Pim and his friends Paul Twigg of Dublin and James Beale of Cork did not need quite so much persuasion, and all became directors of Smith's company. Pim also acted as Smith's agent in Liverpool and for Brunel's *Great Western* in London.[94]

All would-be competitors required vessels of great power and large tonnage. Brunel's *Great Western* (1,775 tons) and British & North American's *British Queen* (2,300) were both building in 1837, and there was great excitement in the spring of 1838 when the first voyages across the Atlantic by these two vessels were due to take place. Brunel's *Great Western* was ready for sea but Smith's *British Queen* was not.[95]

J.R. Pim, ever resourceful, chartered the much smaller *Sirius* (940 tons) – one of his St George Company's new vessels intended for a line to St Petersburg – for British & North American. Dispatched from London and Cork to New York, *Sirius*'s arrival at New York a few hours in advance of *Great Western* created a sensation, and the vessel had the honour of being the first to prove the technological viability of an all-steam crossing from East to West.

Not to be left behind, Charles Wye Williams and Francis Carleton, joint MDs of City of Dublin, set up their Transatlantic Steamship Company in Liverpool. They did not then have a very large ship but they too dispatched a small and reliable vessel – *Royal William* (708 tons) owned by City of Dublin – for at least two voyages to New York later in 1838 until *Liverpool* (1,140 tons) came on to the market. Commissioned for the Atlantic service by Sir John Tobin, a well-known Liverpool shipowner, *Liverpool* was sold in September 1838 to three Irish owners acting for Transatlantic: James Ferrier of British & Irish, Richard Williams (Charles's brother) and James Hartley, partner in Bourne's land and sea enterprises. This 'new splendid and powerful Steamer' made its first crossing in February 1839.[96]

There is no direct evidence that Richard Bourne was involved in this venture or that he intended to bid for the Atlantic contract himself. Towards the end of 1838, however, he asked John Scott, the Greenock shipbuilder, to build a steamer of 500–560 tons (excluding engines) to be launched in August 1839. Scott agreed but when the specification arrived the builder found in it a whole catalogue of features not to his liking. He particularly objected to the fact that the vessel would take double the time and cost twice as much as *Tagus* (built by him for Bourne in 1837); and the new hull would have to be built in a 'system and style of Work . . . so different to what is followed out here in Clyde, that our workmen would take months of practice before they could fall in to a readiness of Working anything like their own accustomed way'. He returned the specification with the hope that Bourne would be sensible and order a vessel 'as the *Tagus* was done'.[97] This tantalising evidence suggests that Bourne had a greater scheme in mind than the middle-distance Iberian service. That the specification was sent to Scott from Liverpool, not London, raises the question of whether Williams had a part in Bourne's scheme. Why otherwise did Hartley take an interest in *Liverpool*? He was very close to Bourne and unlikely to go into such an investment without Bourne's knowledge. Did Bourne mean to become a partner with Williams's *Liverpool* and the new vessel that Scott would not build? There is another mystifying hint about Bourne wanting to take his chance on the Atlantic, this time without Williams. At the end of

1839 he and Hartley published a prospectus for a new company with a capital of £250,000 to fill the gap that existed between Galway, Limerick and London, between which there was not a single steamship connection. It is tempting to surmise that Bourne saw how useful Galway or Limerick could be as a springboard for South America and the West Indies, where his wife had connections.[98] But events on the Atlantic and elsewhere had gathered momentum by that time and no more was heard of this west of Ireland proposal.

Meanwhile Pim, encouraged by the success of *Sirius*, competed on behalf of his St George Company with Brunel for the North Atlantic contract when tenders were advertised in 1838, but in the event the Admiralty rejected both. Samuel Cunard, however, a Canadian merchant and shipowner, was waiting in the wings. In 1831, the first time he crossed the Atlantic, he ordered the first two steamers for his fleet. After that he came to England for a few months every year for business and leisure. He established agents in Liverpool and Glasgow, had a small office in Ludgate Hill in the City of London, and rooms in a hotel at 206 Piccadilly where he was 'inclined to mingle with London's literary set'. A rich man, he also had a number of friends of high rank in Canada and Britain. His home in Canada was Halifax and, some years before, he had made friends with Edward Parry, an official in the Canadian Government.

When Cunard came to London in the summer of 1838, the one man he wanted to see above all his friends was Parry who had been knighted and was the comptroller of steam machinery and packet service in the Admiralty. Returning to his home town full of information about contracts and possibilities, Cunard tried to raise capital there and in Boston, but failed. At first, he was resigned to try again the following year. However, an advertisement in *The Times* arrived in Halifax two weeks after the London paper's date (8 November) stating that tenders had to be deposited in the Admiralty on 15 December, and Cunard suddenly realized that he had no time to lose. Cunard set off for London at once, although he knew that he would be out of time. In London, he was told that two companies had tendered, but Parry did not think either was satisfactory and Cunard was still in the race. Brunel and Pim had offered a monthly service to New York via Halifax, the tender's requirement. Cunard proposed a twice-a-month service to Boston via Halifax, starting on 1 May 1840, for £55,000, and Parry said that he 'might be prepared to entertain a proposition of this kind'. Sir Charles Wood (Chancellor of the Exchequer) and Sir Francis Baring (First Lord of the Admiralty) then 'spent many hours [and] a great deal of pains' with Cunard, helping him for 'a great deal more service than the other parties were to perform' and calculating that he would need £65,000 from the Government.

The next requirement was a builder. Cunard wanted a 'plain and comfortable boat, not the least unnecessary expense for show'. He was introduced by East India Company friends to Robert Napier in Govan, Glasgow, and ordered four big steamers. After that, he was granted the mail contract for seven years, and it was signed and sealed in May 1839. The last and most important step was to find capital. David MacIver, a Scot resident in Liverpool, and his partner George Burns in Glasgow came forward, together with thirty-one others, to form the British & North American Royal Mail Steam Packet Company, a name that was quickly cut down to 'Cunard'. Apparently there were no objections to this contract being granted entirely by private arrangement, nor for having the advantage of being privy to the prices of the other contenders,[99] Pim and Brunel having given the Admiralty some idea of what such a contract should cost.

Although Williams sent *Liverpool* to and from New York on a few more voyages in 1839, the ship was inefficient, and after Cunard got the contract the vessel became unemployable on the Atlantic. In consequence, 'this new Transatlantic Company proving to be a losing concern, was broken up . . . No private association could be sufficient for such a service' unless supported by an adequate public subsidy. A second large companion steamer, *United States* (1,673 tons), intended for the Transatlantic Company and still on the stocks, faced an equally bleak future.[100] Fortuitously, however, Williams's failure to win the North Atlantic contract turned out to be his and Bourne's gain, for arguments about the eastern route reached a decisive point late in 1839. As will be seen in the next section, Peninsular Steam was asked by the Admiralty to draw up a plan for a commercial service between England and Alexandria, thus giving Bourne and his partners the opportunity to shape the operational elements of the Mediterranean contract to suit themselves. Anderson recorded that 'the originators of this Company were enabled to submit to the Government a plan and proposal for an accelerated transmission of these Mails between England and Alexandria, by vessels of such a size and power as would adapt them for the fit commencement of that more extended communication . . .'.

Having himself laid down the size and power of vessels required for the Mediterranean line, Bourne needed large steamers in a hurry. Of the five such steamers in existence, only *Liverpool* and *United States* were available. Williams wanted employment for them; Bourne offered it. A scheme to benefit both parties was quickly drawn up. James Hartley and Francis Carleton appear to have been the active negotiators in bringing about a merger of the two interests they represented, though Bourne and Williams would not have left so important a matter entirely to others. It is not clear when the first overtures were made, but a conclusion was reached in the weeks between the private approval of the plan on 24 February and the first formal meeting in London of the two parties on 23 March 1840. By that date, it was agreed that if the mail contract to Alexandria was secured, the Peninsular Steam and Transatlantic companies would merge to form a new company with a large capital. At this first meeting, two matters of great importance were discussed. One related to 'the pending negotiation for the Admiralty Contract to Alexandria', without which no merger would take place. The other, much more difficult, was how to deal with a rival group that embraced powerful interests in the City of London and in India. With the Governor of the Bank of England Timothy Abraham Curtis as its chairman, the competition was formidable indeed.[101]

The London connection

The origins of this London company lay in the pressure groups organized by merchants and officials in London and India in the early 1820s. Impatient at the constant bickering among campaigners at the Indian end, magnates in the City attempted in 1836 to take charge of the proposed enterprise themselves. Though their preliminary proposals for the Red Sea route were favourably received by the British Board of Control (the government watchdog over Indian affairs) they were unable to go ahead with it. Towards the end of 1836, a second initiative seemed to have a much better chance. A public meeting in the City at the Jerusalem Coffee House on 12 October resulted in the appointment of a committee to make plans for a steam service to India; and at the London Tavern on 18 January 1837 the committee was authorized to carry them out. Both meetings were chaired by Curtis, and he listed a provisional but imposing directorate of merchants and bankers which put forward a detailed scheme for a steam service from London to all three Indian Presidencies via the Red Sea. Supporters of this scheme were dubbed 'Comprehensives', a name taken from the 1837 attempt by Lord William Bentinck and others to keep the many parties together.

Opposition from the East India Company was the main impediment to progress. Curtis insisted on having the Bombay–Suez line, run since 1835 with Indian naval vessels, handed over to him, but if that line were taken away the Indian Navy would become redundant and its loss would strip the East India Company of its last vestige of power. Moreover, in the campaigns that had systematically diminished the East India Company's power in 1813 and 1833, it was the merchants in India and their London correspondents who had called the loudest for the company to be brought down, so there was no reason for the East India Company to help Curtis and his friends to achieve their aims at its expense. In October 1839 he received an uncompromising refusal: the East India Company would encourage 'any well-devised measures' to extend steam communication, but the Bombay–Suez line was not negotiable.[102] Though this lengthy and sterile argument delayed the formal constitution of Curtis's company, the persistent disagreement among the various steam committees in India and their backers in England was a seemingly immovable obstacle, since every step he wished to take had to be approved by Curtis's Indian constituents, some of whom had already put down deposits for shares in the proposed company.

At the end of 1839, high politics intervened to bring the question of an eastern contract to a head. The convention signed by Britain and France in June 1839, a landmark in postal history, allowed mail between England and India to pass unopened through France. This route to India by steam was now confirmed: in the Mediterranean, mails would go in British warships or French steamers from Marseilles to Alexandria, across Egypt to Suez and thence to Bombay or Calcutta by ships of the East India Company. But these arrangements, designed to expedite important official dispatches to and from the East, gave no comfort whatever to the mercantile community at either end. Heavy mails and samples, and small but valuable parcels of specie or merchandise were not carried by warships, and even private correspondence was sometimes refused. This meant that French merchants were able to get trade information several days earlier than their British counterparts, quite apart from the exorbitant cost of French postage.[103]

Complaints from merchants in London gave Curtis reason to press for an 'all-British' sea mail route (whatever that was supposed to mean: if he meant via Egypt, it had to go through Egypt which wasn't British; if he meant the Cape route he forgot about the technical problems) and to reinforce his case by emphasizing the 'patriotic' factor in such an important undertaking. Rumbles of discontent at the number and superiority of French steamers in the Mediterranean also provided grist for Lord Palmerston's mill. Three French steamers to Alexandria each month smacked of 'the French . . . by these Packets getting Possession of the Mediterranean'; this 'must have had a considerable Effect' on the decision of the Government to extend the line to the East in 1835.[104] Despite his much-publicized friendship with France after the Quadruple Alliance was signed, Palmerston remained deeply suspicious of the French, especially in Egypt and the eastern Mediterranean. This area had become particularly sensitive in 1839 because the initial success of a revolt by the Pasha of Egypt against his overlord, the Sultan of Turkey, threatened to upset the interests of the Great Powers. French reactions were carefully watched, while Russia's activity on behalf of the Sultan aroused anxiety about the Tsar's intentions. Britain's capture of Aden early in the year was seen as a defensive bulwark against Russian expansion. Added to these concerns, Britain went to war against China and Afghanistan. An efficient mail service in the Mediterranean was wanted as soon as possible not only to meet the demands of merchants and bankers but for reasons of state. In November, Peninsular Steam was asked if its sailing dates to Spain and Portugal could be changed to harmonise with, and thereby improve, the elaborate arrangements for the naval mail service in the Mediterranean which were clearly not working well.

This was Bourne's chance. He refused to upset the existing Peninsular schedule, but as Peninsular Steam's contract would expire in September, why not instead offer to work the entire line from London to Alexandria, exactly what he and his friends wanted to do? Harassed by delays and complications in the Mediterranean, the Admiralty asked Bourne to submit plans and proposals. Bourne promptly obliged. The Treasury, having seen them, sent them back to the Admiralty to start the process of setting up tenders for a contract. Admiralty officers welcomed the scheme presented to them because, they asserted, they had little experience of passenger traffic, and 'nothing' of insurance, interest, depreciation, wear and tear, cargoes and freights: in the Admiralty there were no mercantile men.[105] Ten days later, the 'Five Principal Officers' were told to suggest conditions for an 'intended Contract' for the England–Alexandria line 'as speedily as possible'. The principal officers were again chivvied 'to hasten [their] report' on conditions, and on 24 February, Peninsular Steam was asked to state terms for conveying mails and passengers. Though this was in order to prepare the tenders that would be put up to public competition,[106] as the Treasury was 'satisfied with the manner in which the Contract [had] been executed' by Peninsular Steam, the company should stand by. This was a good hint to Bourne, supposing that he had not already been privately told that he would get the larger contract.

Consultation between and within the various departments was gone through remarkably quickly,[107] and the rapidity with which the Government acted appears to have taken Bourne by surprise. Anderson said that the contract 'fell, almost by accident, into the hands of the originators' of the provisional P&O. To fend off an open competition with the 'Comprehensives', Bourne first tried to strike a bargain with the Admiralty, but his price was too high. Then Anderson was sent to tell James McKillop, a director in Curtis's company, that Peninsular Steam had a 'junction' with the Transatlantic Company and that the title of the new company was Peninsular & Oriental Steam Navigation Company. Would the 'Comprehensives' like to 'form a junction' with P&O 'by becoming shareholders . . . and appointing some Individuals . . . to be the Directors of it and to represent them in its management'? A distribution of one year's subsidy (at least £60,000, taking the Peninsular and Alexandria contracts together) was to be a sweetener. The letter Anderson wrote a few days after his talk with MacKillop was not answered. Curtis was so tied up with the various steam committees and the East India Company that he was unable to say anything.[108] Thus on 23 March, at the first formal meeting in London of the Peninsular Steam and Transatlantic companies, their merger was confirmed and a discussion held about the urgent issue of what price for the contract the new company should offer when tenders were advertised. It was decided that the price should not go below £30,000 per annum.[109]

That settled, the more intractable problem they faced was what to do about Curtis and the 'Comprehensives'. A three-part merger was still the best solution. If this could be achieved, they would avoid a contest for the contract, and capital already subscribed for Curtis's proposed company could be transferred to the new merged entity.[110] In April it was clear that the London party and their Indian associates, never fully united, had dissolved into irreconcilable factions. Curtis could neither reason with them nor take decisions without them. On 14 April, however, he decided to reject all of Anderson's options. This 'all or nothing' response was taken by the Peninsular Steam and Transatlantic parties to mean that the 'door was shut' as far as a triple merger was concerned, though as it turned out a year-long series of efforts would eventually bring these competitors into the Irish fold.

For the time being, then, the most prudent move was to cement the union of the two Irish companies as agreed in March. Together they would be stronger and better able to withstand any onslaught from Curtis. Bourne convened representatives of the Irish companies for their second meeting in London on 23 April to conclude the essential formalities for their merger. It was agreed that the new company would be named the Peninsular & Oriental Steam Navigation Company, with a capital of £1 million in 20,000 shares of £50 each; that the parties bringing stock-in-ships to the merged company should receive paid-up shares to an agreed value; and that a charter of incorporation should be applied for. Willcox, Anderson and Carleton were appointed MDs under the control of the board of directors.[111]

Advertisements for tenders for the Alexandria mail contract had appeared a week earlier. One of the conditions of the tender was that the service should be carried out by two powerful vessels as stipulated in Peninsular Steam's plan; another was that the contract should start in September. As Curtis and the 'Comprehensives' did not have any vessels at all, they asked the Admiralty for extra time. This request was refused. P&O was later accused of having 'excluded all possibility of a competition' because the conditions in the tender could only be met by themselves. This may have had some truth in it. Bourne and Williams were past masters at using stratagems to avoid competition, and there might well have been an 'arrangement' to ensure that P&O's bid would be chosen. In this case, however, the 'Comprehensives' had been frittering away their time and energy for years and it might take them a few years more to decide what to do. In contrast, P&O's founders had vessels at hand, experience behind them, and the Government wanted a prompt start. There were three other contenders for the contract: J.R. Pim at £51,000, McGregor Laird at £49,000 and a G.M. Jackson at £37,950. In the negotiations after the tenders were deposited, P&O was told that £36,000 would be 'next to certain' but further discussion settled with £38,000 for the first year, £36,000 the second, and each of the next three years £1,000 would be taken off, leaving the subsidy at £33,000.[112] When Southampton became the mail port (at first the Admiralty insisted on Falmouth for two years) the company was given £2,000 for the extra expense; and when P&O stopped calling to the Ionian Islands in 1842, it lost £3,500.

Great progress was made during the spring and summer in setting up the new line – establishment of coal depots and agencies in the Mediterranean, engagement of masters and crews, and fitting out of vessels in readiness for the start of the contract in September. Anderson had taken 'preliminary steps with a view to procuring limited responsibility under a Charter of Incorporation for the shareholders in the proposed amalgamated Company'; he had also been talking to bankers and had 'reason to hope in the event of the Company procuring the Contract to Alexandria that an advance of money by way of a Loan for 6 or 12 months might be obtained thro London Bankers to a considerable amount on the guarantee of the Company and Directors'. Peninsular Steam continued to run to Iberian ports in accordance with the 1837 contract, but from 1 September when all operations came under P&O, the smaller company was subsumed in the larger, and all accounts thereafter were made up jointly. All the 64ths holders in *Iberia*, except de Zulueta who was taken on to P&O's Board, were given cheques for their shares in that vessel and did not have anything to do with the new company.[113] A complicated transaction was necessary before *United States* could be legally sold to P&O, but the vessel was in P&O's hands as *Oriental* in time for it to transport some troops to Malta in August, and to inaugurate the mail service to Alexandria at the beginning of September.[114]

First steps east of Suez

On 2 May 1840, the board (only Bourne, Hartley, Willcox and Anderson were present on that day) decided that 'the speedy establishment of a communication by steam vessels between Suez & Ceylon, Madras & Calcutta is highly expedient as an auxiliary to the line of steam vessels about to be established to Alexandria', and resolved that

> preliminary measures by procuring estimates, specifications & proposals &c be therefore taken by the Managing Directors to enable the Board of Directors of the Peninsular & Oriental Steam Navigation Company to contract for the building & equipment of a vessel of 1600 tons burthen and 500 horse power immediately the pending arrangement with Government for the Alexandria Mail Contract shall have been completed in order to commence with such vessel a communication on the other side of the Isthmus with the Eastern Presidencies of India & Ceylon in connection with the line to Alexandria.

The founders were determined to succeed against all obstacles.[115] Anderson was deputed to open negotiations with Admiralty, the Treasury and the East India Company about an extension east of Suez.[116]

Throughout these months of intense activity, the envy and anger of the 'Comprehensives' dogged P&O's progress, the various factions busily pursuing their own interests in India and Britain. In April 1840, one large group of Calcutta merchants with London support decided to build their own steamer, *Precursor*, in Glasgow so that they could run an independent line east of Suez as soon she was ready. This in itself constituted a threat because that vessel might be stationed on the Indian side before P&O was able to forestall her. A smaller consortium of merchants trading in India bought *India*, launched in 1839 and completed by its builders after the original owners had gone bankrupt, and sent the vessel out in September with the same object in view. The third faction, the City magnates, appeared to be adrift, masters without men. However, in April they wrote a prospectus for their East Indian Steam Navigation Company and, although it was in an embryonic state, it was they who posed the real danger. Cunard after all had had his coterie of friends who helped him to get the North Atlantic contract, and the South Atlantic contract had been won with even greater ease, by Royal Mail. Charles Wood, Secretary to the Admiralty, told the House of Commons in August 1839 that 'certain persons' had come to the Treasury and the Admiralty and said they would perform the duty (of the West Indies and the whole northern part of South America and of the southern USA) for £240,000; and this was agreed to. The 'certain persons' included Sir Francis Baring and the Rothschilds, not persons to argue with, and, like Cunard, they were granted the contract before they had either company or ship. Curtis attached a copy of Wood's statement in a letter to the East India Company declaring that 'a service of that kind can be much better carried out by a private company'; Royal Mail 'had no existence until the terms of the contract were settled', and he wanted *his* 'prospective company' treated in the same way.[117] 'It must be admitted', Willcox and Anderson wrote to their agent Samuel Briggs & Co. in Alexandria, 'that [P&O] possess both in means and in experience very great advantages over any other party who yet appeared in the field'. Nevertheless, P&O's fear was that Curtis's influence as governor of the Bank of England would be enough to bring about a coup similar to the Royal Mail's for the Indian portion of the route; he might even dislodge P&O from the Mediterranean.[118]

In April 1840 Curtis and his 'Comprehensive' friends had refused to discuss a merger with P&O. In July, P&O tried another approach to Curtis. Having resolved to build a suitably large and powerful vessel for the Suez leg of the route, the founders proposed a scheme whereby Curtis, Larpent and their associates in India would contribute to the cost. This would ease the financial burden and ensure that P&O had a stake in working the line east of Suez. It was rejected by Curtis, and to show that he could fight with 'intelligence, energy and opulence' Curtis intended to go his own way. That Curtis did not have a 'way' of his own, however, and therefore could never act, is shown by his handling of a chance he let go in January 1839, when P&O was not even on the horizon. Captain James Barber retired from the Indian Navy and became a member of Curtis's provisional directorate with the title of superintendent of steam vessels (although there were no vessels to look after). He played a key role in trying to bring together the disparate interests among the 'Comprehensives' by organizing 'a numerous and highly respectable meeting' in London with Curtis in the chair. Various resolutions about a line to India were accepted, but Curtis could do nothing until he had the opinions of all the factions in Britain and India. It took *eighteen months* – until July 1840 – after the meeting before Curtis could announce his East Indian Steam Company, indicative of the many obstacles he had to confront, but also of his poor business instincts.[119] By this time P&O was about to sign the contract to Alexandria, so if the rival company was hoping to frighten off P&O, it was clear that Curtis had not yet taken the measure of his adversaries.

Nothing was left to chance in the P&O camp. As soon as the closing date in May for tenders had passed without a bid from Curtis, P&O told the Admiralty that plans to extend the line of communication to India were in train, thus putting down a marker in advance of the lengthy negotiations that this expansion would involve. By November 1840, many unresolved problems remained, but the Government agreed in principle to P&O's proposals. The charter of incorporation, ready to be sealed, confirmed the commitment that enjoined the company to start a service to and from India within the next two years.[120]

On 19 November, Sir John Nicholl Robert Campbell, KCMG, was 'to be invited to become a Director of the Company', and the next week, as a director, was 'put on the proceedings'. Also in November, with P&O's prospectus about to be published and shares issued, directors judged that the time had come to make another overture to Curtis and his friends. Anderson, 'acting in [his] individual capacity, and on [his] responsibility' published *A Letter to the Directors of the Projected East Indian Steam Navigation Company*, apparently in a fit of impulse. This pamphlet reproduced letters between MacKillop and P&O from February and April, embellished with a scathing commentary. Reminding the 'Comprehensives' and other factions of opportunities lost, Anderson was contemptuous of the feeble and inept management displayed by those 'respectable names'. All that they had done, apart from trying to obstruct P&O, was to quarrel among themselves. He taunted them for having failed to achieve 'the formation of a vessel or pin of an engine' in the seventeen years since the question of steam navigation to India had first begun to discussed. A 'numerous body of wealthy individuals, now resident in this country ... have derived their fortunes from ... India', but were incapable of providing the communication for which India was crying out. Obstruction from the East India Company was no excuse: 'the route is open to all'. Inability to get anything done was due to their projects 'having never before fallen into *practical* hands, conversant with Steam Navigation on a large scale' – an oblique reference to Bourne and Williams who, though 'unconnected with India', would in little more than a year bring Calcutta within six weeks of London because they had 'great practical knowledge' to back up their 'extensive means'. P&O had taken the lead, for 'its direction is in the hands of individuals possessed of such ample practical experience in conducting Steam enterprises of magnitude, as to guarantee the judicious and beneficial extension of its operations'. Those were the men 'who will build ships and construct engines instead of entering into interminable discussions'. It was still not too late to join P&O: 'a seat in the Direction of an undertaking of such a magnitude and character, is an object not beneath the ambition of a commercial man, however high his standing'.[121]

Perhaps Curtis did not see this 'Letter to the Directors'. If he did, its barbs made no difference to the November discussions. They began with a friendly token: Willcox wrote to Curtis telling him that 'very probably' George Larpent or John Studholme Brownrigg, MP (also of Cockerell & Co.), would be P&O's chairman 'if he comes forward in such manner as to entitle him to that compliment'. Then Curtis, East Indian Steam's chairman, J.P. Larkins, its deputy, and two directors – Captain Alexander Nairne and Alderman John Pirie – started negotiations 'officially'. P&O's board offered seats for three directors, one of them kept for Curtis because his 'respectable name' would afford proof 'of a union of all parties'. But Curtis evidently failed to appreciate how strong P&O's position had become, for he tried to lay down conditions: he wanted more seats, and alterations to the deed of settlement. Willcox told him that the deed was settled and it was 'impractical in the present advanced state of the undertaking' for him to have more seats. P&O's directors did 'not desire to couple [the undertaking] with any conditions'. Willcox made light of the contentious issue of transferring capital from East Indian Steam to P&O. He and his colleagues felt 'independent . . . and competent to carry out the further objects of the undertaking', though an injection of 'Indian' money would consolidate the union, and P&O 'would consider it more satisfactory' that a board of directors in Calcutta should be 'in conjunction with parties connected with India'. Correspondence carried on the arguments but showed that there was still no meeting of minds. Willcox was surprised that Curtis could not open his eyes and see that he had lost the game. The purpose of the talks even at this late date was 'in the hope of *eventually* joining these jarring views into one of harmony', not to lay hands on East Indian Steam's capital, for 'there is no difficulty in raising [capital] here upon a well governed Plan, already at work in experienced hands with Government Contracts & a charter of Incorporation; we seek *Indian* Capital, because its proprietors would be our best customers in the traffic between the two countries'. Willcox was sure that London subscribers 'who really wish to see Steam Communication with India will join us'. Indian subscribers, however, were a different case: these potential shareholders were being deliberately prevented from joining P&O by hostile agents directed by 'Comprehensives' whose aim was to undermine P&O's credibility. Although 3,000 P&O shares had been earmarked for Indian subscribers earlier in the year and advertised in local newspapers, very little had reached P&O. 'To speak frankly', wrote Willcox in a letter of clarification, 'it is a matter of public notoriety that the subscriptions here from India . . . [are] nearly all, if not all, interdicted from participations in the Mediter[ranean] part of the line'. Willcox had nothing more to say to Curtis except that he could 'join or not as you may approve or disapprove it'. As to Curtis's wish to call in legal experts to resolve the differences between the two companies, Willcox confessed that 'having perhaps peculiar notions upon the Subject . . . but I have my misgivings how far a reference to Lawyers will contribute to the immediate union of all parties'.[122]

These were fruitless negotiations and Curtis bowed out, leaving Pirie, Nairne, Robert Thurburn (another East Indian Steam director) and George Larpent to make a final decision. Thurburn had been invited to join the board of directors in November but first he wanted to see what the others would do. The MDs then proceeded with their plans on the assumption that P&O would get neither the 'Comprehensive' vessel *Precursor* nor a significant tranche of its capital. As a matter of policy, the board 'did not wish to burthen' the company with a vessel of 'inferior quality'; the MDs rather chose to take advantage of the 'great advances . . . only recently made . . . [in] the science of steam ship building'. Thus the first call on P&O's issued capital in January 1841 was earmarked for 2 ships of 2,000 tons and 520 hp, as the charter demanded.

No ships could be built, however, without an intimation that a contract would be forthcoming. In the cold light of day (Anderson was out of the country), the MDs realized that P&O must merge with East Indian Steam, partly to stamp out its remnants and partly to bring its *Precursor*, building in Glasgow, into P&O, because very few such vessels – some said there were only five in being – could be purchased.

In February 1841, then, a deputation made up of P&O's MDs and Nairne, Pirie, Thurburn and Larpent went to India House in Leadenhall Street, the City headquarters of the East India Company. They reminded the 'Court' (the East India Company's board of directors) that Curtis had petitioned it for financial help in 1839 and was turned away because of the chaotic state of his and the other factions. Now the deputation declared that there was still 'a chance of . . . amalgamating', while P&O assured the Court that in the course of the next year the communication between Suez and Calcutta [would] be opened' by two expensive vessels and other necessaries. This enterprise was 'not one of an experimental character'; it would cost nearly £500,000. The Court was convinced, and in March granted P&O £100,000 over 5 years. The first tranche of £20,000 would be paid to P&O as soon as the first vessel reached Calcutta from Suez. If P&O obtained a mail contract from the British Government, the remaining tranches would be subsumed in it.[123]

With this guarantee, P&O commissioned *Hindostan* (2,017 gross tons, 520 ihp) and the following year its sister *Bentinck* was ordered. Their hulls were built in Liverpool by Thomas Wilson and the engines by Fawcett, Preston & Company, all under the expert eye of Charles Wye Williams and his engineer John Shaw, to accommodate 102 first class passengers plus their servants. Their boilers were fitted with his patent smoke condensers, another of his inventions that was generally adopted later. Both were made of wood and propelled by paddle wheels and well able 'to contend against the monsoons in the Indian Seas', for the MDs held 'firmly to the opinion [again, from Williams] that none but vessels of the largest size and power can be depended upon'.[124] These vessels were the first of the 'splendid ships' that were to become famous all over the world.

Both steamers were dispatched in style, with important personages invited in 1842 to a *déjeuner* on *Hindostan* and in 1843 to an 'entertainment' for *Bentinck*. For the latter, the MDs invited the Duke of Buccleuch, cabinet ministers, directors of the East India Company and 'such other influential parties' as were appropriate. The occasion was intended to present the inauguration of the regular service between England and India as an important event in the life of the nation, and made much of P&O's 'patriotic efforts to shorten the distance between Europe and the East' (from 4–5 months to 40 days, Southampton–Calcutta) and to confer a 'vast benefit' on the country and its commerce. *Bentinck* was a showpiece for luxurious travel in the age of steam. Her interior was 'especially elegant, commodious and complete', each cabin having its marble-covered basin stand, mirrors, drawers, writing apparatus and venetian blinds; the gilding in the saloon was 'gorgeous', all the fittings 'correspondingly superb'; hot and cold shower baths and a 'well selected library' added to passengers' comfort; and, for their safety, the ship was fitted with water-tight iron bulkheads, another of Williams's contributions to early steamship construction.[125] *Hindostan* was on station in Calcutta in December 1842, just in time to fulfil the charter's stipulations, having arrived in 91 days (only 63 of which were under steam), and began to ply to and from Suez every 2 months. *Bentinck* followed in 1843, and in that year P&O ran the first regular two-month steam service on the Calcutta–Suez line.[126,127]

The end of East Indian Steam

Now we must pick up the story of the crumbling East Indian Steam Company after Curtis left the scene. Following the deputation of February 1841 to the offices of the East India Company, not only that company but Pirie and Nairne were convinced that P&O's plans for a Suez–Calcutta service were more than mere words, and on 2 March, J.P. Larkins sent a message 'recommending a Union' with P&O; and a week later, after further exchanges, P&O concluded that 'the spirit of the request . . . had been so satisfactorily responded to . . . [and] the conditions upon which the proposed union was based [had] been complied with': the end was near. Before the union could come about, however, there had to be an 'official dissolution' of East Indian Steam; the two directors who would be received into P&O should be named, and the subscription list should open again so that Indian Steam money could be transferred to P&O. In the event, Larkins managed to get three directors (Nairne, Pirie and Thurburn) on to P&O's board, all of whom had been on the deputation in February. Between them, according to Captain Andrew Henderson, they had 789 £50 shares out of P&O's first issue of 6,300 shares. Thus on 31 March 1841, the struggle with the 'Comprehensives' was over and East Indian Steam had come to an end. In December, P&O received a cheque for £12,500, the balance of funds remitted from those persons who had put money into the defunct company.[128]

In March 1841, Larpent was very anxious not to be left out in the cold. On 30 March he and Mr Small (of Small, Colquhoun & Co.) begged Willcox to wait for an answer from the 'Indians' in Calcutta before P&O 'finally completed the Directory'. Next day, Willcox wrote to say that 'not without regret' the board was 'unable to comply' with their wishes. P&O had tried very hard for nearly a year 'to maintain the best understanding with the *Precursor* party in India' and with Larpent personally:

> We sought the junction because it would tranquillize the minds of that large portion of the public interested in this great national undertaking and because we think that it is one of so gigantic a nature that to carry it through efficiently to their satisfaction all parties must unite into *one* . . . In a mere pecuniary point of view . . . it would best suit the interests of our Company to keep aloof from the *Precursor* . . . We are willing to concede that you and Mr Small's entry into our Directory does not bind [Indian Steam] to bring in their vessel or form any junction . . . In short the whole matter has at length arrived at a point of maturity which will not brook a further delay to 4 months.

Small backed down and let Larpent be unanimously elected by the board as P&O's first chairman on 11 May 1841,[129] though it was not until 1844 that *Precursor* was sold to P&O, for a knock-down sum.

Subsequently, P&O had to bear two sources of irritation for many years. The first was Captain Henderson of the *India* group, the last remnant of the opposition, who also required a drawn-out settlement. P&O bought *India* at a low price, too, and Henderson, a part-owner and *India*'s agent in London, vented his resentment at this by making mischief for P&O. His constant complaint was that British shipowners in India were ignored by the Admiralty while P&O was showered with favours, and at every opportunity he hinted at the company's malfeasance and shady schemes, their getting of contracts, for example, 'by agitation, newspaper agency and fallacious statements'.[130] His was the longest witness testimony at the Select Committee on Contract Packets in 1849, much of it spent in spewing his venom on P&O, but though the committee listened, its members took little notice of him.

The second source was Captain James Barber, though Anderson was the real culprit, not Barber. Barber was in the East India Company for 23 years, then for 12 in command of a sailing ship,[131] and in 1840 was the superintendent of steam vessels on East Indian Steam's directorate (although there were no ships in East Indian Steam). Though the director of East Indian Steam most eager to enter P&O, because of a rash promise from Anderson, he was the man *least* wanted on its board. In February 1840, Anderson wrote a memorandum after his conversation with MacKillop, urging Curtis to join P&O by inviting him to nominate a few individuals for the board. No doubt Anderson was so excited about a triple merger that he spoke carelessly, saying that one of the individuals should '*represent them in its management*'. But P&O did not want a fourth MD, and after several polite refusals, everyone hoped that Barber would go away. But in March 1841, East Indian Steam gave Barber a glowing reference and was 'so strongly in favor [*sic*] of Capt Barber . . . [that] he should be appointed to a seat in your Board of Management'. As P&O's board did not have 'the pleasure of being acquainted with Capt Barber', secretary James Allan replied that it would be 'premature to disturb the existing stipulation of the Deed of Settlement, limiting the Number of Managing Directors to three Members as at present'. Larkins soon realized that P&O was disregarding its 'recorded pledge' and doing an injustice to Barber. P&O was failing to honour its promises, and Barber was given £1,400 in 1842. During 1842–44, he was indirectly employed by P&O, which sent him around the kingdom, organizing meetings, memorials, interviews and speeches to chambers of commerce, to urge the Government to grant a mail contract for the Calcutta–Suez line. Having helped P&O to get the contract, Barber showed how 'useful out of doors' he could be. However, it was clear that P&O would 'not avail themselves of [his] services as originally intended'. He demanded 'some lucrative post of employment under the Company', but had to bring his solicitor in before he was appointed superintendent of passengers and parcels in London, starting in 1847. He earned £10,000 – £5,000 from the board and £5,000 from the MDs – over 5 years, and the board then had to give him a further £6,000 to get rid of him (and he may have had a similar sum from the MDs).[132] Anderson's careless words turned out to be very costly.

Looking back to February 1841, everything seemed provisional and unstable, with many things to be worried about. But Bourne and Williams were not the sort of men to lose their heads; step by step, the fledgling P&O became stronger and watched the magnates in the City lose theirs. Nor did 'enthusiasts' in India have much to be proud of. The risks taken by P&O were enormous. Risks were always taken in any venture, but at that time, there were no risks so high as P&O's in the Mediterranean and the Red Sea, the latter having not yet been surveyed and being subject to monsoons and violent hurricanes. The founders knew what they wanted to do and they did it well. They and their shareholders were convinced of the national importance of their undertaking, but they were primarily men of business for whom the mail contract was a key with which to open the ultimate new markets in the East. The founders had 'a large capital', and 'great arrangements' with which to exploit them. Without Bourne and Williams, as Anderson gracefully acknowledged in November 1840, 'the question of "Steam Communication with India" might have either remained in abeyance for another seventeen years, or continued an embryo project to the end of time'.[133]

Notes

1 The phrase is from *PP*, 1849, 12 (571), *SC on Contract Packets*, q. 2169.

2 These two are usually credited with being the founders of P&O (see below, n. 63), even if – as I show – that could be due to their having outlived Bourne and having remained in senior positions in P&O long after Williams had left the company.

3 This and the following section owe much to F. Harcourt, 'Ownership & Finance 1820–1850: The Case of Ireland', in J.R. Bruijn and W.F.J. Mörzer Bruyns (eds), *Anglo-Dutch Mercantile Marine Relations 1700–1850: Ten Papers* (Amsterdam: Rijksmuseum 'Nederlands Scheepvaartmuseum', 1991); and F. Harcourt, 'Charles Wye Williams and Irish Steam Shipping', *Journal of Transport History*, 3rd series, 13:2 (1992), pp. 141–50.

4 See L.M. Cullen, *An Economic History of Ireland since 1660* (London: Batsford, 1972), ch. 3.

5 *PP*, 1830, 7 (667), *SC on the State of the Poor in Ireland, Third Report*, q. 6753.

6 21, 22 Geo. III, cap. xlvi (Irish Parliament), *An Act to Promote Trade and Manufacture, by Regulating and Encouraging Partnerships*; Cullen, *Economic History of Ireland*, pp. 95ff.

7 For the life and work of Charles Wye Williams, see F. Harcourt, 'Charles Wye Williams', and also 'Williams, Charles Wye', in H.C.J. Matthew and B. Harrison (eds), *Oxford Dictionary of National Biography* (Oxford: Oxford University Press, 2004); see also J.F. Petree, 'Charles Wye Williams, a Pioneer of Steam Navigation', *Liverpool Nautical Research Society: Transactions*, 10 (1961–71), pp. 14–21, and 'Charles Wye Williams (1779–1866), a Pioneer in Steam Navigation and Fuel Efficiency', *Transactions of the Newcomen Society*, 39 (1966–67), pp. 34–45.

8 *PP*, 1830, 7 (667), *First Report of Evidence*, q. 3112.

9 This passion is evidenced by Williams's own 'plain story', related as the Preface to his *On the Steam-Generating Power of Marine Locomotive Boilers* (1862), pp. ii–x.

10 For a list of shareholders see F. Neal, 'Liverpool Shipping, 1815–1835', MA thesis, University of Liverpool, 1962, Appendix 10, no. 102.

11 Williams, *Steam-Generating Power*, p. vii.

12 *Dublin Mercantile Advertiser* (henceforth *DMA*), 2.8.1824.

13 *Ibid.*, 20.2.1826.

14 POST 34, 549/1828, Arrangement, 30.6.1826.

15 *PP*, 1830, 14 (647), *Twenty-Second Report of the Commissioners of Revenue*, q. 722, referring to the agreement made in March 1818 and which lasted until 1843; see also CST/38/2.

16 *Parliamentary Debates* (hereafter *PD*), 3rd series, vol. 32, c. 1187.

17 S. Palmer, '"The Most Indefatigable Activity": The General Steam Navigation Company 1824–50', *Journal of Transport History*, 3rd series, 3:2 (1982), p. 3.

18 The three Acts are 9 Geo. 4, c. lxvi (*Local and Personal Acts* 1828, vol. 2, pp. 1461–90); 3, 4 Will. 4, c. cxv (*Local and Personal Acts 1833*, vol. 3, pp. 2593–618); and 6, 7, Will. 4, c. c (*Local and Personal Acts* 1836, vol. 4, pp. 3841–5). The City of Dublin Company was incorporated in 1860 by 23, 24 Vict., c. xcviii (*Local and Personal Acts* 1860, vol. 2, pp. 1343–50, which recited the previous three Acts.

19 *PP*, 1830, 7 (667), qq. 1184 and 3213ff.

20 Williams, *Steam-Generating Power*, pp. vi–vii.

21 Petree, 'Charles Wye Williams, a Pioneer of Steam Navigation', pp. 14, 16.

22 Williams presented a paper on the merits of iron bulkheads to the Dublin meeting of the British Association for the Advancement of Science in 1837. The full text was printed in *PP*, 1839, 47 (273), *Report on Steam Vessel Accidents*, pp. 58–61, in which Williams states: 'It occurred to me that the only practicable expedient for preventing the sinking . . . of the entire vessel would be by confining the effect of the injury sustained to that portion or section of the vessel . . . The plan is not restricted to any patent, and all are free to adopt it.'

23 *PP*, 1836, 28 (–), *Sixth Report of Commissioners to Inquire into the Management of the Post Office Department*, Appendix H, Examination of Mr C.W. Williams, 18.11.1834, p. 242.

24 *DMA*, 5.10.1829.

25 *PP*, 1830, 7 (667), qq. 3165–6.

26 C.W. Williams, *Reasons in Favor* [sic] *of the City of Dublin Steam Company's Bill for an Increase of Capital* (London, 1836), pp. 6–7.

27 *PP*, 1828, 11 (501), *Post Office Steam Packets, Steam Communication*; for Pim's application in 1824 see p. 1; for Williams's in 1826 see p. 2.

28 T1/3958, Statement by C.W. Williams, 18.7.1837.

29 *Ibid.*; see also P. Bagwell, 'The Post Office Steam Packets, 1821–36, and the Development of Shipping on the Irish Sea', *Maritime History*, 1 (1971), pp. 10, 13–14.

30 *PP*, 1836, 28 (–), pp. 3, 17.

31 ADM 2/1289 fos 250, 298–9, 512 and ADM 2/1290, fo. 48; T1/3958 11.10.1838.

32 *PP*, 1839, 47 (273), p. 50.

33 *DMA*, 19.7.1830.

34 C.W. Williams, *Observations on the Inland Navigation of Ireland* (London, 1833), Dedication.

35 *DMA*, 24.5.1830 and 5.7.1830.

36 *DMA*, 20.2.1826 and 10.5.1839.

37 Cf. *PP*, 1833, 6 (690), *SC on Manufactures, Commerce and Shipping*, q. 6921, on unprofitability in shipping, 'except for some very large ships'.

38 *PP*, 1834, 14 (478), *SC on Steam Navigation to India*, q. 524.

39 *DMA*, 19.7.1830.

40 In 1828 and 1833, City of Dublin's directors were Williams, his brother Richard, James Jameson, brewer and distiller, James Ferrier of Ferrier Pollock & Co., wholesalers for silk and haberdashery, and J.R. Pim, all of Dublin, and William Dixon, Sir John Tobin and George Parsons, all of Liverpool; J.C. Ewart came on the board later in the 1830s, as did Paul Twigg, also of Dublin, a close associate of Pim.

41 Williams, *Steam-Generating Power*, p. iv. Very little information about Carleton's background has been found; his father may have been George Carleton, a Dublin merchant and director of various companies.

42 *Dublin Almanac & General Register of Ireland* (1837), pp. 49–51.

43 *PP*, 1829, 12 (353), *Nineteenth Report of Commissioners of Revenue Inquiry*, Part II: Ireland, pp. 145, 487, 725 and throughout; *ibid.*, 1831–32, 17 (716), *SC on Post Communication with Ireland*. These sources, together with *ibid.* (645), *SC on Turnpike Roads*, and 1837, 20 (484), *SC on Turnpike Roads, Ireland*, give details of the Bourne family as road and mail contractors, and their relations with the Post Offices in Ireland and England.

44 Registry of Deeds, Dublin, vol. 741, no 504715: Marriage Settlement, 21.12.1816; PROB 11 2143: Richard Bourne's Will, 20 December 1851; ADM 21/393, Lieutenant's Certificate, from which the usually attached baptismal certificate is missing; W.R. O'Byrne, *A Naval Biographical Dictionary* (London, 1849), p. 103; F. Boase, *Modern English Biography* (London: Cass, 1965), vol. 4, p. 464.

45 Registry of Deeds, Dublin, vol. 741, no 504715: Marriage Settlement, 21.12.1816. The Bourne property was charged with a settlement of £5,000 for Louisa and Richard, while she brought £2,000 to the marriage from her grandfather's estate.

46 W.H. Bourne, George Darling and John Birch, all Irish 'Gents', were the trustees: BT 107/361, no. 80, BT 107/363, no. 27; *DMA*, 4.7.1827 and 20.8.1827.

47 *DMA*, 17.3.1828, p. 1, and 19.8.1829; BT 107/195, no. 128 (Pim owned 38/64ths and Fawcett 26/64ths); 'Captain Bourne RN, Obituary', *Illustrated London News* (hereafter *ILN*), 1.11.1851, vol. 19, p. 539.

48 Dublin & London was formed in 1826 under the 64ths rules, probably because those would be in line of London rules, and Richard kept to them until P&O was set up in 1840.

49 *DMA*, 30.5.1831, 4.7.1831, 6.2.1832 and 17.9.1832.

50 In 1830, Pim had fourteen vessels under the St George flag: *PP*, 1830, 14 (647), *Twenty-Second Report*, p. 722. In 1832, his empire was broken up, with several vessels sold off and some registered in single-vessel companies: BT 107 series, Liverpool and Dublin, 1832; see also Harcourt, 'Ownership and Finance', Appendix B. A new St George Company ('Company of the proprietors of the "St George"') was constituted in that year: BT 107/371, no. 8.

51 *PP*, 1831–32, 17 (716), *SC on Post Communication with Ireland*, pp. 5067, 5092, 5099.

52 *Ibid.*, q. 5092; 1831–32, 17 (645), *SC on Turnpike Roads*, qq. 2255, 2886, 2917–19; and 1837, 20 (484), pp. 6–7 and q. 202, Appendix 7.

53 H.D. Inglis, *Ireland in 1834: A Journey Through Ireland* (London: 1835), vol. 2, pp. 249–51.

54 *PP*, 1833, 6 (690), *SC on Manufactures, Commerce and Shipping*, qq. 6860, 6862, 6895, 6908, 8825; *PP*, 1830, 7 (667), *SC on the State of the Poor in Ireland*, qq. 3130ff; *PP*, 1831–32, 17 (716), *Report*, p. 21; *PP*, 1836, 28 (–), *Sixth Report*, Appendix H, pp. 244–5.

55 *PP*, 1837, 20 (484), *Turnpike Roads, Report*, pp. 1–8, Appendix 1, pp. 38, 40; this inquiry urged payment of compensation by arbitration to end the monopolies as soon as possible: p. 8. *PP*, 1829, 10 (353), *Nineteenth Report*, pp. 64ff., Examinations, especially nos 97, 112; *PP*, 1831–32, 17 (645), *Turnpike Trusts, Report*, pp. 10–15. Richard and William claimed £44,500, and Frederick £10,400. Post Office Archives (hereafter POST) 36/6, 1835, shows that the Bournes asked for 'further periodical Extra Toll as Lessees of the Limerick Turnpike', making a total of more than £7,000. The money was paid: *ibid.*, minute 105, 9.3.1835, 447, 10.9.1835; POST 36/7, Minute 61, 10.2.1837; POST 1/46, fo. 270, 12.3.1838.

56 POST 36/8, minute 519, 13.12.1837; *PP*, 1843, 51 (358), *Mail Coach Contract (Ireland)*, pp. 31–33 for Richard's connivance with Peter Purcell in bidding for the building contract.

57 F. Harcourt, 'British Oceanic Mail Contracts in the Age of Steam, 1838–1914', *Journal of Transport History*, 3rd series, 9:1 (1988), pp. 1–18; S. Palmer, '"The Most Indefatigable Activity": The General Steam Navigation Company 1824–50', *Journal of Transport History*, 3rd series, 3:2 (1982), pp. 11–12; *PP*, 1836, 28 (–), *Sixth Report*, Appendix (H), pp. 227, 251, 263.

58 K. Bourne, *Palmerston: The Early Years 1784–1841* (London: Allen Lane, 1982), ch. 8. The meeting at Münchengrätz in September 1833 between Russia and Austria confirmed his suspicion that the balance of power in Europe was tilting towards Russia.

59 *Times*, 19.7.1833, p. 6, col. 1 and generally in July–August.

60 His daughter's marriage to John Bourne, Richard's son from his first marriage, confirmed the friendship. After a short time in a shipyard in Glasgow, John turned to railways in India, and wrote several books about them.

61 W.S. Lindsay, *History of Merchant Shipping and Ancient Commerce* (London: S. Low, 1876), vol. 4, p. 379.

62 *Times*, 3.8.1833, p. 5, col. 5.

63 Willcox and Anderson did not act as London agents for Bourne's regular Dublin–London line, nor were they engaged as agents by Williams before 1837.

64 M. Stenton (ed.), *Who's Who of British Members of Parliament: A Biographical History of the House of Commons* (Hassocks, Sussex: Humanities Press, 1976), vol. 1: *1832–1885*; S. Rabson and K. O'Donoghue, *P&O: A Fleet History* (Kendal: World Ship Society, 1988), p. 13; J. Nicolson, *Arthur Anderson: A Founder of the P&O Company* (Paisley: A. Gardner, 1914), generally; Lindsay, *History of Merchant Shipping*, vol. 4, pp. 378–9.

65 The former has been suggested without the benefit of any evidence by B. Cable, *A Hundred Years History of the P&O: The Peninsular and Oriental Steam Navigation Company, 1837–1936* (London: I. Nicholson & Watson Ltd, 1937), where 'Messrs Bourne' are mentioned once and Williams not at all; and by D. Divine, whose garbled account of 'legends' in *These Splendid Ships: The Story of the Peninsular Line* (London: F. Muller, 1960) refers to Bourne as a director of the City of Dublin Company and gives Willcox and Anderson leading roles at all stages.

66 See Harcourt, 'Ownership and Finance', pp. 77ff.; Palmer, '"The Most Indefatigable Activity"', pp. 8–9.

67 *Herapath*, 12.6.1854, p. 595.

68 There is a copy of that prospectus in the British Library, shelf mark 1890.6.3 (132).

69 Customs, London, Bills A and B, 1835–36. *Royal Tar* made 4 northern voyages in 1835, it and *Glasgow* making 8 between them in 1836.

70 *ILN*, 'Captain Bourne', p. 539.

71 *Ibid.*

72 *Shipping Gazette*, 4.1.1837; Customs, London, Bills A and B, 1836. The new vessels cost £21,000, £28,000 and £48,000 respectively; they were owned in the same proportion of 64ths as Bourne's other vessels, he having the biggest portion of 38/64ths.

73 P&O/91/2, Letter to Mendizabal, 30.5.1835.

74 *PP*, 1836, 28 (–); the *Sixth Report* recommended this change which was executed in 7 Will. 4, c. iii; *PP*, 1849, 12 (571), *Contract Packets*, qq. 936ff., 1268–74, 1297, 1750.

75 ADM 1/3807, Treaty, 12.7.1837; Commercial Steam's bid was £400 less than Peninsular Steam's.

76 CST/38/5, Articles of Agreement, 16 October 1837. The three parties were (1) Richard and Frederick Bourne, James Hartley, Simeon Boileau and William Henry Fortescue (Peninsular); (2) James Ferrier, John McDonnell,William Willans, Francis Carleton, Joseph Boyce, John Jameson and John Ennis (British & Irish); (3) Charles Wye Williams, Richard Williams and George Roe (City of Dublin). All were of Dublin though Williams resided in Liverpool.

77 *Shetland Journal*, 12.11.1836, advertisement. The journal, published in London by Anderson, did not survive beyond its first year.

78 P&O/15/1, no. 135, 30.10.1838.

79 Presumably Bourne was not dissatisfied either, as Engledue was given another command. He later became a senior manager for P&O in the UK and in Calcutta, and ultimately joined the board in 1868. He died in 1888.

80 P&O/30/1, An Abstract of the Proceedings of the House of Commons to Inquire into the Contract Packet Service, November 1849, no. 1, Peninsular Service; *ILN*, 'Captain Bourne', p. 538; P&O/15/1, letters, nos 111, 213, 242, 299.

81 *Shipping Gazette*, 22.12.1836, 3.6.1837.

82 P&O/15/1, fo. 224, 25.2.1839; fos 396 and 398, 26.11.1839; fo. 135, 30.10.1838.

83 The ramifications of the Indian connections are set out from different points view: *PP*, 1849, 12 (571), *Contract Packets*, evidence of A. Henderson, generally; J.H. Wilson, *Facts Connected with the Origin and Progress of Steam Communication between India and England* (London: W.S. Johnson, 1850); C.R. Low, *History of the Indian Navy (1613–1863)* (London, 1877), vol. 1, pp. 521ff.; D. Thorner, *Investment in Empire. British Railways & Steam Shipping Enterprise in India, 1825–49* (Philadelphia: University of Pennsylvania Press, 1950), ch. 1.

84 *PP*, 1837, 6 (539), *Steam Communication with India*, qq. 1911 and 1954; and Statement by Sir John Hobhouse, p. 15.

85 William Jolliffe, a London shipowner, took the lead at this meeting (Wilson, *Facts*, p. 5), but saw that it was more practicable to ply on coastal routes in England and the Continent. He was a founder of General Steam in 1824 (Palmer, '"The Most Indefatigable Activity"', pp. 2–3).

86 H.L. Hoskins, *British Routes to India* (New York: Longmans, Green & Co., 1928), pp. 87–96. On arrival in Calcutta, *Enterprize* was sold to the Indian Government for war service against Burma and was subsequently employed in India waters.

87 Wilson, *Facts*, pp. 7–9.

88 Hoskins, *British Routes*, pp. 108ff.; Wilson, *Facts*, p. 31.

89 M. Greenberg, *British Trade and the Opening of China 1840–42* (London: Cambridge University Press, 1951), p. 74 and chs 1–4 generally; *PP*, 1831–32, 12 (735–II), *SC on the Affairs of the East India Company*, Appendix 25; *PP*, 1840, 7 (353), House of Lords (hereafter HoL), *SC on the Petition of the East India Company*, q. 146.

90 *PP*, 1850, 53 (693), *Correspondence . . . regarding the Establishment of . . . Steam Communication* [with India], pp. 1ff.

91 *Ibid.*, pp. 7–8. Major C.F. Head (he had made the journey by the Red Sea route) and Mr Hutt, MP for Hull, had charge of this project. There was a long delay before they put forward a precise proposal, and when they did the Post Office rejected it, in February 1837: *PP*, 1837, 6 (539), *Steam Communication*, pp. 15–20.

92 *PP*, 1837, 6 (539), *Steam Communication*, qq. 1936ff., 1569ff., and Report, p. iii; *PP*, 1849, 12 (571), *Contract Packets*, q. 1876; Hoskins, *British Routes*, pp. 121–5; A. Anderson, *Steam Communication with India: A Letter to the Directors of the Projected East Indian Steam Navigation Company* (hereafter *Letter*) (London, 1840), p. 20.

93 *Shipping Gazette*, 4.1.1837.

94 *New York Herald*, 19.9.1839; *Shipping Gazette*, 21.3.1838, 25.5.1839.

95 G.H. Preble, *A Chronological History of the Origin and Development of Steam Navigation* (Philadelphia, PA: L.R. Hamersley, 1883), pp. 126–8. Bankruptcy of the Glasgow engineers led to a long delay for *British Queen*; her hull was built in London. *Sirius* was built in 1837 and plied on the London–St Petersburg later in 1838: *Shipping Gazette*, 2.7.1838.

96 *Liverpool* is registered in 1838 (BT 107/254, no. 59), as having three owners (21/64ths each for Ferrier and R. Williams, 22/64ths for Hartley), and is registered again in 1840 in the same way (BT 107/268, no. 162). But *Shipping Gazette*, 18.8.1838, announced that this vessel had been bought by the Transatlantic Steam Ship Company, and advertised its departures: see *ibid.*, 3.1.1839.

97 Glasgow University Archive, GD 319, Scott's Shipbuilding Co., letters no. 136 (20.10.1838) and no. 195 (10.12.1838). The engines intended for the vessel were 'lying finished in Mr Sinclair's workshop'.

98 *DMA*, 29.11.1839. Twenty years later the Lever line made Galway the port to North America but it was short-lived: *PP*, 1860, 14 (328), *SC on Packet and Telegraphic Contracts, Report*, pp. ivff.

99 H.K. Grant, *Samuel Cunard, Pioneer of the Atlantic Steamship* (London: Abelard–Schuman, 1967), pp. 73ff; *PP*, 1849, 12 (571), *Contract Packets*, qq. 2048–101 for Cunard's own account of the competition; F.E. Hyde, *Cunard and the North Atlantic 1840–73: A History of Shipping and Financial Management* (London: Macmillan, 1975), pp. 3–6. The contract for the South Atlantic route to the West Indies and South America was awarded to the last of the three long-distance enterprises, the Royal Mail Steam Packet Company, for ten years starting from 1841, also by private negotiation: see *PP*, 1849, 12 (571), qq. 2427ff.

100 Williams, *Steam-Generating Power*, p. viii. *United States*, renamed *Oriental*, was bought on the stocks by the Dublin & Liverpool Building Company which leased and then sold it to P&O: Harcourt, 'Charles Wye Williams', pp. 155–6.

101 P&O/2/1, 23.3.1840. Among Curtis's interests was his partnership in Thomas Vernon & Co., the Liverpool iron founder and shipbuilder concern: BT 107/299, no. 184.

102 *PP*, 1850, 53 (693), *Correspondence*, pp. 28ff. Curtis broached the subject in February and sent his answer on 14.10.1839.

103 ADM 2/1291, fos 124–45, 21.10.1839; *Shipping Gazette*, 19.1.1839.

104 *PP*, 1850, 53 (693), *Correspondence*, pp. 35, 39; *PP*, HoL, 1847, 5 (225), *SC on . . . the Post Office*, qq. 161–62; *Shipping Gazette*, 19.1.1839; Hoskins, *British Routes*, pp. 135ff.

105 *PP*, 1849, 12 (571), *Contract Packets*, qq. 1273, 1279, 1297, 1537, 1750, 1752.

106 *Ibid.*, q. 1812; Anderson, *Letter*, pp. 5–11.

107 ADM 2/1291, fos 267–78, 25.11.1839; fos 273–4, 27.11.1839; fos 471–2, 27.1.1840; fo. 497, 7.2.1840 fo. 527, 18.2.1840.

108 P&O/20/5, nos 87, 89, 90, 91, 104, Correspondence with Captain James Barber; P&O/51/2, Agreement.

109 Anderson, *Letter*, pp. 5–6; P&O/2/1, 23.3.1840. The comptroller of the victualling, charged with drawing up the contract, was told that 'public tenders are to be called for, & not to . . . offer any particular party already made': ADM 2/1291, fos 542–4, 24.2.1840.

110 By September 1839, shares to the value of £122,000, 10 per cent paid, had been subscribed, *c.* 10 per cent of the capital Curtis wanted. It rose to £134,000 in 1840, mostly from India: *PP*, 1849, 12 (571), *Contract Packets*, q. 1811; *PP*, 1850, 53 (693), *Correspondence*, p. 40.

111 Anderson, *Letter*, pp. 8–13. This letter was published as a pamphlet in November. For an account by Captain A. Henderson, a 'Comprehensive' on Curtis's provisional directorate who did everything he could to bring P&O down, see *PP*, 1849, 12 (571), *Contract Packets*, q. 2238. He tried to buy *United States* but Carleton refused and told him to persuade the 'Comprehensives' to join P&O: *ibid.*, q. 1923.

112 *PP*, 1847, 36 (117), *Copies of the Contracts*, Articles of Agreement, 26.8.1840, pp. 6–14. *PP*, 1849, 12 (571), *Contract Packets*, q. 2033, shows that P&O's tender was £35,200, but negotiations afterwards brought the price up to £38,000. Jackson has not been identified, and one of Pim's names was transposed so that its reads J.P. Robinson.

113 P&O/15/2, fo. 193, 8.2.1841.

114 P&O/2/1, 21.11.1840 refers to the payment for *United States*; P&O wanted to pay in shares but Williams's associates objected. Meanwhile *United States* was registered as P&O's property under the new name of *Oriental*. In 1842, P&O mortgaged *Oriental* to Royal Exchange Assurance Co for three years – the mortgage was not recorded on the Certificate of Registry, P&O/20/5. Transatlantic's *Liverpool* was renamed as *Great Liverpool* to distinguish her from Bourne's much smaller and older *Liverpool*, occasionally referred to as 'Little Liverpool' or 'Liverpool no. 2'.

115 P&O/15/1, fos 482–3, 15.4.1840; P&O/2/1, 2.5.1840, 6.6.1840.

116 P&O/2/1, 6.6.1840.

117 *PP*, 1849, 12 (571), *Contract Packets*, qq. 1811–14. Capt. A. Henderson said the promoters of Indian Steam broke into three at the end of 1839; this explains why the publication of Indian Steam's prospectus was held back until April 1840: *ibid.*, q. 1811. *Shipping Gazette* did not publish it until 22.7.1840.

118 *Ibid.*, qq. 2433ff.; *PP*, 1850, 53 (693), *Correspondence*, pp. 40–1; Wood's 'actions' appeared in *The Times*, 28.8.1839.

119 P&O/2/1, 8.7.1840; *Shipping Gazette*, 19.1.1839 and 22.7.1840; *PP*, 1850, 53 (693), *Correspondence*, Paper A, pp. 1–6. Henderson said that Curtis was supported by a 'small section of the London shareholders': *PP*, 1849, 12 (571), q. 2208.

120 ADM 2/1292, fos 432–43, 23.5.1840; P&O/2/1, 8.7.1840, 4.8.1840; P&O/15/2, 31.10.1840, 4.11.1840; P&O/1/100, 6.11.1840. The charter was dated 31.12.1840.

121 Anderson, *Letter*, generally.

122 P&O/15/2, fo. 89, 4.11.1840; fo. 97, 13.11.1840; fo. 104, 18.11.1840; fos 112–13, 25.10.1840; fo. 118–19, 26.11.1840.

123 *PP*, 1849, 12 (571), qq. 1803ff; *PP*, 1850, 53 (693), pp. 42ff; P&O/15/2, fo. 118, 26.11.1840; P&O/1/100, 24.3.1841.

124 P&O/6/1, Report, 29.11.1843.

125 P&O/1/100, 18.7, 1.8.1843; *ILN*, 12.8.1843, p. 107; Harcourt, 'Charles Wye Williams', pp. 141–162.

126 *PP*, 1850, 53 (693), *Steam Communication . . . all Correspondence between HMG and the East India Company . . . the Peninsular & Oriental Steam Navigation Company . . . Suez and Bombay . . . Suez and Calcutta, Ceylon and Hong Kong, and with the Australian Colonies* (*Correspondence* hereafter), begins in 1834, goes up to July 1850 and reveals much of the history of East Indian Steam's rise and fall (1837–41) and P&O's ascendancy; references in this and the following paragraphs are at pp. 42ff.

127 P&O/65/157; *ibid.*; P&O/65/185.

128 P&O/1/100, 7.12.1841.

129 P&O/15/2, 31.3.1841; P&O/1/100, 31.3.1841 and 3.4.1841.

130 P&O/1/100, 31.8.1841, 30.4.1844, 14.1.1845 and 27.5.1845; *PP*, 1849, 12 (571), *Contract Packets*, Henderson's evidence, generally; *PP*, 53, 1850 (693), p. 115. *India* was never employed on any of P&O's routes but was kept as a reserve vessel at Calcutta until, riddled with dry rot, it was sold as a hulk in 1849.

131 *PP*, 1837, 6 (539), *SC on Manufactures, Commerce and Shipping*, qq. 1021–2, 1037.

132 P&O/20/5, fos 87, 90, 91, 104; P&O/51/2.

133 *PP*, 1849, 12 (571), *Contract Packets*, q. 2169; Anderson, *Letter*, p. 22.

CHAPTER TWO

Full steam ahead: west and east of Suez, 1840–45

'It is the business of the Government to open and to secure the roads for the merchants.'[1] The dictum is Palmerston's, but it could have been a motto for P&O as the company pressed the State to subsidize long-distance steam navigation by presenting the profitable business it ran for its shareholders as a national mission for the public good. The first phase of the company's operations saw new lines opened to steam first in the Mediterranean, then east of Suez, thereby increasing the mileage covered and the tonnage at work and creating the infrastructure needed for expansion. The three MDs – Willcox, Anderson and Carleton – had a clear strategy: first, expansion was to be supported by mail contracts; and, second, to aim for monopoly. The Government discriminated between major routes that had to have a subsidy and minor lines which were supposedly profitable enough without public support. This set limits in practice to how far the first part of the strategy could be fulfilled, though mail contracts, where granted, did lead very naturally to monopoly. But P&O was content to run minor lines either as feeders to the main lines or in order to pre-empt predators.

P&O's success in the early years gave it a sound base. The 1849 gold rush in California and, more directly relevant to P&O, the discovery of gold in Australia in 1851 had a marked effect in creating a more truly global economy; and, since Britain was the most advanced industrial country, its interest in overseas trade was largest. An existing tendency towards distant markets was confirmed when, after the abolition of the Navigation Laws in 1849, universal free trade did not come about and Britain's closest neighbours and North America remained rigidly protectionist.[2] Success was also guaranteed because P&O's lines led to the areas that promised, or were already known, to be profitable.

Yet the company found itself in a dilemma of its own making. A mail contractor was in practice a monopolist: no long-distance line could be worked by more than one operator and P&O intended to be the one. But during most of the period 1840–52 demand for steam communication in the Mediterranean and in the East ran ahead of P&O's provision of tonnage. Critics were therefore justified in complaining that the company was unable to supply sufficient tonnage while refusing to allow others to do so: the monopolist was cramping the development of steam navigation while generating envy among other companies which were trying to break into its lines.

P&O had a dual identity: it was a company under contract to government and at the same time a profit-seeking business. These two activities were not always compatible. Because the contractual side of the company had to take first place, its wider interests could not be fully protected. The numbers and quality of the ships were geared to the mail service, not to commerce: P&O built expensive steamers because the Admiralty would not allow it to carry mails otherwise, and each vessel had to be able to carry arms. Again, when the economy was at a low ebb, mail steamers could not be laid up; and when trade was prospering, the company could not supply the space and tonnage for which the mercantile community called. Investment in new vessels, indeed, relied on the assurance of a long-term relationship with the State, not on commercial needs. This made the company exceptionally subject to public and political scrutiny. P&O's MDs had always to tread carefully when decisions were taken, and they quickly learned the art of public relations. On the other hand, the utility of subsidies provided ammunition for aspiring competitors to question the rising cost of the contract system in general and, in particular, P&O's monopoly. From 1847 onwards, P&O had constantly to defend the territory it occupied, for the company could not count on automatic renewal of the mail contracts. By the end of 1852, however, almost all of the strategy envisaged in 1840 had been carried out.

From England to Egypt, 1840–52

As chapter 1 showed, Peninsular Steam's 1837 contract to Spain, Portugal and Gibraltar was the first stage on the way to the East. Three years later, Bourne, Willcox and Anderson were joined by Charles Wye Williams and Francis Carleton to create P&O and reached the second stage, a contract for the Mediterranean as far as Alexandria, the key to the overland route to India; and 1845 took P&O triumphantly to the third stage, a contract for the Red Sea route to India by steam.

Steam shipping in the Mediterranean had many built-in advantages for P&O. Britain's strategically placed bases at Gibraltar and Malta provided emergency facilities and convenient coaling depots free of the heavy costs levied at foreign ports. Again, it was well known among mariners that 'there is no part of the world' where a vessel met with 'such variable winds as in the Mediterranean', a feature that made voyages by sail in this area particularly unpredictable.[3] P&O's 'floating taverns', with their fixed timetables and rapid voyages in all seasons and all weathers, built up the company's reputation for efficiency and reliability. Earnings were governed by the design and technology of early steamships. *Oriental*, the largest of P&O's steamers in 1840, could carry no more than 150 tons of cargo after allowing for space for coal, even though the 2,000 mile voyage from Southampton was broken at Gibraltar and Malta for coaling. Space was also taken up by the mails. These grew year by year: on one voyage in May 1851, about twenty-seven tons of mail were carried, three times the amount in May 1848. Only small packages and light but valuable goods could be taken as cargo. Passage money therefore was the best source of revenue for all early steamship enterprises. Though the Admiralty did not usually concern itself with the commercial side of a contractor's business, officials appreciated the importance of passenger traffic: the greater revenue from it, the smaller the subsidy required. Thus, every facility 'shall be afforded for the conveyance of Passengers that will not materially interfere with the conveyance of the Mails'; and on P&O's behalf the Admiralty remonstrated with

> the Lords of the Treasury [who] must be aware that the sum now paid for the performance of this Service is altogether inadequate, unless the Contractors receive a large return from the passengers to and from Alexandria & that unless the arrangements for the public Service are such as to allow the Contractors this source of emolument a much larger remuneration must be paid to them for the conveyance of the mails or a larger expenditure incurred for the same service in Vessels belonging to the Public.[4]

Passenger traffic, however, was slow to develop. *Oriental*, with berths for over 100 passengers, and her companion *Great Liverpool* conveyed 573 persons to and from Alexandria in the first year, and 800 in the second. Scarcity of suitable steam tonnage east of Suez was responsible for this disappointing result. The MDs, however, were confident that 'the whole tide of passengers to India [would] flow through Egypt' as soon as its own regular steamers were stationed east of Suez. Sure enough, passengers increased when *Hindostan* (January 1843) and *Bentinck* (December 1843) began their two-monthly service from Calcutta to Suez, and in 1845, the first year of monthly service, over 2,000 passengers were carried: *Bentinck* arrived at Suez in April 1846 with 170 passengers 'besides servants'.[5]

A contractor was obliged to keep a few berths, at one-third below the ordinary fare, for military and civil officers, their families and servants. In busy times, government passengers became a loss-making nuisance because they had to be victualled and accommodated (according to rank and status) as if they were full-fare travellers. Admiralty agents were a greater nuisance. A contract ship had to take one of these personages on every voyage. He had charge of the mails and full authority in all matters pertaining to the strict execution of the contract and of every other eventuality on board. His decisions were 'final and binding', though he did not have 'the power of compulsion'. These officials were paid by the Admiralty, but the company had to provide them with a first-class cabin, accommodation for servants, food and drink, all at the company's expense. Agents were not above complaining that a cabin was 'not sufficiently commodious' and demanding another in 'a more respectable situation'; and occasionally they had to be reprimanded by the Admiralty for 'most unbecoming and indecorous' behaviour.[6] Resented by masters and officers, these watchdogs were, in the company's view, trouble-makers and a drain on resources.

Until the 1850s, P&O took only first-class passengers. Though space was reserved for servants and non-commissioned officers, it was not referred to as second class, and as common soldiers and sailors were detailed to sleep on deck (provided that there was adequate cover), the servants' quarters may well have been not much better than that. European servants, however, must have had somewhat better quarters because their fares were that much higher. An awkward question was posed in the case of 'educational persons' and missionaries. They could not afford the first-class fare, but neither could they be relegated to the lower classes where 'society' might not be congenial. The problem was solved by allowing individuals in these categories to travel first class but at two-thirds of the ordinary fare. A limited number of young cadets, going out to India to begin their careers in the Indian Army or Civil Service, were also carried at a reduced fare from 1846. In the 1850s, a discreet second class catered for artisans who were sent out to work in India on government projects and railways, but it was not advertised.

Passenger traffic to and from India was seasonal according to the monsoons east of Suez. Year after year, the prime season for residents of India to come home was from May to July or August, and voyages outwards were nearly always booked for October, November and December. After allowing for margins, this meant that P&O's vessels were full or overflowing for 8 months of the year, and in the other 4 months were more than half-empty. Having paid a large sum for their first class berths, passengers expected to have ample space. Yet every high season produced a constant stream of complaints. Some disliked having to sleep on deck (though the heat of the Red Sea was an encouragement to do that voluntarily); others were outraged to find themselves squeezed into any old corner. Since steamships were not elastic, the MDs could only apologize to dissatisfied passengers and smooth ruffled feathers with cash rebates. Though these hand-outs often totalled over £1,300 a voyage,[7] they did not solve the problem.

And problem it was. If P&O could not provide enough space on the Alexandria–Southampton line, there were other steamers whose owners were eager to fill the gap. French vessels ran a frequent and direct line between Alexandria and Marseilles. This popular route enabled 'Indian' passengers to spend some time in Paris before crossing the English Channel; or, if they could put up with the discipline and spartan quarters of a warship, they could get to Marseilles at low cost by the British naval vessel that landed and picked up mail at Malta. These various options were taken up as soon as *Hindostan*'s Calcutta service to Suez began in January 1843. Two years later the problem became acute when the monthly contract service began. Because of seasonality it was not possible to spread the load: few passengers would willingly travel in the off season – reduced fares for off-season travel made little difference – and P&O probably lost some passengers, to whom speed was not important, to one of Richard Green's (much less costly) 'splendid sailing ships going round the Cape'.[8] As no statistics were kept it is impossible to quantify the passenger trade; nor is it possible to identify passenger earnings, either on individual lines or in total between 1840 and 1846. What is certain is that P&O's monthly Alexandria–Southampton service could not meet passenger demand in high season and revenue was lost in consequence.

Seepage of passenger money was compounded in 1845 when the Austrian Lloyd's (AL) started a line between Alexandria and Trieste, its home base.[9] Now there were choices by sea and also by land: a French steamer to Marseilles and through France to the English Channel; or an Austrian vessel to Trieste and the North Sea through the Austrian empire, Switzerland and the German states. Though none of those states had continuous lines of rail, their construction was increasing rapidly, and even British naval commanders on the Marseilles mail line, aware of a sharp drop in their passenger earnings, were instructed to make their service more appealing.[10]

One remedy for the problem would have been for P&O to double the service by plying between Southampton and Alexandria every fortnight. The MDs, anticipating the need, put this proposal to the

Admiralty in 1842, but the Government saw no necessity, and without a subsidy the extra service could not be undertaken. At the end of 1844, however, when the monthly Calcutta–Suez service was about to start, there was concern that mails from Bombay would suffer severe disruption if extra tonnage was not provided: the existing Alexandria line (the 'Calcutta' line) could cope only with mails from Calcutta and China. Accordingly, a second line from Alexandria to Southampton was opened in May 1845, designated the 'Bombay' line. This was an arrangement made by the Admiralty with P&O, not a formal contract, so it could be terminated at three months' notice. For this service P&O had to accept – 'with reluctance, after much negotiation, and a pertinacious refusal by the Government of their previous proposals' – the much lower subsidy of £15,525 per annum, a mileage rate of 4*s* 6*d*, 'the lowest rate of any existing Mail Steam Contract'. Hard-nosed officials in the Treasury were 'of [the] opinion that this offer still exceeds the amount' for which the service might be performed.[11] Indeed, the 1840 contract, which reached its 5-year term in 1845, had started at £37,000 – 10*s* per mile – but, with various diminutions, had come down to £29,500 (8*s* a mile). This contract was continued on an annual basis from 1845 at the lower rate of £24,000 (6*s* 10*d*), diminishing by £500 a year, at 12 months' notice. At the same time, the Peninsular service was reduced to 3 calls a week and the subsidy for that line adjusted to £20,500 per annum.[12]

Before these arrangements were made, however, the board of directors decided to take action of its own by establishing a line that would have two functions: one to help with the seasonal overflow and the other to act as a feeder to the main line. This was the Constantinople branch, opened in 1845. It was to be an important part of P&O's trade for the next few years.

The Constantinople branch

In the summer of 1840, when the MDs were preparing for P&O's advent in the Mediterranean, they considered how best to make the Alexandria line profitable and to guard the company against competitors. It was agreed that branch lines radiating out from Malta or Gibraltar would be the most efficient way to achieve both aims. The company's policy, which played an important part in P&O's expansion strategy, was based on 'the principle of occupying lines now requiring the benefit of steam navigation not solely in the expectation of realising large profits, but in order to prevent those lines being taken up by other influential parties . . . who might hereafter become powerful rivals to the P&O company on their existing lines'.[13]

Anderson, dispatched to the Admiralty in August to discuss ways and means of setting up branches, reported to the board in November 1840 that the Government 'was prepared to entertain' P&O's proposals.[14] One extension was thrust on the company without more ado. This was the spur from Malta to the Ionian Islands (then under British rule): the Admiralty included this service in the Alexandria contract although there was little enthusiasm in P&O for it.[15] Of greater importance for the company were two other branches from Malta: one to Marseilles, replacing the Royal Navy's steamers, and the other to Constantinople. A subsidy for the Marseilles branch was ruled out by the Admiralty: the India mail via France was faster than P&O's sea service, and naval vessels could bear the cost of high speed between Malta and Marseilles. It may also have been expedient to have naval vessels in French waters at that time for political reasons.[16] But as there seemed to be no impediment to opening a Constantinople branch, the MDs expected that it would soon come under contract, for they did not consider setting up an unsubsidized branch. Indeed, the charter prohibited the company from opening any lines in the Mediterranean that were not under contract or for which a contract was not intended.[17]

While waiting for a decision from the Admiralty, Anderson went on a tour of the Mediterranean. One of his charges was to gather information about the Constantinople line and any others that might be of interest to P&O. Just after his departure, in December, word came from the Admiralty that there would be no contract for the time being. As far as St Mary Axe was concerned, this meant that any extension would have to be postponed, and a letter to that effect was sent on to Anderson. He claimed that he had not received it, for on reaching Constantinople in the summer of 1841 he was so enthusiastic about the line's potential that he advertised the imminent arrival of P&O's steamers. The board knew nothing of this step until it appeared in the English press. It caused great consternation among directors and shareholders. Infringement of the charter might cause trouble with the Government and would certainly provide ammunition for the 'hostile parties' who were still smarting from P&O's success in getting the Alexandria contract. Anderson's advertisements were quickly withdrawn, and shareholders were assured that P&O's main object was to increase communication with India, not to divert resources to the Black Sea.[18]

Anderson's estimate of the commercial value of trade in the eastern Mediterranean, however, was carefully noted by the board. In 1839 a commercial treaty between Britain and Turkey opened the whole of the vast Ottoman empire to British manufactures, making Britain Turkey's leading trading partner. In the early 1840s, the Black Sea region was the biggest market in the world for British textiles. Outward cargoes of fine cottons and woollens were complemented on return voyages by silks, carpets and fresh and dried fruit. Thriving business stimulated demand for speedy delivery of bills of exchange, specie and bullion. Though passenger space was taken up by merchants and by adventurous tourists in search of Greek temples, Byzantine churches and shrines in the Holy Land, this was 'chiefly a cargo trade'. And though French and Austrian steamships were already at work in the eastern Mediterranean, the best of all the favourable features of this area was that no British steamship company had yet arrived there: P&O would be the first to occupy the line.

Several applications for a mail contract were made between 1841 and 1843 but all were rejected, although the MDs reduced the price with each offer. The Treasury reckoned that postage revenue from that area would not be large enough to justify a contract; in any case it was clear that there were profits to be made on that line and it did not need state support.[19] Leaving the line unoccupied was a hazard, but so was venturing into a new area without a subsidy, even if the prohibition in the charter were to be removed. The question was whether the volatile Anderson's assessment could be believed. By chance, the company was able to make an experimental voyage eastwards without attracting any attention. In the summer of 1842, P&O gave up the branch from Malta to the Ionian Islands. The line was commercially useless and awkward to run, and after two years P&O was glad to drop it and to accept an abatement of contract money.[20] *Iberia* was thus available to make a circumspect voyage eastwards from the Ionian Islands instead of returning to base. Calling at several ports on the way to Constantinople, *Iberia* showed that the line 'was likely to be remunerative'.[21] This was confirmed in the following spring when *Tagus* undertook a more extensive investigation that included Sinope, Samsun and Trebizond in the Black Sea, and Smyrna, an important Levantine port and the centre of the Turkish opium trade.[22] Making his only known long voyage in a P&O steamship,[23] Captain Bourne sailed in *Tagus* to make his own assessment of the Black Sea region, an indication that the company was seriously contemplating working the line without subsidy.

In January 1844, another rejection of a much reduced offer came from the Admiralty. A decision had to be taken, for if the Constantinople line was not occupied in the near future, P&O might lose it altogether. So, at the AGM in November, the board announced that a regular monthly steam service would start in the new year to 'benefit the interests connected with that extensive market for British manufactures, and at the same time afford a reasonable return' to the shareholders. As the charter's prohibition was not yet expunged, the directors' boldness was tempered with 'much apprehension' in case 'certain parties . . . create[d] a decided opposition'. In the event, the prohibition was removed without incident in 1845.[24]

The Constantinople venture prospered. Conceived as a feeder to bring trade to the Alexandria line and to pick up and land passengers between Malta and Southampton, it soon turned into a line busy enough to stand alone and run directly to and from Southampton. Ports in the Black Sea and the Levant, including Trebizond, Samsun and Smyrna, were added to the schedule, and within two years of operation much larger and more powerful ships were needed to cope with the demand for space. Because trade was so active, more effort was required than a simple occupation of the line: it had to be developed. The MDs were aware that if 'this lucrative Trade' fell into other hands it would be 'not only to the diminution of the Company's profits but to the prejudice of British interests'; and a sombre picture was painted of the consequences if 'other parties' came to the line, 'especially if such were originated' in Britain. Shortage of tonnage, however, hampered the progress of the line. In 1847, it was 'but imperfectly carried on by three ships' whose primary function had to be to help with the overflow of passengers at Malta. The Black Sea traffic paid '*remarkably* well', and though 'only in its infancy . . . the elements of profit and success [were] . . . palpably evident'. New 'distinct vessels' could meet demand and fend off the 'positive injury' of competition. The board was told that

> to protect the Company's interests and to meet the urgent demand which exists for extending its operations in order to guard those interests, it is essential that several new ships should be put in hands, and contracts entered into, for the completion of the same in . . . 1848; and that this Company must either adopt this course or anticipate the possibility of the other capitalists entering the field as competitors.[25]

Of the two objectives – taking in passengers and mail at Malta and carrying on a 'cargo trade' in the Black Sea – there was no question which had priority. State support for the mail line became all the more necessary when P&O's second Alexandria line (the 'Bombay' line) was discontinued in May 1848, and vessels bound for Constantinople became responsible for taking in and landing all the 'Bombay' heavy mails at Malta. Not surprisingly, the company could not do justice to the Black Sea trade. Free conveyance of mails enabled P&O to rebut some of the criticism voiced about its subsidies, but this free service 'subjected the company to a considerable additional expense'[26] through lost cargo revenues.

The commercial crisis in late 1847, followed by political upheavals all over Europe the following year, gave P&O a clear run for a short time, but the disruption of trade and shipping due to revolutionary outbreaks in France and Austria provided opportunities for other British shipowners too. The 'injury' of competition that had been staved off began to make itself felt as financial confidence was restored, and several Liverpool owners, and the General Screw Steam Shipping Company in London, established lines to the Black Sea in 1849. Of all these newcomers, the most potentially dangerous for P&O was Charles MacIver, one of Samuel Cunard's partners. But, as mail contractors, Cunard and P&O had equal privileges, so one company could not intimidate the other. Whether by independent choice or by arrangement – and there is no evidence of the latter – the two companies refrained from meddling with each other, the one keeping to Liverpool, the other to London. MacIver ran a steamer to the Black Sea on his own account in 1849, and when the venture proved profitable Cunard and George Burns, the third partner, joined him to form the British & Foreign Steam Navigation Company (B&F) in 1851.[27] The most important feature of the Black Sea trade at that time was that, thanks to its medium distance from Britain, a shipping company did not need a subsidy, now that the more efficient screw steamers were in general use.

P&O's main backers were the Greek merchants in London who 'steadily and liberally supported the Company's interest in the Levant and the Black Sea'. New and fast vessels were needed for the Constantinople line, so that older steamers could ply in the Black Sea, acting as feeders for the main line. These intentions were difficult to fulfil. New tonnage was urgently required to meet contract requirements east of Suez as it was not possible to charter steamers in those seas. To achieve any kind of balance, the MDs had to resort to expensive charters for the Mediterranean services or the purchase, second hand, of such older and not very suitable vessels as *Jupiter*, *Tiger* and *Achilles*.[28] Of P&O's own steamers, *Erin* (built 1846) replaced the much older *Tagus* on the line from Constantinople to Trebizond in 1849 to meet the 'views' of the Greek merchants. To keep up the momentum, their loyalty was acknowledged by an exceptionally lavish entertainment, with a concert, ball and supper for the merchants and their ladies in Willis's rooms.[29] But shortly afterwards, *Erin* was dispatched eastwards for the Bombay–China line; *Euxine*, built in 1847 and specially designed for the Southampton–Constantinople trade, was moved into the Black Sea in 1850 as an 'extra' because of 'the unusual activity of the Turkey trade' when room in the regular steamers 'greatly exceeded the quantity [of cargo] the vessels [could] take'; and in 1852, the newly built *Madras* made one voyage to the Black Sea, after which it was sent east of Suez without delay, leaving only one ship on the Constantinople line. Once again, vessels had to be chartered.[30] In July 1853 a blunt report to the board stated that the Constantinople line 'has for some time past been carried on at a heavy expense by unsuitable vessels, and to maintain it profitably against the competition now established on it, Screw vessels arranged for carrying large cargoes and to run twice a month are indispensable'.[31]

Opened with such good prospects in 1845, P&O's Constantinople line was close to collapse. Competition was clearly a factor, but it was not the only and certainly not the main reason for this deterioration. Rather, as a mail contractor operating in two hemispheres, P&O inevitably had exceptional difficulty in apportioning tonnage, and contract obligations always came before unsubsidized lines. Mails had to be picked up and landed regularly no matter the season or the state of trade. In 1853, as we shall see, P&O added an enormous contract tonnage to its existing lines. This alone would have made the Constantinople line a very doubtful survivor. In the event, it was the Crimean War that ended the company's commercial connection with the Black Sea. Every available steamship was taken up by the Government's transport needs when war broke out in March 1854. A few months later, there were no British mail packets in any part of the Mediterranean apart from those on P&O's Southampton–Alexandria line.

But the war was merely the occasion, and not the root cause, of the line's demise. For the war did not deter the French Government from setting up a second line to Constantinople, giving a twice-weekly service later in the year;[32] and French expansion on this scale did not stop Cunard from resuming the trade after the war. P&O made a gesture in that direction by advertising a steamer in May 1856, but when this failed to attract any cargo the company abandoned the line for good.[33]

The rise and fall of P&O's Constantinople line points up the restrictive side of the mail contracts. Commercial feeders could not be fully exploited unless they were specifically tied in with mail lines, as Cunard's Mediterranean feeder was with its Atlantic trade: immigrants from Southern Europe were conveyed to Liverpool for shipment to America, while employment in the Black Sea brought in revenue when trade was slack on the Atlantic. By contrast P&O's India and China lines became the main focus of the company's operations from 1853 and the Black Sea trade was peripheral to these despite yielding such good returns. Vigorous competition in the Black Sea region, the chronic shortage of tonnage and the stern discipline of the contracts east and west of Suez made it impossible for P&O to continue the line.

The Italian branch

The only other branch that P&O began in the Mediterranean in this period was a line to Genoa. During his tour of the Mediterranean in 1841, Anderson stopped off in northern Italy. His inquiries led him to believe that a branch from Gibraltar to Genoa would both serve to protect P&O from competition and prove lucrative in its own right. From the outset the board was sceptical about the proposition and considered it only because of Anderson's persistence. He based his argument on the Lombardy silk trade. Silk from this region was conveyed to Britain through Switzerland and France at the high rate of £15 a ton.[34] High in value but low in volume, silk was eminently suited to steam. Anderson was confident that merchants could be persuaded to ship it out of Genoa instead. The board was not convinced by his enthusiasm in 1841, and no action was taken. In 1844, after Anderson had initiated another survey of silk prospects and dispatched *Iberia* on a trial run to Italian ports, a rumour that 'Capitalists in England and Italy' were waiting in the wings to set up a line if P&O did not act promptly nudged the board into looking at the line with more interest. Aside from the charter's prohibition on unsubsidized branches and the speculative nature of this proposition, there was no tonnage available. An option put to the board by the MDs – to join prospective competitors so that the Italian branch could be worked together – was considered but firmly rejected:

> The danger of inviting others to occupy the line and of inducing them to seek the cooperation of the Company . . . as an alternative is too obvious to be entertained except in an extremity because the traffic seems to be of that improvable [*sic*] character that any independent party would soon become our avowed opponents and rivals. They would neutralize the exclusive priviledges [*sic*] which we now enjoy . . . and as experience added knowledge to their operations, their opposition & rivalry would meet us throughout the Mediterranean & Levant.[35]

It was just as unwise, however, to allow a competitor to be installed too close to P&O's interests. So, with some reluctance, it was agreed to send occasional steamers to call at Genoa 'if only to warn others of the P&O's ulterior intentions . . . to obstruct or perhaps entirely subvert' the competition and to protect the Peninsular line. [36]

To avoid an infringement of the charter James Hartley, part-owner with Francis Carleton of *Queen*, placed that vessel on the line in his own name. It made the first voyage to Genoa on charter to P&O in the summer of 1844, and he and the MDs in their own names hired *North Star* for further voyages. They showed a loss, but calculations indicated that results would have been better if carried out by P&O's

own steamers. If enough tonnage could be spared, it seemed that a feeder between Gibraltar and Genoa might be 'capable of responding' to the gradual introduction of 'our name & influence'; and 'a practical knowledge of the regularity & efficacy of our operations' would keep predators away. In 1846, after being 'strongly urged' by the MDs to set up a more 'creditable' service in the following spring, the board sanctioned arrangements to work the line more systematically, with agents and a superintendent. But the difficulty with tonnage remained. Three vessels were needed, but there was no chance that so many would be available. Again, the company resorted to costly charters. Misfortunes made the situation worse. *Tiber*, designated for the Italian line, was wrecked on her maiden voyage in 1847, and *Ariel*, which replaced *Tiber*, was lost in the summer of 1848. At the end of 1847, the MDs admitted that P&O's ships had taken nothing but 'the coarser kinds [of cargoes] like straw hats', and 'not one bale of silk' had been brought by the steamers. Despite unrest in the Italian states in 1847–48, an effort was made to stimulate trade in silk by advertising a regular monthly service, but regularity could not be maintained. A sudden increase in demand was generated by refugees fleeing from revolution to England. Then trade to Italy stopped altogether. Erratic service by the steamers had much to do with the lack of interest in steam at Genoa; but Anderson did not see that the poor land transport from Lombardy made it difficult to send silk to Genoa. He tried to resuscitate the Italian line in 1853 when P&O began to operate out of Marseilles, but high prices of coal wiped out any profit, and the line was formally abandoned in January 1854.[37] P&O was not again to take up an Italian line for twenty years, but then in very different circumstances.

Though the two Mediterranean branches were quite different in their potential for profitability, both were abandoned. Success on the Italian line was always doubtful, whereas the Constantinople line bade fair to remain a money-spinner. But the lesson learned was that branches had to be integral to the company's main objectives. Its orientation had always been eastwards, and from 1853 even the mail lines in the Mediterranean were increasingly regarded as branches to the far more important lines east of Suez. We must now turn, therefore, to the company's eastern strategy.

The India contract, 1840–45

In January 1845 'the long talked of Scheme of Steam Communication with India' under government contract became a reality. Jubilation at 51 St Mary Axe was unbounded. P&O's principals had set their sights on the route to the east and never wavered in their determination to reach that goal. Seventeen months earlier however, when *Bentinck* was about to be dispatched to India in August 1843, there was still no sign of a mail contract. The MDs calculated that coal for a single voyage between Suez and Calcutta cost £7,000,[38] and they were justifiably anxious to know how the line could be maintained without a much larger subsidy than the original £20,000 each year. But the East India Company's earlier benevolence towards P&O had evaporated, to be replaced by a negative and ultimately hostile attitude.

However, in view of recent events in the east – the ending of war with China, the annexation of Sind (both in 1842) and a massacre of British troops (in 1843) in the aftermath of the first Afghan War[39] – the British Government wanted steam communication with India properly established as quickly as possible, and P&O acquired the support of such men as the Earl of Haddington at the Admiralty and the Earl of Ripon, president of the Board of Control (the India Board), to intercede on its behalf with the East India Company. J. Emerson Tennent, the senior official at the India Board, and his colleague Charles Hood Chicheley Plowden, who was in charge of marine affairs, were particularly helpful.[40] The MDs therefore adopted a much bolder approach.

The new scheme they set out in August 1843 was designed to make Bombay the principal port, thus giving P&O the Bombay–Suez and Alexandria–Marseilles lines on which the fast mail via France was conveyed, while subordinating the Calcutta–Suez line which was to be worked in connection with Alexandria–Southampton's 'heavy' mails service. Since Bombay was the nearest port to England,[41] this was a 'perfectly feasible' plan. The cost of the existing Bombay–Suez line worked by the East India Company's warships worked out at 30*s* a mile, with little revenue from passengers and none from commercial sources to set against it. P&O offered to work the whole 'comprehensive' scheme for 22*s* a mile, saving £30,000; the 2 lines running alternately would give a fortnightly mail service with India, bringing India into communication with England in 27 days.[42]

An ominous silence from the East India Company over the next three months led the MDs to modify the scheme, reinstating a monthly service from Calcutta and proposing to take over only a section of the Bombay–Suez line – the 'expensive' portion between Aden and Suez.[43] The letter detailing that modification, which expressed the 'hopelessness' of carrying on such a costly communication without proper support, was ignored. The MDs wrote again in March 1844, thinly disguising 'any appearance of a desire to precipitate the deliberations of the Honourable Company', but clearly anxious and impatient[44] since a contract was 'the *only* prospect which existed of remuneration for such a heavy outlay' as had already been spent on vessels for the eastern station.[45]

There was no comfort in the curt note that came two months later, to the effect that P&O's plan was unacceptable and that the company had better look to the Government in London for a contract.[46] The refrain was always the same: the East India Company would have nothing to do with this or any other plan that meant giving up any portion of the Bombay–Suez line, since it was adamant that this line was required to provide employment for the Indian Navy.[47] Steam communication with India had apparently run into an immovable obstacle.

In the spring of 1844, all the relevant departments in the British Government decided to go ahead with a contract based on P&O's plan if that obstacle could be removed. It could not. Exasperated, Ripon had to give way, conceding the East India Company's argument that the Indian Navy acted as insurance against a complete failure of P&O's operations east of Suez. The East India Company could therefore keep the Bombay–Suez line, though there were conditions: the Indian Navy must run fast steamers that would serve as warships but provide adequate space for passengers, to do away with 'the painful inconveniences' to passengers and 'the manifest deprivations inflicted' on merchandise.[48]

No sooner was this – from P&O's point of view unsatisfactory – agreement concluded than a new stumbling-block was raised that nearly wrecked the whole enterprise. This was the all-important question of who was to pay for the contract. The Treasury insisted that the cost must be shared equally between the British and Indian Governments; the latter refused to pay more than one-third.[49] Ripon could hardly contain his anger at the East India Company's narrow view of steam communication. It seemed that it could see nothing beyond the Bombay–Suez line and the Indian Navy, while the British Government had 'objects more extended than the communication with India alone'. But those objects were 'so interwoven . . . with Indian interests' that any part of the plan should be considered only as 'parts of one comprehensive system'. P&O's proposals had been aimed at improving and accelerating the existing Bombay–Suez line, yet the East India Company concentrated on petty matters, spreading innuendoes about P&O that had been leaked to losers of the prize in 1840 and designed to cast doubt on the company's ability to carry out a contract east of Suez. The British Government had already bowed to the East India Company's wish to keep the Bombay line; as to P&O's means and ability, the company was 'remarkable' for its 'punctual performance' and inquiries into its means had been 'entirely satisfactory'. Whatever the views of the East India Company, Ripon said that the British Government intended to make a contract with P&O for the Calcutta–Suez line which, together with the 12 Bombay–Suez voyages by the Indian Navy's vessels, would provide 24 communications between India and England each year. For the Calcutta–Suez line, and for the connection from Ceylon to China – dealt with in detail in chapter 3 – P&O had calculated that £170,000 would be a fair subsidy: 20*s* a mile for the Indian line, and 12*s* for the China line.[50] Also reasonable was P&O's request for a term of 7 or 10 years, and the cost would have to be shared equally by the London and Indian Governments.[51]

Still the East India Company refused to compromise. The contract was far too expensive. P&O should not get such a large sum 'merely for the conveyance of mail upon a line which has been established for mercantile purposes and upon which a considerable return on freight and passage money may be expected'. And why should India be burdened with 24 mails when 12 were onerous enough? Besides, P&O would never be able to carry out its expensive scheme. Further defamatory suggestions about P&O incidentally revealed that some of them emanated from 'other parties desirous of competing for employment of their vessels, at least on the China portion of it', one of whom was Captain Andrew Henderson, always ready to slander P&O.[52] He decried the 'efforts made by a London Steam Company to obtain a monopoly of all the Government assistance to steam navigation in the East Indies, as well as of all the passengers by that route', and alleged that through public meetings and the press P&O had deliberately put it about that the Indian Navy's vessels were inefficient, so that the company could make way for its own steamers.[53]

Ripon ignored these poisonous remarks. He was more concerned about removing the financial obstacle put up by the East India Company. Unable to persuade it to pay more than £70,000 towards the subsidy, and that only for a 5–year term, Ripon managed to wheedle an extra £5,000 out of the Treasury, and then looked to P&O to bridge the gap by sacrificing £10,000 of its asking price. To avoid any more delays the MDs 'very hesitatingly accepted the Reduction',[54] but were able in return to negotiate a 7–year term, arguing that it was 'somewhat unreasonable' to expect the outlay of about £250,000 on vessels constructed for this service 'upon so very brief a tenure as a contract for five years only'.[55] Thanks to Ripon, East India House was obliged to accept the longer term. Even after the major problems had been ironed out, the details of the contract were not finalized until the end of 1844. To the last, the East India Company persisted in besmirching P&O, predicting that the company would not be ready to begin the

Calcutta line in January nor to open the line to China in August 1846, thus disappointing the public and embarrassing the Post Office.[56]

But P&O had not yet failed to start a service on the contract date, and the MDs had no intention of giving East India House the satisfaction of fulfilling its dismal forecast: both lines east of Suez started on schedule. The 'superior manner' in which P&O had carried out the Peninsular and Mediterranean contracts was tantamount to a guarantee of the company's competence east of Suez.

This record of reliability, and the tenacity and tactical skill of Willcox, Anderson and Carleton, who altered their play as the game opened out, won the contract for the company. Throughout the months of negotiating for the contract, the board placed 'unlimited confidence' in those three men, 'leaving them free to act on emergencies daily arising to the best of their judgement'. Their 'unwearied exertions', so 'highly beneficial to the interests of the Company', had at last reached a triumphant conclusion. Exulting in their victory, the MDs could not resist a final barb aimed at Curtis and his *Precursor* friends, 'the parties who tho' most respectable were not conversant or experienced in Steam Navigation'. In 1841, Curtis vented his spleen when he knew he had lost: 'whether any underhand plot was laid . . . by which commission or advantages of a pecuniary nature were to be obtained, I do not know; but it seems very remarkable' that P&O had won the contract. As working shipowners, P&O's principals had placed their company in a 'proud & independent position'[57] that was to become the envy of the shipping world.

Notes

1 From a letter of 1841, quoted in Bourne, *Palmerston: The Early Years*, p. 625.

2 S. Palmer, *Politics, Shipping and the Repeal of the Navigation Laws* (Manchester: Manchester University Press, 1990), pp. 167ff.

3 *PP*, 1860, 18 (480), *SC on Transport Services*, qq. 371–4.

4 ADM 2/1293, fos 156–9, 25.6.1840; 1295, fo. 419, 19.8.1841.

5 P&O/15/2, fo. 87, 31.10.1840; fo. 89, 4.11.1840; P&O/6/2, Report, 30.11.1842, p. 9; *ibid.*, ch. 2, p. 22, table 1a; *Times*, 27.7.1846, p. 5, col. 4.

6 *PP*, 1847, 36 (117), *Copies of Contracts*, pp. 8–9; ADM 2/1287, fo. 507, 3.7.1838; ADM 2/1295, fo. 444, 8.9.1841.

7 Among many, see P&O/1/100, 19.5.1846 (£1,146), P&O/1/101, 12.5.1848 (£1,300), P&O/1/103, 9.7.1852 (£1,322).

8 *PP*, 1851, 21 (605), *Second Report, SC on Steam Communication to India &c*, (*Second Report*), qq. 4798–805.

9 See pp. 33–4 above.

10 ADM 2/1310, fos 344–5, 23.5.1849.

11 P&O/1/100, 7.2.1845, 22.4.1845, 6.5.1845, 27.5.1845; ADM 2/1297, fo. 207, 24.9.1842; ADM 2/1300, fos 430–2, 23.12.1844, fo. 543, 5.2.1845; ADM 2/1301, fo. 172–3, 30.4.1845, fos 214–5, 23.5.1845 and 28.2.1845; *PP*, 1849, 12 (571): Contract Packets, q. 1735.

12 £1,000 was deducted annually; in 1842, P&O's withdrawal from the Ionian Islands line reduced the subsidy by £3,500: P&O/1/100, 26.4.1842, 2.8.1842; ADM 2/1300, fo. 546, 8.2.1845; ADM 2/1301, fo. 25, 24.2.1845, fos 214–5, 23.5.1845; *PP*, 1849, 12 (571), *Contract Packets*, q. 2047, p. 132; *PP*, 1851, 21 (605), *Second Report*, Appendix 4, p. 368; ADM 2/1301, fo. 546, 8.2.1845; P&O/1/100, 11.3.1845.
13 P&O/1/100, 23.4.1847.
14 P&O/2/1, 4.8.1840; P&O/1/100, 6.11.1840.
15 *PP*, 1849, 12 (571), *Contract Packets*, qq. 1728–30.
16 France sided with the ruler of Egypt, while all the other Great Powers supported Turkey in a clash between suzerain and vassal.
17 P&O/30/25, [First] Charter, 31.12.1840, p. 4.
18 P&O/6/2, First Annual Report, 30.11.1841, p. 8.
19 P&O/1/100, 6.11.1840, 23.12.1840, 7.9.1841, 26.4.1842, 17.5.1842, 24.10.1843, 21.11.1843, 5.12.1843, 30.1.1844; ADM 2/1294, fo. 310, 9.12.1840, fos 490–4, 9.2.1841; ADM 2/1296, fo. 290–1, 22.2.1842, fo. 458, 10.5.1842, fo. 500, 23.5.1842; ADM 2/1297, fo. 101, 29.7.1842; ADM 2/1298, fo. 357, 29.5.1843; ADM 2/1299, fos 51–5, 21.9.1843. P&O's first offer of £20,000 was pushed down to £12,000, but the Treasury still thought it was too high.
20 See n. 15 above.
21 P&O/1/100, 26.4.1842 and 2.8.1842.
22 *PP*, 1851, 21 (605), *Second Report*, qq. 4116–17.
23 P&O/1/100, 17.1.1843 and 7.3.1843. Bourne left Southampton on 4 April and returned early in July.
24 *Ibid.*, 9.12.1845; supplemental charter, 23.12.1845, pp. 2–3.
25 P&O/1/101, 23.4.1847 and 25.5.1847.
26 *PP*, 1851, 21 (605), *Second Report*, Appendix 4, p. 376–7.
27 Hyde, *Cunard*, pp. 16–19; Hyde names the Moss, Bibby and Dixon lines as newcomers to the Black Sea, p. 17. General Screw ran steamers to Holland and the Mediterranean in 1848: J.M. Maber, *From North Star to Southern Cross* (Prescot, Lancashire: Stephenson, 1967), p. 52. The young Donald Currie was B&F's manager, displaying the competence that led to his later successful career in South African shipping: see A.N. Porter, *Victorian Shipping, Business and Imperial Policy: Donald Currie, the Castle Line and Southern Africa* (Woodbridge: Boydell Press, 1986), pp. 26–7.
28 *Achilles* (built 1839, 820 tons) was rejected by P&O as unsuitable in 1844, but was bought in 1845: see S. Rabson and K. O'Donoghue, *P&O: A Fleet History* (Kendal: World Ship Society, 1988), no. 28, p. 32; *Tiger* (built 1835, 620 tons) was hired for 16 months at £150 per week: P&O/1/101, 10.11.1846 and 8.10.1847; *Jupiter* (built 1835, 610 tons) was hired in June 1847 at the same rate for 18 months, with an option to buy which was taken up: *ibid.*, 4.6.1847 and 31.12.1847.
29 P&O/1/102, 2.3.1849; the cost of £440 was met by the company because it gained from the loyalty of these merchants; lesser feasts for shippers would have been at the expense of the MDs.
30 *Ibid.*, 28.9.1849 and 14.6.1850; P&O/1/103, 23.11.1852 and 21.12.1852.
31 P&O/1/103, 12.7.1853.
32 *PP*, 1854–55, 20 (–), *First Report of the Postmaster-General on the Post Office*, pp. 27–8.
33 P&O/15/5, 12.5.1856, 23.5.1856 and 31.10.1856; P&O/1/104, 12.8.1856.
34 P&O/1/100, 26.11.1844, 17.12.1844, 14.1.1845, 4.2.1845, 8.4.1845, 9.12.1845 and 12.5.1846.
35 The 'capitalists' were the proprietors of the Neapolitan Steam Navigation Company; it traded with Naples and Sicily in 1846: *Times*, 12.11.1846, p. 5, col. 1; *ibid.*, 24.12.1846, p. 7, col. 5.
36 P&O/1/100, 13.11.1844, 17.11.1844, 14.1.1845 and 4.2.1845.
37 P&O/1/101, 16.11.1847, 19.11.1847, 14.4.1848, 30.6.1848, 11.7.1848, 25.8.1848, 10.11.1848; P&O/1/103, 11.1.1853, 26.4.1853, 9.9.1853 and 24.1.1854.
38 *PP*, 1850, 53 (693), *Correspondence*, pp. 42–6, 16.2. (April) 1841.

39 P.E. Roberts, *History of British India under the Company and the Crown* (London: Oxford University Press, 1958), pp. 321ff.

40 Scion of an old East India Company family, he was given a seat on P&O's board in 1862 after his retirement: P&O/1/105, 14.11.1862.

41 The distance between Bombay and Suez is 2,900 miles, and from Calcutta to Suez 4,800 miles.

42 *PP*, 1850, 53 (693), *Correspondence*, pp. 56–7, 24.10.1843. The scheme was more economical because, while Bombay was to have a monthly service, Calcutta, connected to the Bombay–Suez line at Aden, needed only two-monthly calls.

43 *PP*, 1850, 53 (693), pp. 59–61, 11.1.1844.

44 *Ibid.*, pp. 61–2, 30.3.1844.

45 P&O/6/2, Half-Yearly Report, 30.5.1843, p. 8.

46 *PP*, 1850, 53 (693), *Correspondence*, pp. 59–62, 11.1.1844, 23.4.1844, 29.5.1844.

47 *Ibid.*, pp. 53–61, 22.8.1843, 24.10.1843, 11.1.1844.

48 *Ibid.*, pp. 62–3, 23.4.1844.

49 *Ibid.*, pp. 61–2, 28.3.1844, 29.5.1844, pp. 65–9, 22.5.1844, 3.7.1844.

50 *Ibid.*, pp. 62–4, 23.4.1844.

51 *Ibid.*, p. 71, 25.7.1844.

52 See above, p. 59.

53 *PP*, 1850, 53 (693), *Correspondence*, pp. 87–8.

54 P&O/1/100, 23.7.1844.

55 *PP*, 1850, 53 (693), *Correspondence*, pp. 69–73, 11.7.1844, 13.7.1844, 22.7.1844, 23.7.1844 and 25.7.1844.

56 *Ibid.*, pp. 79–80, 12.12.1844, 24.12.1844 and 31.12.1844.

57 P&O/1/100, 23.7.1844 and 7.1.1845.

CHAPTER THREE

From India to China: P&O and the opium trade, 1845–57

Service on the second part of the 1844 contract, the Ceylon–China line, began in 1845 and placed P&O on the trunk routes to the Far East. Further extensions – Bombay–Hong Kong and Calcutta–Hong Kong – were ready in May 1846, and a third line from Hong Kong to Shanghai was in view. P&O regarded all three extensions as '*absolutely necessary* to protect the interests' of the company.[1] The 1844 contract also enabled the company to introduce steam transport to the opium trade. Opium played such a significant part in P&O's history and prosperity in the nineteenth century that the company's expansion in the Far East needs to be placed in the context of the opium trade more generally.

Black gold[2]

Indian opium had a unique status: apart from small quantities of the Persian product exported to Europe through Smyrna (Izmir), India was the sole supplier. The drug was widely prized for self-medication and for the temporary sense of well-being it produced.[3] During the Moghul era in India, the Emperor's monopoly of opium brought him a handsome revenue from exports to China. As Moghul India declined, the monopoly fell into abeyance, but it was reinstated at the turn of the nineteenth century by the East India Company and taken over intact in 1858 by the Government of India after the Mutiny. From about 1820, the opium industry in British India was consistently expanded to provide revenue from exports. Opium was cultivated, manufactured and sold by the Government for foreign consumption on an increasing scale, and more moderately for domestic use. Only in the sphere of sea transport did the Government distance itself from the trade, handing this function over to private merchant shipowners.[4]

China was a peculiarly vulnerable recipient. With a self-sufficient domestic economy, the empire had no need to trade and had been closed to foreigners for centuries, except for very limited access through the tiny Portuguese settlement of Macao. Opium was the only article that did not compete with any of China's domestic products,[5] and the Chinese were willing to pay high prices for it. On the other side of the globe, tea – at that time grown only in China – had become *'a necessity of life in England'*.[6] For the East India Company, the opportunity to make opium pay for tea was irresistible. Moreover for British and American merchants, eager to exploit China's enormous closed market, opium was the key that would unlock it.[7]

Thus a 'triangular web' was spun between Britain's imports of tea, China's payments for opium and India's financial obligations to the metropole.[8] As late as 1881, the Government of India had no doubt about the efficacy of this arrangement:

> One of the elements which regulates exchange between England and India is the balance of trade between the two countries. In proportion as the exports from India exceed in amount the imports from England, exchange will be favourable to India. The China trade, however, exercises a very important influence on exchange. England owes China a large sum of money annually, which represents the excess of imports from China over exports from the United Kingdom. China, on the other hand, owes India a large sum annually, mainly for opium. This debt is, in a great measure, paid by transferring to India a portion of England's debt to China.

Between 1853 and 1881 imports of tea and silk cost Britain £323 million while exports from Britain to China were worth only £121 million. Britain's annual deficit, on average about £4 million, was wiped out with money earned each year from opium and sent to Britain from India by way of tribute in the guise of 'Home Charges'.[9]

Indirectly, opium revenue was a convenient alternative to the imposition of additional taxes on India's overwhelmingly poor population. In 1832, the East India Company justified the 'very large revenue' derived from the excess of the sale price over the first cost of the drug by asserting that 'such a tax . . . would be hopeless to get by any other device', and that it would not be prudent 'to abandon so important a source of revenue . . . which falls principally upon the foreign consumer, and which appears, upon the whole, less liable to objection than any other which could be constituted'.[10] Opium thus ranked high among the principal sources of revenue in British India. In the early decades, the land tax was the main source, with the salt monopoly second and opium third. Opium replaced salt in the 1860s with 17 per cent of the total, and did not fall below 6 per cent even when the trade was in decline.

The opening of China to opium

Lord Palmerston, the Foreign Secretary, declared that 'though in regard of the quickness of the returns, markets nearer home might be better, yet on a political point of view it must be remembered that these distant transactions . . . employ our manufacturers'.[11] Both he and the merchants were at one in wanting the supremely rich trade in opium to be drawn into British hands.

In the 1820s and 1830s, two obstacles were perceived to hinder the development of a reciprocal trade with China. First, the importation of opium was officially prohibited by the Chinese Government, and foreigners were not allowed to establish settlements on the coast or to go into the interior. Second, China's ancient commercial regime was such that trading according to British practice could not be carried on. Aware that the Chinese Government was too weak to enforce its prohibition edicts, private merchants who transported opium to China and sold it to the Chinese grew bolder: they moved up the coast, made bases for themselves on islands off Canton, and in the 1830s ventured occasional voyages as far as Tientsin (Tianjin) and Manchuria,[12] selling the drug to Chinese dealers off shore from receiving vessels on a cash-and-carry basis. But trading under these conditions was unsatisfactory. If reciprocal commerce was to be properly nurtured, the old ways in China would have to be changed and the interior opened to the West.

In 1833, the Act of Parliament that deprived the East India Company of its monopoly of the India–China trade encouraged private merchants to crowd in on the opium trade. But this increased the pressure on the confined market, and the resulting invasion of newcomers upset the old-established pioneers. Their anxiety intensified in the later 1830s when the Imperial Government issued an edict of prohibition on opium which was executed with unusual vigour. Unless fundamental changes were wrought in China, the opium trade might wither away and any chance of penetrating the closed empire would be lost.[13] William Jardine, senior partner in Jardines (Jardine, Matheson & Co.), by far the most successful and influential of all the firms in China, launched a campaign for the destruction of China's antique method of trading, calling for action from the British Government to bring about the desired result.[14] It was not difficult to pick a quarrel. China became more determined to maintain the old ways as the Western merchants became more aggressive. Almost inevitably, war broke out in 1839 over the confiscation and burning of opium worth more than £2 million. The outcome was defeat for China. In 1842, the Treaty of Nanking opened five ports – Canton (Gwangzhou),

Amoy (Xiamen), Foochow (Fuzhou), Ningpo and Shanghai – to foreign trade, allowed British consuls to reside in them, gave Britain a secure base in Hong Kong and deprived China of her customs autonomy.[15] Although opium had everything to do with the war, it was not once mentioned in the treaty and in theory remained contraband. In practice, greater quantities of opium were brought to the coast, with Chinese officials not even pretending to intervene.

The opium trade under sail and steam

Among the numerous foreign flags plying the China Sea, Americans were strong competitors. But Jardines, formed in 1832 out of a succession of partnerships that began in 1782, towered over all the other firms.[16] Before the advent of steam in the China Sea, opium was carried in a variety of locally owned sailing vessels. Though British merchant–owners dominated, Parsees had a significant share of the dealing and carrying trade. Specially designed clippers, with several coasters and receiving ships besides, made up the combined 'opium fleet' of more than 100 vessels.[17] But even the fastest clippers could make only 2, or at most, 3 voyages each year, for none of them could withstand the adverse north-east monsoon. A voyage by clipper from Bombay to China could be made in 40–50 days in fine weather, but took twice that time when caught by the monsoon.[18] Again, sailing vessels carrying opium were subject to piratical violence; this necessitated arms for defence and a large complement on board, thus adding to costs. Moreover, Eastern seas were inadequately surveyed, and unpredictable typhoons made insurance expensive. Investors in Britain could not expect a return on their capital within the year. All these drawbacks of sail account for the great interest taken in steam navigation in India in the 1820s and 1830s. Steam committees sprang up in Bombay, Calcutta and Madras to demand steam communication, and many unworkable schemes were put forward to hasten its arrival. By 1837, marine technology made it possible to navigate on long-haul routes by steam and the British Government yielded to public pressure by placing naval steam vessels on both sides of Suez to carry mail.[19] Government contracts to private steam companies, among them P&O, followed shortly afterwards.

In 1847, P&O began to transport opium from Bombay to China. This was a propitious moment for the company. The Opium War was over; though limited to the five Treaty Ports, foreigners now had access to the maritime provinces north of Hong Kong as far as Shanghai; and changes in commercial practice in China raised expectations of a promising trade.[20] The only regular and reliable commercial steam company in the East, P&O reduced the time for communication between Britain and India to about 6 weeks – P&O's best time in 1851 from Southampton to Calcutta was 37 days – and 7 weeks to China. As engines became more efficient, voyage time was pared down further: in 1867, Bombay was reached in under 4, Calcutta in under 5 weeks.[21] P&O was fortunate, too, in that it had already occupied routes in the East by the time the British Navigation Laws were abolished in 1849, thus giving British steamships the advantage over any foreign predators.[22]

The low volume and high value of opium made it the ideal cargo for steamships, and the impact of steam on the opium trade was felt in many ways. In the early 1800s, the East India Company held two public sales of opium each year in Calcutta. Increased from time to time, there were nine sales a year by the time P&O's steamers arrived on the scene. Shortly after P&O had carried its first cargo of opium in 1847, the Government decided to have a sale every month, to achieve its policy of 'an annually increasing . . . supply'.[23]

Table 3.1 shows the recovery of the opium trade after the 1839–42 war and, from 1845, the impact of P&O's regular monthly overland communication from London via Suez. The fall in value in 1847–48 can be attributed to the general lack of confidence following the commercial crisis in Britain and India. Better times in 1848–49 coincided with P&O's steam transport from Bombay and the increase of sales at Calcutta to twelve per year. From 1848, Bombay exports, though they advanced erratically, were more likely to go by P&O than by sail, though because space for cargo was very limited in early steamships, and their cost very high, P&O could not carry all the opium that could be shipped from Bombay each month. At Calcutta, the government-controlled output went by sail until steam was established there in the 1850s (see below). Table 3.2 shows how steam affected the volume of opium exported to China by each outlet.

Mercantile houses and investors gained from steam communication in other ways too: the safety, speed and reliability of P&O's steamships reduced insurance costs and interest on loans. Millions of pounds were turned over each year in opium alone. Under steam, sea-borne trade moved into a much higher gear simply by the regular and safe delivery of bills of exchange, indents for merchandise and shipments of specie and bullion, and indirectly by encouraging investment and enterprise in the East.[24] Back cargoes on the China line to Bombay consisted largely of gold, silver and specie. Silk began to be exported from China by steam in quantity in the late 1850s and tea in the late 1860s, but those cargoes were taken to Europe, not India.

Table 3.1 Quantity and value[a] of chests exported from India to China, 1836–37 to 1857–58

Year	*Chests*	*Value*
1836–37	31,375	3,934,459
1837–38	26,484	2,904,284
1838–39	31,852	2,791,132
1839–40	3,948	191,422
1840–41	17,839	1,267,887
1841–42	25,695	1,839,401
1842–43	30,108	2,820,352
1843–44	32,341	4,229,542
1844–45	29,594	4,133,591
1845–46	40,965	5,541,735
1846–47	30,057	4,271,320
1847–48	34,349	3,507,804
1848–49	49,262	5,345,719
1849–50	47,509	5,543,588
1850–51	48,030	5,074,078
1851–52	58,089	6,082,307
1852–53	56,412	6,470,916
1853–54	60,054	5,802,469
1854–55	69,910	5,684,978
1855–56	63,427	5,592,532
1856–57	66,305	6,505,586
1857–58	68,004	8,241,032

Source: *PP*, 1859, session 2, 23 (38), p. 11.
Note: [a] Value = current £s sterling derived from the monthly proceeds of opium sales at Calcutta and export duty at Bombay.

Bengal and Malwa

There were two distinct varieties of opium cultivated in India – Bengal and Malwa. Bengal, or 'monopoly', opium was the common name of opium produced at Patna and Benares in British India. Quantity and quality were regulated by the Government. Regarded as superior to any other, the two Bengal strains were at the luxury end of the trade and usually fetched high prices at the public sales and in China. Only licensed dealers were allowed to take part in the sales, and the opium had to be shipped within a period laid down by the Government. Export opium was carefully packed in wooden chests in 2 layers, each with 20 sculptured lumps of about 3.5*lbs*. Eight chests made a measured ton,[25] but the drug was priced, sold and carried by the chest.

Table 3.2 Number of chests exported from Bombay & Calcutta, 1844–45 to 1857–58

Year	*Bombay*	*Calcutta*
1844–45	20,660	18,792
1845–46	12,635	20,553
1846–47	18,602	24,990
1847–48	15,485	23,877
1848–49	21,392	32,902
1849–50	16,513	35,093
1850–51	19,138	32,902
1851–52	28,168	32,306
1852–53	24,979	36,178
1853–54	26,113	40,795
1854–55	25,958	51,421
1855–56	25,576	44,938
1856–57	29,846	42,441
1857–58	36,125	38,613

Source: *PP*, 1865, 40 (94), pp. 4, 10–12.

Officials regulated the number of chests to be sold at each auction in order to gain the maximum price; and in the second half of the century, a proportion of the manufactured article was held back each year to act as a reserve to meet future demand or to compensate for a poor crop. All Bengal opium was shipped from Calcutta.

Jardines dominated the carrying trade, with Apcars in second place. In 1842, Jardines made its headquarters in Hong Kong, and set up Jardine, Skinner & Co. (Skinners hereafter), to manage its shipping business in Calcutta. Jardines bought and sold on commission whatever its clients required, but the company had a special and often personal interest in opium. In collaboration with other mercantile houses in Calcutta and Bombay, Jardines owned a fleet of clippers, and an array of coasting and receiving vessels in China. The Apcars were Armenians who had been prominent in the China trade since the early 1800s; they also had their own vessels, and dealt in opium with constituents all over the East. They had an intimate relationship with native dealers, and could call on small shipowners to help out when necessary.[26]

Malwa was the other strain of opium, cultivated and manufactured as a private enterprise in the native states of central India and Rajputana. Gwalior and Indore states had the biggest stake in Malwa; another was Bophul; Baroda stopped exporting the drug long before the official end. Different in taste and consistency from Bengal opium, Malwa was described as 'black gold' because of the hue it took on during its manufacture.[27] It was different, too, in that it was grown in areas not under British governance and produced at will by local landowners. Before 1820, Malwa was carried to Macao via Diu and Daman, two Portuguese settlements on the west coast of India.[28] Compared with the Bengal strain, Malwa's quality was questionable and its packaging sloppy.

Having failed to establish a monopoly in Malwa in the 1820s, the East India Company decided instead to levy a tax on opium exported at Bombay. To avoid this imposition, or 'pass', dealers smuggled the drug through Sind to Karachi and thence to China, and they were not won back by a reduction of the tax. But in 1842, Britain went to war with Sind and annexed it. From 1843, opium in that province was prohibited, the leakage at Karachi was stopped and Malwa opium was thereafter exported from Bombay. Government policy was to tax Malwa as heavily as possible 'short of killing the trade'.[29] Demand from China was buoyant, and in the 1860s cheap rail communication with Bombay encouraged licit exports.[30] Because Malwa opium went through many hands on the long journey to the coast, its cost was much higher than that of Bengal opium, and the high export tax was said to have 'often caused losses to the trade and much discouraged the cultivation'. Those factors account partly for Malwa's lower output.[31] In addition, Malwa opium's only market was China, whereas Bengal's was distributed from Singapore and Hong Kong to the Straits, the Dutch East Indies, the Philippines and other places.[32]

Dealers bought, sold and shipped opium from Calcutta or Bombay depending on demand and price, so that the two varieties were in constant competition with each other. When Charles Skinner (of Skinners) heard that the Malwa crop in 1847 was 'deficient in quantity and *worse* in quality than usual', he knew that Bombay dealers would buy in the Calcutta market instead and so push Bengal prices up. William Jardine, however, did not want Malwa to sink in value. He appointed T.G. Beaumont as 'Inspector of Drug for Jardine Matheson & Co'. Other firms followed this practice. By the 1850s the Malwa variety had become more standardized after the enforcement of 'very stringent regulations'. Chests for export from Bombay were passed only if the drug had been properly prepared.[33]

P&O and the Malwa trade, 1847–53

William Jardine did much to develop the trade in Malwa and pioneered its distribution far beyond Canton in the 1830s. He also formed a syndicate with some of the leading firms in Bombay which together made the best deals for their clients and themselves. In 1847, the syndicate consisted of Jardines and three other firms: R.F. Remington & Co.; Colvin, Ainslie, Cowie & Co.; and Sir Jamsetji Jeejeebhoy & Sons. The syndicate owned opium clippers in common, pooled resources for operations in Bengal and Malwa, and divided profits annually. There was constant communication between the members, either by letter or in person, and between China, Calcutta, Bombay and London. In 1847, for example, Robert Crawford (of Crawford, Remington & Co.) expected Alexander Matheson to come to Bombay where they would 'lay their heads together' to plan the syndicate's strategy for the next season's crop.[34] Both Crawford and Matheson left Bombay for London in 1847, the former (whose firm did not survive the commercial crisis of that year) to replace his father (who had earlier spent many years in India) as senior partner in the newly formed Crawford, Colvin & Co. in London; the latter to take over Magniac, Jardine & Co., the ailing merchant bank that had been Jardines' financial arm, and, with the help of his uncle James Matheson, to recreate it as Matheson & Co. for the same purpose.[35] Jardines had more than fifty correspondents in Bombay and about the same number in Calcutta.[36] Sir Jamsetji Jeejeebhoy, affectionately known as 'Sir J.J.' and famous for his charitable munificence, was the richest and most important of several Parsee family concerns. These were the principal players in the trade in Malwa opium when P&O came on the scene in 1847.

According to Anderson's *Letter* of 1840,[37] P&O's founders were 'unconnected with India' when they won the mail contract in 1840, and, as late as 1851, George Braine, promoter of a rival company, sought to belittle the company by asserting: 'I do not find a single name [on P&O's board] that has anything to do with the India trade at all . . . excepting the chairman, Sir James Matheson, who, I believe, has a mere honorary appointment but who has nothing to do with the direction of affairs'.[38] In fact, the directors were well aware of the importance of the opium trade and knew it would add the 'advantage of an enormous trade already existing upon which to found [their] calculations and expectations'.[39] To acquaint themselves with the intricacies of the trade, the founders gathered a succession of men whose knowledge of the trade would help them to make the best of this opportunity:[40] Larpent had chaired the influential East India and China Association since its inception in 1836;[41] Campbell had mercantile experience with India; Sir James Matheson was the senior partner in Jardine, Matheson & Co. in China until he retired to Britain in 1842 and retained an interest in the China trade through his investment in Matheson & Co., his nephew's merchant bank; and John

Abel Smith, MP, once a partner in Magniac, Smith & Co. (Jardine, Matheson & Co.'s predecessor) had in 1844 'taken a good deal of pains to forward' the 'great and comprehensive plan' for the long-awaited steam communication that P&O put to the Government.[42]

Less distinguished though no less knowledgeable were the men chosen to sit on the P&O board, the policy of the company being that there should always be at least one director with personal experience in the opium trade. Patrick Douglas Hadow had 'many connections and friends' in the East 'where his father and other relations had for a long time been involved'; the family partnership was hard hit in the 1847 collapse, but one of his relatives, J.R. Hadow, remained in Bombay for a few years in the reconstituted partnership of Colvin, Ainslie, Cowie & Co., a member of Jardines' syndicate. P.D. Hadow's own interest in P&O dated from the company's foundation: he bought shares in the first issue of capital in 1841 and made himself useful to the company before joining the board in 1849, becoming deputy chairman in 1861 and chairman in 1868.[43] Thomas Stock Cowie, a partner in Colvin, Ainslie, Cowie, had over twenty years' experience of the trade before his retirement in 1868, and was then given a seat on the board.[44] He was succeeded in 1881 by Montague Cleugh Wilkinson who had lived in India since 1858 and also became a partner in Crawford, Colvin & Co. in London. A vacancy on the board created by the death in 1888 of Captain J.R. Engledue[45] made room for Edward Ford Duncanson, one of the 'leading merchants in the China trade, and the head of one of the oldest and most valued firms' with which P&O dealt.[46] The last of these 'thorough men of business' to become a director was William Adamson whose firm, Adamson, Gilfillan & Co., had large interests in the Straits Settlements and valuable experience at Singapore, an important entrepôt for the distribution of opium.[47] But this list would not be complete without Thomas Sutherland, the man who had entered the company as a clerk at the age of 18, acted first as agent and then superintendent at Hong Kong for over a decade, founded the Hong Kong & Shanghai Bank in 1864, returned to London to see P&O through its most difficult period in the late 1860s, became an MD in 1872 and chairman in 1881, dominating the company and the shipping fraternity until 1914.

It was not possible for P&O to enter the opium trade in 1845, for neither Bombay nor a direct line between Calcutta and Hong Kong was included in its 1844 mail contract, and a request to the Government to subsidize the Bombay–Galle section of the opium route to China was refused.[48] It was imperative for the MDs to find a way into Bombay, for they calculated that freight on opium and specie on the Bombay–China line would be 'not less than two millions sterling' each year 'when the traffic [became] duly developed'. Moreover they were confident that, sooner or later, the East India Company would have to surrender the Bombay–Suez route: vessels of the Indian Navy would never be able to compete with private contract vessels. Some of the naval vessels had 15 very small cabins which accommodated 30 passengers; all the other travellers had to sleep in the saloon or on deck where 'there [were] no conveniences whatever; there [was] no place even for them to dress in'. One captain 'did not wish to be troubled with having any ladies on board'; and only in about 1850 were beds, bedding and food supplied.[49] With the Indian Navy out of the way, P&O would occupy the route as part of the company's overall strategy to monopolize all the main lines east of Suez: there was 'scarcely a doubt of this Company at no very distant period having the mail contract' for it. Furthermore, because it was 1,000 miles nearer than Calcutta to London, Bombay was certain to become the mail port for India. It was only a matter of time before the 1843 plan would be put into practice, so, 'looking to the vast importance of this line as it affects the Company's operations and interests on this side of the Isthmus', the fleet should be strengthened and ready 'to take it up at the shortest notice'.[50] Meanwhile, for practical reasons, the company needed dock and repair facilities at Bombay in case of accidents at the Suez end of the Suez–Calcutta mail route. P&O was thus able to install itself 'under official sanction' at Bombay. By 1847, the company had acquired a dock and repairing establishment at Mazagon, and was ready to test the opium trade 'commercially' (without a contract on the Bombay–Galle section of the line to Hong Kong) by dispatching *Erin* (798 gross registered tonnage [grt]) on an experimental voyage in March 1847 with 400 chests of Malwa opium on board. Consumption of coal in the contrary north-east monsoon was the critical factor: if too high, the venture might not pay.[51] A favourable result removed all fears, because, apart from coal, costs were covered by the mail subsidy, since the vessels carrying opium came under contract at Galle. Bombay became the terminus of the opium line; a regular monthly service began in August, and the company undertook to carry mail without expense to the Government from Bombay to Galle.[52] Though many firms went out of business in the commercial crisis that began in October 1847, the opium trade was not seriously affected.

For the first time, shippers in Bombay experienced the advantages of a reliable specialist steamship company. P&O did not care who bought or sold the drug; the company's only interest was in carrying it. The superiority of steam transport made it an instant success. A monthly voyage of about twenty-three days to China made sail redundant. Clippers quoted Rs20 (£2 per chest, £16 per ton), and to begin with, it appears that P&O either kept to that rate for a short time or asked for a percentage of the value of the cargo.[53] In 1851, when P&O advertised Rs30 (£3 per chest, £24 per ton of 8 chests) for *Pacha* (548 grt), the vessel failed to get a cargo, but 2 years later, Rs28 and Rs30 were accepted. On return voyages, gold, silver and specie were carried at the rate of 2.5 per cent from Shanghai.[54]

Bombay members of the syndicate, with substantial interests in the opium trade, welcomed steam transport. J.R. Hadow remarked on the 'eagerness to ship [opium] in the Steamer', and he anticipated that 'the Steamers here will get everything in the N.E. Monsoon'.[55] *Pekin* (1,182 grt) and *Achilles* (820 grt) arrived late with the mails at Hong Kong because they were carrying 'excessive cargoes, especially opium': the former had 1,500 chests on board; the bunkers and hold of the latter were filled with opium, and coal was stored on deck.[56] Though the poppy crop was seasonal, steam transport allowed opium to be exported throughout the year. The trade was most buoyant at the beginning of the new season, which coincided with the north-east monsoon – 'the Bombay Steamers [were] quite *full* of Opium for 6 months in the year' – but smaller shipments were carried in the other months.[57]

Within a short time, steam transport on the Bombay line was well established, and its effect was felt in Hong Kong, Shanghai, London and in Calcutta. The monthly public sales in Calcutta expanded the trade, and Skinners reckoned that 'a clipper every month' would be needed if Bengal was to keep pace with Malwa. Could their Bombay friends do without *Mor* and *Lanrick* (two of the syndicate's clippers) 'now that the P&O are about to put a [regular] Steamer on the line from Bombay to China'? The answer, repeated several times, was that the syndicate was 'very anxious to get rid of [*Mor*], as they think the Steamers have entirely destroyed the Clipper trade to Bombay'. Sir J.J. & Sons insisted that Jardines 'should relieve them of their interest in these vessels, or dispose of them to someone else'. Skinners was advised to try to sell them outright, for no one in Bombay would buy a share in them. Two clippers were in a bad state and had to be withdrawn in turn for repairs. With only three clippers at any time, it was impossible for Jardines to be represented at every sale in Calcutta. Building a new clipper was considered but ruled out: 'with the certainty of the P&O Com[pan]y having sooner or later steamers between . . . [Calcutta] & China, it would perhaps not be desirable'. Despite the frustration of the syndicate members, Jardines still hesitated to sink capital in steamships. David Jardine's idea of cooperating with Dent & Co. was rejected.[58]

However, Bombay merchants who had quickly accepted the advantages of steam were disappointed to find that much of the Malwa export still had to go by sail, because for some years to come P&O's contract obligations meant that it could provide only a limited amount of tonnage. In 1851, a group of bankers and merchants in London, in association with several India and China houses involved in the opium trade, conceived an ambitious project which, among other things, would put more tonnage on the India and China lines, and at the same time compete with P&O and bring down the company's rate of freight. At least one former member of the syndicate now in London, Robert Wigram Crawford, was party to this scheme, as was George Braine, mentioned above. A new firm, the Eastern Steam Navigation Company, was to be set up to run in parallel with P&O, doubling voyages and tonnage.[59] With envious eyes on the opium trade, the promoters hoped to get a share of 'an immense amount of valuable traffic' that would otherwise give P&O 'a perfect monopoly of the trade' and the freedom 'to charge the public any rates they please'. Monopoly would prevent the full development of a trade that required 'a great extension': 'So very large a communication, involving so many interests in various parts of the world, ought not to be any longer in the hands of single company.'

These entrepreneurs accused P&O of failing to develop the trade more rapidly, asserting that it was 'not in its interest' to do so 'beyond a certain extent' because a monopolist would not 'push the traffic beyond what the present steam accommodation is barely adequate to supply'. 'Wholesome' competition, much in vogue in the wake of the abolition of the Navigation Laws, was seen as the solution to these problems.[60] Crawford and his friends organized parliamentary debates and lobbied for select committees in the Lords and the Commons, aiming to make a public attack on P&O before the 1844 mail contract, due for renewal at the end of 1852, was put out to tender. With Parliament's sanction, the recommendations of the select committees were incorporated in the tenders for the new contract.[61] But competition at that stage in long distance steam navigation was a fanciful notion, not a reality, and the new contract, to begin in 1853, was awarded to P&O.[62]

The failure of Eastern Steam to wrest the mail contract from P&O in the 1852 competition led the Bombay members of the syndicate to think of going into steam on their own in 1853. Inspector Beaumont had great doubts about the plan: 'No doubt several parties here think well of the idea on account of the large Freights which the P&O's vessels earn, but I am not sure that they take into consideration the enormous expenses. Without very powerful support, I don't think the scheme would answer, but we should not object to go into it with our above named friends, and other influential men.'[63] Three months later, the syndicate dropped the idea: prices had risen and coal was in very short supply. A new small company competing with P&O would fare badly, for P&O was able to keep ample stocks on hand and was 'always provided with spare articles of Machinery besides having a large establishment of workmen and a dockyard provided with all necessary appliances in Bombay'. Anyway, the immensely rich 'Sir J.J.' and his Parsee friends did not favour the proposal.[64]

In 1853, then, with P&O's bigger steamers specially built for the new contract, opium shippers expected to have more opportunities to send their opium by steam and hoped that freights would be cheaper. But the number of ships that could be spared for the opium line could not keep up with this expanding trade. Bombay was reasonably catered for, but Calcutta merchants complained that 'at present the steamers from Bombay are so filled that they refuse to take any of our Bengal opium down to Ceylon [for transhipment at Galle]; they have not got room'.[65] This was not surprising: contract mileage was almost doubled in 1853 because mails had to be carried fortnightly instead of monthly on the Suez–Calcutta and the Galle–Hong Kong lines, and the new steam line from Singapore to Sydney added many thousands of miles to the total. As before, the Bombay–Galle section of the Malwa line was not subsidized. But these facts were overlooked by the mercantile community: the company continued to be charged with inhibiting the development of trade and demanding exorbitant freights.[66] We shall see in the section after next how difficult it was for P&O to satisfy the demand for space on the Bengal opium line.

The 'direct' opium line and the Hong Kong–Shanghai connection

The second 'direct' opium line,[67] connecting Calcutta to Hong Kong via Singapore, was mooted in 1846,[68] and appears to have been discussed in some detail in London during the contract negotiations in 1843–44. One of the East India Company's criticisms of P&O's plans was that there was no provision for this opium line. A separate line would have to be established, therefore, necessitating a further subsidy. Ripon countered this view, pointing out that the Board of Control and the East India Company had 'lately' agreed

> in intimating to a private Company their desire to encourage the establishment of a regular line of steam communication for mail purposes, as well as others, between Singapore and Calcutta, – a project which, if

> carried out by private enterprize, will, in connexion with the line now about to be undertaken by the two Governments, give to Calcutta . . . direct communication with China . . .[69]

This discreetly worded statement mentions neither opium nor P&O. There is no doubt about opium being among the 'other' purposes; and which 'private Company' could it have been if not P&O? Captain Henderson? He sold *India*, the only steamer in which he had an interest, to P&O only in May 1845[70] after P&O had secured the contract for China, so it is possible that in 1844 he thought there was still a chance for him to get hold of this short but important line. His failure would account for his bitterness towards P&O. As it happened, no one could have made a fortune from *India* – P&O found it to be in such bad repair that it was never put to sea.[71]

Lady Mary Wood was to have opened the Calcutta extension in 1847; the MDs had always regarded the Calcutta line as 'indispensable', but neither this nor the extension from Hong Kong to Shanghai could be occupied as planned because of the commercial and political uncertainties of 1847–48. These were 'disastrous in an extraordinary degree, to nearly every branch of commercial interest and enterprise' in Europe, and several mercantile houses in Bombay and Calcutta failed. All P&O could do was to put down a marker for future occupation by building a small steamer for the Hong Kong station. Armed against pirates, *Canton* (400 grt) arrived at Hong Kong in 1849 and was employed to take Malwa opium on to Canton. The vessel was also profitably hired out to local firms, and its presence deterred Jardines and Dents from building their own small steamers for that purpose.[72]

With the recovery at the end of 1849, demand for a mail service from Hong Kong to Shanghai took priority over Calcutta–Hong Kong. If achieved, the Shanghai extension would 'complete the whole line of communication between Southampton and the Northern ports of China'. The MDs hoped that the Government would be 'compelled' by public opinion to place this extension under contract,[73] but subsidies had been severely criticized in Parliament and were not granted on the nod.[74] However, Shanghai was rapidly developing into the main centre, after Hong Kong, for the distribution of opium, and was becoming an important silk *entrepôt* as well. The Hong Kong–Shanghai run was to be worked 'as a merely commercial and passenger line, in such manner and at such seasons as the traffic may require, and as may be found most advantageous to the Company, unfettered by any contract'.

For her first voyage on the Shanghai run, *Lady Mary Wood* was dispatched from Bombay to Calcutta to take in a cargo of Bengal opium; then round to Singapore to pick up Malwa opium from Bombay, consigned to Shanghai (brought to Singapore by the contract steamer); off to Hong Kong to land the Calcutta opium, and finally to Shanghai with the Bombay opium, 'having for some time past been urged, by merchants and others connected with the trade' to do so. She was 'efficiently armed' against pirates; the company's small coastal steamer *Canton*, that ran between Hong Kong and Canton, had recently destroyed a number of 'piratical junks'.[75]

A few months later, *Lady Mary Wood* became embroiled with the Chinese and British authorities as a result of the ambiguities of the Treaty of Nanking and the jealousy of merchants running sailing ships. Sir Henry Pottinger, the British plenipotentiary, had warned British merchants after the end of the Opium War that opium was still contraband, that it was not subject to the duty on legitimate articles, and that British subjects engaging in the opium trade could not look to the protection of the British consul. Regardless of this warning, opium cargoes were discharged into heavily armed receiving vessels stationed just beyond the assumed limit of the British consul's jurisdiction in the Treaty Ports; dealers from the mainland brought the drug from these receiving vessels in a variety of small craft and carried it off for distribution in the interior. Foreign consuls purported to have no cognizance of this illegal but very visible trade.[76] In reverse, bales of silk, a legitimate and valuable cargo, were similarly smuggled out to the receiving ships by stealth and transferred into sea-going vessels for their ultimate destinations, thereby escaping port dues and export duty.

Lady Mary Wood's entry into this smugglers' paradise was an experiment. To trade competitively with the sailing ships, it would have to do as they did – avoid dues and duties by discharging opium and taking in silk at the receiving vessels. Its first few voyages were reported to have been 'remunerative' and 'highly appreciated by most of the merchants . . . in China, as a means of facilitating commercial intercourse, as a check to price, and as a postal communication'. Owners of sailing ships, however, did not welcome this steamship, and it was not 'piratical junks' that spoiled the trade for *Lady Mary Wood* and led to its withdrawal from China, but

> the resident partner, at Shanghae [*sic*], of an extensive mercantile firm in China, largely interested in the ownership of these sailing vessels, [who competed with her and] sent a large quantity of silk from Shanghae on board the 'Lady Mary Wood' at Woosung [the anchorage 13 miles out to sea], upon which it appeared the Chinese export duty had not been paid. The transaction was conducted in so open a manner, that the Chinese Custom House authorities felt themselves obliged, as it appears, to claim the interference of the British Consul at Shanghae . . .[77]

The shipper was fined for a breach of the port regulations and *Lady Mary Wood*'s master was not only fined but ordered to discharge and load at Shanghai in future. As a result, the vessel suffered a double punishment: its outgoings rose considerably and the amount of cargo taken in dwindled rapidly. The loss could not be sustained. After failing to collect funds from Hong Kong merchants to pay for its fuel bill,[78] *Lady Mary Wood* was withdrawn. The MDs appealed to the Foreign Office to discipline the consul at Shanghai. He was accordingly instructed 'to prevent a repetition of such partial interference' as had forced *Lady Mary Wood* to abandon the line, while the Supreme Court in Hong Kong returned the fine.

For a short time, the Hong Kong–Shanghai line was again without steam transport; Bombay shippers responded at once by demanding its restoration.[79] No doubt the MDs had wind of the syndicate's pressure on Jardines to replace clippers with steamships. The attempt by Crawford and his associates to set up their own company was a warning that the opportunity to be the first steam company in the Bengal opium trade might soon be lost. In 1851, therefore, *Shanghae* (550 grt),[80] the first screw-propelled sea-going steamer owned by P&O, was advertised to run from Calcutta to Hong Kong and Shanghai. As with the Bombay–Galle section, the Calcutta–Hong Kong–Shanghai line had no subsidy, but P&O's policy was to occupy lines 'now requiring the benefit of steam navigation not solely in the expectation of realising large profits, but in order to prevent those lines being taken up by other influential parties who could not be limited in their operations and who might hereafter become powerful rivals to the P&O Company on their existing lines'.[81]

With the curve of opium exports climbing upwards, as can be seen in table 3.3, and screw-driven steamers coming into general use, competition would soon have to be faced. All three opium branches were now in place, and two of them – Bombay–Hong Kong and Hong Kong–Shanghai – were prospering, but as it turned out the Calcutta–Hong Kong line could not sustain competition against the 'owners' of that line, Jardine, Matheson & Co., who were too deep-rooted to be removed.

P&O and the Bengal trade, 1851–57

A chorus of discontent from the syndicate met the appearance of P&O's first steamer on the direct line. The Calcutta David told his cousin in Hong Kong:

> With a large Steamer every month carrying some 1600 [chests], Clippers must sail at a loss. As they will get no Drug beyond that belonging to parties interested in them, and not always that, they will carry a mere

Table 3.3 Number of chests of opium exported, 1847–57

Year	*Bengal*	*Malwa*	*Total*
1847	21,648	18,602	40,250
1848	23,877	15,485	39,362
1849	32,902	16,509	49,411
1850	35,093	18,062	53,155
1851	32,902	19,138	52,040
1852	32,306	28,168	60,474
1853	36,178	24,979	61,157
1854	40,795	26,113	66,908
1855	51,421	25,958	77,379
1856	44,938	25,576	70,514
1857	*42,441*	*29,846*	*72,287*
Total	*394,501*	*248,436*	*642,937*

Source: *PP*, 1865, 40 (94), pp. 4, 10–12.

> nothing, particularly the *Mor* and *Rover*. This subject of Clippers requires the serious consideration of yourselves & Bombay friends, for it is evident they will lose money every voyage.[82]

To which J.R. Hadow, writing from Bombay, added, on behalf of his own partnership: 'You are advised by your Calcutta Friends that there is no chance of the Clippers being run any longer with advantage, and for our own parts we are of the same opinion, and we should not be sorry to hear that you could get a fair offer for either of [them]'.[83] The Calcutta cousin feared that 'clippers for the future will make a positive loss at every voyage, and . . . you should take into your consideration, what is best to be done'. R.F. Remington doubted that *Lanrick*, another of the syndicate's clippers, would be taking any more remunerative cargoes.[84] News that P&O had won the 1853 contract and would be running fortnightly services intensified the syndicate's concern. It was probably at about this time that Jardines was persuaded to order two steamers to be built in Liverpool.

However, P&O's decision to enter the Calcutta drug trade, though bold, did not turn out well, because the company did not have enough tonnage to establish anything like a regular service. With only 3 voyages made in 1851 and 10 in 1852, P&O's advent did not arouse any great enthusiasm.[85] T.S. Cowie predicted that 'the line can surely not pay the P&O Comp[an]y'.[86] But the MDs did not anticipate the resistance that would be put up by the sitting tenants, the Jardines and the Apcars.

Each of these two firms had a distinct clientele: Jardines' clippers conveyed cargo for their co-owners and for their wide circle of correspondents in both Bombay and Calcutta; Arratoon and Gregory Apcar attracted the custom of a large number of small native dealers for their two sailing vessels, *Arratoon Apcar* and *Catherine Apcar*. The Apcars' rates were much lower than Jardines' – only Rs8 or Rs10 per chest – while Jardines' fast clippers could command Rs28 or more. Skinners suspected that Apcars also offered monetary inducements to the native community that were not related to shipping, and believed that this practice gave the Apcars a 'positive claim' on their loyalty, turning them into dependents rather than constituents.[87] There was a certain tension between the two firms, but little open rivalry.

The impact of steam on the Bengal trade, then, was slight when compared with its impact on Malwa. In 1852, Dents was the first of the 'old hands' to add a steamer to its opium fleet, *Paou Shun*, which tracked P&O's vessels to and from Calcutta, but as neither company could offer a regular service, little competition was generated.[88] At the end of that year, P&O's situation looked better: two ships came on the berth in quick succession, *Pekin* taking 1,500 chests and *Erin* 1,100, and with improved engines the voyage to China could be made in 17 days. The syndicate's clippers had still not found buyers, and no one knew when Jardines' steamers would arrive from Liverpool.[89] In January 1853, the syndicate made it clear that as 'the prospect is small of getting even a moderate quantity of drug' for clippers, they should not again be sent to Bombay.[90]

At last, in February 1853, Jardines' *Larriston* (472 grt) reached Bombay after a very long voyage punctuated with mishaps. For that reason, it was 'on every account important that there should be no failure on the first trip', and Hadow assured the Hong Kong David that 'we have made a shipment of Malwa Drug to your Coast friends by your Steamer *Larriston* . . . principally with the view of assisting the good ship on this her first voyage on the Trade for which she is destined.[91] But *Larriston* was unlucky. A few months later she was wrecked with Joseph Jardine (another cousin) on board, though he escaped unhurt.[92] *Mor*, in a different accident, was lost too, just as the syndicate members were congratulating themselves on having found a buyer.[93] Jardines was again thrown back on to the clippers for the next two years.[94]

P&O was not inclined to cooperate with Jardines in that company's predicament, as Charles Skinner grumbled in a plaintive letter to Hong Kong:

> I observe you limit us for the most part to *shipment by Steamers*, and as we can never rely on getting even 100 Chests by these, it practically

> nullifies your instructions. I was led to expect at least 150 Chests by the *Formosa* [613 grt] but we were put off with only 70 Chests, & as the P. & O. Co[mpan]y's people know your Steamers are to be here next year, they will not stretch a point to oblige us.[95]

In 1855 Jardines' two new steamers, *Lancefield* (1,055 grt) and *Fiery Cross* (1,059 grt), arrived from Liverpool. Apcars also acquired two steamers, *Lightning* (673 grt) and *Thunder* (947 grt).[96] Yet the vigorous competition with P&O that might have been expected at this point failed to be ignited. For from January 1853, when the new mail contract came into force, circumstances beyond P&O's control upset the company's plans.

First, in January, unusual shipping activity in the Mediterranean, partly due to squabbles between Russia and Turkey in which Britain and France were involved, forced coal prices to double. Attracted by high freights, colliers preferred the Mediterranean to India. This caused an 'unprecedented and extraordinary scarcity' of colliers in the East. When the expected replenishments of coal failed to arrive, P&O had to solicit all and sundry to collect enough fuel to keep the mail ships going.[97] Then, later in the year, the East India Company was forced to give up the Bombay–Suez line. The Admiralty offered it, under contract, to P&O. This put P&O in a very awkward situation: from its inception, Bombay–Suez was a key line in P&O's overall strategy, but for the time being the company was struggling with its current commitments and could not undertake any more. If the offer was refused, however, the line might be lost to others. The MDs prevaricated for almost a year and only completed the contract after an ultimatum from the Admiralty.[98] Moreover Britain and France were by this time at war against Russia and several of P&O's steamers had already been taken up as transports for the Crimea in March 1854. These extra burdens almost brought the company to breaking point. The Australian line was abandoned,[99] and changes had to be made on the opium lines. Instead of a fortnightly service on the Bombay–China line, the company reverted to monthly calls; this was the only way a regular monthly steamer could ply between Calcutta and Shanghai.[100] But it was not until peace was restored in Europe that P&O was able to make a determined bid for the Bengal opium trade.

In April 1856, rumour had it that P&O was about to advertise a rate of freight of Rs22 per chest (less Rp1 for the shipper and Rp1 for the broker), instead of the Rs28 (less Rp1 for the broker) or more that had been current for steamers. P&O's Calcutta superintendent, Captain E.C. Lovell, was said to have had permission from London to lower the rates whenever he thought the right time had come. If true, George

Robertson (now in charge of Skinners) warned Jardines that a fierce rate war was about to begin:

> The P. & O. Company have just given the operations of the steamers a more severe blow than they have yet perhaps suffered . . . Under the promise of this reduction [of freight] the *Pekin*, which is the present vessel on the berth, secured a larger share of drug than she would otherwise have got . . . It is likewise said, but I cannot at present state with what truth, that the P. & O. Coy are determined to continue reducing till they drive their rivals from the line, and to test this it occurred to us, that it might be advisable to advertise to take cargo at one rupee per Chest below their rate whatever it may happen to be, for as they have already gone so far in this ruinous cause, perhaps the sooner we can know the worst they are capable of the better . . .[101]

Robertson tried to protect *Lancefield* from P&O's lower rate: 'We shall of course demand the former rate of Rs28 or higher if we think we can get it, and nothing but compulsion will cause us to reduce. I hope we shall not have an increase in the present competition, but the Peace [in Europe] will release a very large fleet of Steamers seeking employment where they can.'[102]

By June 1856, it was 'only too true' that the former rate of Rs28 had to be abandoned. But that was not all: a very worried Robertson told Joseph Jardine in Hong Kong that

> altho' hardly credible the P&O Coy people have further stated that they have positive instructions from Headquarters at home to reduce their rate if they should see fit, to Rs5 per Chest, and in case of further reductions, or their actually proceeding to the above extremity, I should be glad to secure your views and wishes for our guidance . . . The present rate [without a steamer on the berth] is Rs22, returning Rs1.[103]

Robertson also wrote 'as strongly as [he] could' to Charles Skinner, suggesting that he and David Jardine, both in London, should call on the directors at P&O's headquarters in Leadenhall Street and ask them to stop the competition. Meanwhile, Robertson hoped that 'the P&O Coy will never be so insane as to reduce to a figure which will drive us to the alternative of laying up the steamers for even a single trip'.[104]

Placatory news came from London. P&O's directors promised Skinner and Jardine that the Calcutta office would be instructed to return to the old rate of Rs33 per chest, and told them that the Calcutta agent and his staff had been 'severely wigged' for departing from that figure. In a second interview, James Allan, one of the MDs, said that an inquiry would be held on the working of the direct China line, and if it was not 'a paying one' P&O would give it up.[105]

Relieved that the competition was about to end and hoping to raise the rate for the next steamer, Robertson called at P&O's office to arrange with Lovell a date on which the new rate would be advertised. Unaccountably, Lovell was not at the office on this or two further visits, but a junior clerk said that P&O would be satisfied with Rs28. Having made this rate known to his shippers, Robertson was furious when he discovered that P&O was actually taking opium at Rs24 (less 2Rs). Lovell denied that he had ever agreed a fixed rate, asserting that Rs28 had been mentioned only 'to sound the shippers'; when they had demurred, he brought the rate down. A bitter correspondence between the two men followed while the 'senseless competition' continued. Lovell's parting shot, couched in a high and mighty tone, was especially offensive. He rejected Robertson's version of events, and, claiming that he was the victim and not the instigator of the intrigue, demanded an apology:

> I am so little versed or practised in the varieties of underhand trickery, that have been so notoriously current in the opium trade, both long before and since the establishment of the steamers, that I should only fail, & be taking in myself if I were to attempt to follow any of them. They are moreover utterly foreign to my nature, and therefore I seldom, unless obliged, have anything to do or say respecting the shipment or shippers of opium, except in private consultation with Mr Stewart [his chief assistant].[106]

Nothing was achieved by these exchanges. The rate of Rs24 could now not be raised because, as Robertson had predicted, many other steamers had arrived from the Mediterranean in search of a cargo. Jardines wanted Robertson to keep to Rs28 even if a steamer had to be dispatched with a half-cargo. This did not meet the case. Robertson pointed out that

> if we had the field to ourselves like the P&O Coy before they were opposed, we could command the Opium and dictate the Freight, but the case is now completely altered, we are beggars, not choosers, and if we try to exact more than what [Apcar's] *Lightning* and P&O Coy's vessels are now supposed to be content with, we shall assuredly be made to suffer for it . . .[107]

Then, suddenly, P&O withdrew from the direct line. The last steamer to appear was *Rajah* (537 grt), at first announced to leave for China in April 1857, but instead ordered to stop at Singapore.[108]

Why did P&O back out? One obvious reason was that the company was bound to give up its steamers for national emergencies. Scarcely had P&O's last steamer been released in 1856 than tonnage was required for the Persian Expedition, from October to February 1857. A month later, trouble 'of a pressing nature' in China – the preliminaries of the Second Opium War – had to be dealt with. The Indian Government approached Jardines and Apcars for transports as well, but they had the choice of refusing to give up their ships. Robertson had already engaged a full cargo of opium from which he could not be released, but 'if *Fiery Cross* had been free, & we [could] have got a sum . . . equivalent to a cargo of Drug to China, it is possible the emergency of the case might have caused us to let Govt have her . . . *Lightning* was also applied for but [could] not alter her present destination for the same reason'.[109]

P&O did not have this freedom of choice. In August, the company's *Ava* (1,313 grt) was hired to take Lord Elgin and his suite from Calcutta to China, but Lovell's application for permission to take a cargo of opium on board was refused.[110] If this was an attempt to regain a footing in the Calcutta market, the company could not have sustained it. Unrest in Central India soon became mutiny, and all available tonnage was required for that emergency.

An equally good reason for giving up the direct line was its unprofitability. It is not possible to calculate the profit and loss on any of P&O's lines individually because it was company policy not to reveal those details. A rise or fall in the total revenue could be due to a variety of factors.

Table 3.4 shows that revenue rose significantly in the years that cover P&O's occupation of the Calcutta–China line (see numbers in bold). A large proportion of this increase must be attributed to the doubling of mileage in the mail service and to the rapid expansion of trade world-wide. Unfortunately, expenditure climbed even more rapidly between 1853 and 1857, reaching 90 per cent of revenue. Though the Calcutta–China line's costs cannot be identified, given the more favourable circumstances on other lines it is probably safe

Table 3.4 Operating costs as percentages of revenue (£000s)

Year	*Revenue*	*Operating cost*	*% of revenue*
1851	728	576	79.1
1852	775	597	77.0
1853	**925**	**766**	**82.8**
1854	**1,216**	**1,095**	**90.0**
1855	**1,309**	**1,218**	**93.0**
1856	**1,426**	**1,294**	**90.7**
1857	**1,695**	**1,458**	**86.0**
1858	1,594	1,535	96.3

Source: P&O/6/52 and P&O/3/25, annual accounts.

Table 3.5 Earnings on freights of treasure by P&O on the Malwa & Bengal lines, 1854 and 1855

Year	*£000s carried*	*No. of voyages*	*Rate of freight %*	*Earnings (£000s)*	*Earnings per voyage*
A Bombay–Shanghai					
1854	5,482	24	2.5	137	5,708.00
1855	3,014	13	2.5	75	5,769.00
	Calcutta–Shanghai				
1854	195	16	1.5	3	187.50
1855	59	10	1.5	90	90.0
B Shanghai–Bombay					
1854	290	23	2.5	7	304
1855	808	13	2.5	20	1,538
	Shanghai–Calcutta				
1854	157	13	1.5	2	154
1855	430	11	1.5	6	545

Source: *PP*, 1857, session 2, 43 (2221), pp. 67–9.

to conclude that P&O's losses on that line made a bad situation worse. P&O ceased to compete on the Bengal line just after the first half of the financial year (October 1856–March 1857), and this might in part account for the almost 5 per cent reduction in total costs in 1857: not before time, certainly, given the alarming increase in total costs in 1858.

Losses on the direct line were certainly due to the lack of return cargoes. An account of bullion and specie carried between India and China from both opium ports in the calendar years 1854 and 1855, is shown in table 3.5.

At Bombay, P&O took large quantities of treasure to China – £5.5 million over 24 outward voyages in 1854, and £3 million over 13 voyages in 1855 (after P&O had reverted to monthly calls) – at a rate freight of 2.5 per cent to Shanghai; much less was taken on the return voyages – £232,000 and £647,000 respectively. At Calcutta, however, the amount of treasure carried by P&O was very small, and apart from a few bales of silk there was nothing on this shorter route that could not be brought from China more cheaply by sail. As one Calcutta merchant put it, 'if the Steamers, returning empty as they do, would make the rates of freight moderate, we think that mode of conveyance preferable to the small sailing craft wh: almost in all instances cause damage more or less, tho' seldom to such an extent as to enable us to recover loss from the Ins[uran]ce office'.[111] We may assume, too, that Jardines took great care to see that bullion and specie on this line was carried in its steamers, not P&O's.

P&O intended to capture the Calcutta line before any opposition steamers arrived. Having failed to do so, the MDs then counted on a show of strength to make Jardines give way and beg for a peace treaty which would enable P&O to have a share – perhaps the major share – of the Bengal exports. The gamble did not come off. P&O's resources, given the commitments to government service, were inadequate. But the MDs also misjudged the strength of the opposition. Jardines had no intention of surrendering: its shipping interest was concentrated on this opium line, but its main concern was the highly successful agency and commission side of the company's business. Jardines could afford to fight on; P&O could not.[112]

Notes

1 P&O/1/100, 19.5.1846.

2 For a more detailed account of the importance of the nineteenth-century drug trade for P&O, see F. Harcourt, 'Black Gold: P&O and the Opium Trade, 1847–1914', *International Journal of Maritime History*, 6:1 (1994), pp. 1–83.

3 T. De Quincey, *Confessions of an English Opium-Eater* (London, 1823), pp. 6, 7, 87; *PP*, 1895, 42 (C. 7723–I): *Royal Commission on Opium* (hereafter *Royal Commission*), vol. 7, Appendix A, p. 5; V. Berridge and G. Edwards, *Opium and the People: Opiate Use in Nineteenth-Century England* (New Haven, CT: Yale University Press, 1987), Introduction and chs 1–6; 80–90 per cent of imports to England came from Smyrna: p. 3.

4 *PP*, 1894, 41 (C. 7397), *Royal Commission*, vol. 2, Appendix 11, paras 2ff.

5 *PP*, 1895, 42 (C. 7723–I), *Royal Commission*, vol. 7, Appendix A, pp. 5ff., which states that opium was probably an item of trade from the eastern Mediterranean with India and China very early in the Christian era, though not in large quantities. G. Watt, *Papaver Somniferum: Opium* (Calcutta, 1891), pp. 2ff. ('History'), agrees that opium poppies had been grown in a few of the most remote provinces of China in early times, but states that 'native' opium was not well known in the coastal areas until about 1860. Native opium was inferior and was often mixed with Malwa opium to make it palatable: *PP*, 1857, session 2, 43 (2221), *Opium Trade in China, 1841–1856*, enclosure 1 in no. 26, 6.11.1855, pp. 42–4.

6 Quoted in Greenberg, *British Trade*, p. 211; italics in original.

7 Several important facets of the impact of opium on China are set out in W.O. Walker III, *Opium and Foreign Policy: The Anglo-American Search for Order in Asia, 1912–1954* (Chapel Hill and London: University of North Carolina Press, 1991), ch. 1. These include the serious damage done to China's economy and the changes wrought on society and domestic politics, all of which contributed to the Chinese revolution in 1911 and the instability thereafter in East Asia; he also asserts that demand in China for opium encouraged supply from India.

8 Greenberg, *British Trade*, especially pp. 13–16 and ch. 5.

9 *PP*, 1894, 41 (C. 7397), *Royal Commission*, vol. 2, Appendix 11, para. 57, quoting dispatch of 19.12.1881. Home charges covered the cost of the administration of Indian affairs in Britain, pensions for government servants and military stores. Silk was not taken to Europe by steam in bulk until the 1860s.

10 *PP*, 1840, 7 (359), *SC on Trade with China*, Appendix 1, pp. 163, 166; extract from *Report* of 1832.

11 Quoted in C.K. Webster, *The Foreign Policy of Palmerston 1830–1841: Britain, the Liberal Movement and the Eastern Question* (London: Bell, 1951), vol. 2, p. 751.

12 Greenberg, *British Trade*, pp. 10ff., 137ff.

13 Much of this paragraph has been taken from *ibid.*, ch. 7.

14 J. Matheson, *The Present Position and Prospects of the British Trade with China; together with an outline of some leading occurrences in its past history* (London, 1836), generally.

15 The other Treaty Ports were Amoy (Xiamen), Foochow (Fuzhou), Ningpo (Ningbo) and Shanghai; 5 per cent was to be paid on all dutiable imports: see S.F. Wright, *China's Struggle for Tariff Autonomy 1843–1938* (Shanghai: Kelly & Walsh, 1938), ch. 1.

16 Kwang-Ching Liu, *Anglo-American Steamship Rivalry in China 1862–74* (Cambridge, MA: Harvard University Press, 1962), pp. 3ff.; Russell & Co. and Augustine Heard & Co. were the two most prominent American merchants: F.H.H. King, *The History of the Hong Kong and Shanghai Banking Corporation* (Cambridge: Cambridge University Press, 1987), vol. 1, p. 48; Greenberg, *British Trade*, pp. 53–6, 72–3, 84, 159–65, 168–70, 186, and generally; J.K. Fairbank, *Trade and Diplomacy in the China Coast* (Cambridge, MA: Harvard University Press, 1953), vol. 2, Appendix A, pp. 56–7, for Jardines and its predecessors.

17 B. Lubbock, *The Opium Clippers* (Glasgow: Brown, Son & Ferguson, 1933), pp. 3ff.

18 *PP*, 1851, 21 (605), *Steam Communication*, q. 4169.

19 The vessels were from the Royal Navy in the Mediterranean and from the East India Company between Bombay and Suez: H.L. Hoskins, *The British Route to India* (New York: Longmans, Green & Co., 1928), pp. 87ff.

20 Greenberg, *British Trade*, pp. 212–15.

21 *PP*, 1849, 12 (571), *Contract Packets*, p. 124; *PP*, 1851, 21 (605), *Steam Communication*, q. 4029; *PP*, HoL, 1851, 10–II (187–II), *SC on Steam Communication to India* (*Communication to India*), q. 4788; POST 51/40, Articles of Agreement, 27.2.1866.

22 Fairbank, *Trade and Diplomacy*, p. 361.

23 Jardine–Matheson Archive (hereafter, JMA), Cambridge University Library, Reel 71, Calcutta, nos 3254, 3373, 2.1.1847, 27.7.1847. I am most grateful to Mr. Alan Reid, the custodian of these papers, who kindly allowed me to see them.

24 As the trade surged to its peak in the 1860s, the scale of capital employed in the opium trade was such it could not be handled by individual houses in China. Thomas Sutherland rounded up most of the merchants in Hong Kong in 1864 and persuaded them to found the Hong Kong and Shanghai Bank and to open a branch in Shanghai: King, *History of the Hong Kong and Shanghai Banking Corporation*, pp. 47ff.

25 Bengal chests weighed 160*lbs*, Malwa 140*lbs*.

26 Greenberg, *British Trade*, pp. 114–15; B. Lubbock, *Clippers*, p. 334. W.H. Coates, *The Old 'Country Trade' of the East Indies* (London, 1911), p. 151, states that Arratoon and Gregory Apcar's partnership began in 1819.

27 *PP*, 1895, 42 (C. 7723), *Royal Commission*, vol. 7, Section 2, paras 86, 113, 115.

28 *PP*, 1894, 41 (C. 7397), *Royal Commission*, vol. 2, Appendix 11, paras 7ff.

29 *PP*, 1895, 42 (C. 7723–I), *Royal Commission*, vol. 7, Appendix A, pp. 24–43.

30 Watt, *Papaver Somniferum*, pp. 2ff.; *PP*, 1894, 41 (C. 7397): *Royal Commission*, vol. 2, Appendix 11, para. 11.

31 *PP*, 1895, 42 (C. 7723–I), *Royal Commission*, vol. 7, Appendix A, p. 15.

32 *PP*, 1914–16, 49 (Cd. 7766), *Review of the Trade of India in 1913–14* (*Review*), p. 25.

33 JMA, Reel 71, Calcutta, no. 3426, 11.10.1847; *PP*, 1894, 60 (C. 7313): *Royal Commission*, vol. 1, Appendix 1, p. 135; Jardine Skinner Papers (henceforth JSP), Cambridge University Library, File 5, 17.4.1848. Mr Alan Reid kindly drew my attention to the Jardine Skinner Papers.

34 Greenberg, *British Trade*, pp. 139–40, 146, 150; JSP, File 5, 24.1.1848; JMA, Reel 71, Calcutta, nos 3436, 3458, 6.11.1847, 11.2.1848; Reel 127, Hong Kong, no. 1526, 28.9.1847.

35 M. Keswick (ed.), *The Thistle and the Jade: a celebration of 150 years of Jardine, Matheson and Co.* (London: Octopus, 1982), pp. 24–7; Greenberg, *British Trade*, ch. 2 and Appendix 2.

36 Greenberg, *British Trade*, pp. 146, 150; JSP, File 5, 24.1.48; JMA, Reel 71, Calcutta, nos 3436, 3458, 6.11.1847, 11.2.1848; Reel 127, Hong Kong, no. 1526, 28.9.1847.

37 See above, p. 54.

38 *PP*, 1851, 21 (605), *Steam Communication*, q. 5685.

39 Anderson, *Letter*, p. 9.

40 *PP*, 1851, 21 (605), *Steam Communication*, q. 4159.

41 *PP*, 1840, V (353), *SC on the Petition of the East India Company for Relief*, qq. 146–7; Stenton (ed.), *Who's Who*, vol. 1. Cockerell, Larpent & Co. in London was associated with the Bombay house of Cockerell & Co. Larpent had large interests in the East: *PP*, 1833, 6 (690), *SC on Manufactures* qq. 2063ff.; 1840, 7 (359), *SC on Trade with China*, qq. 146ff.

42 JMA, Reel 463, London, p. 75, 6.4.1844.

43 *Herepath*, vol. 18, 8.12.1849, p. 552; P&O/1/105, 15.1.1861, P&O1/107, 17.3.1868. William Dent of Dent & Co, was also a large shareholder in P&O but was not offered a seat.

44 *Herepath*, vol. 80, 11.12.1880, p. 1406.

45 See above p. 54.

46 *Herepath*, vol. 96, 15.12.1888, p. 1372. Duncanson, who had worked in Shanghai and later joined the bankers T. & A. Gibbs & Co, was elected to the London committee (formed in 1875) of the Hong Kong and Shanghai Bank: King, *History*, vol. 1, p. 181.

47 *Herepath*, vol. 96, 16.12.1893, p. 1312. Adamson, a manager in the Borneo Company in the 1860s, was for a short time a director on the provisional board of the Hong Kong and Shanghai Bank in 1864–65: King, *History*, vol. 1, pp. 54–5.

48 P&O/1/100, 19.5.1846, 16.6.1846, 1.12.1846.

49 *PP*, HoL, 1851, 10–I (187–I), *Steam Communication*, qq. 5916–40.

50 P&O/1/101, 23.4.1847.

51 *Ibid.*, 4.12.1846, 11.2.1847.

52 P&O/1/101, 4.12.1846, 11.2.1847, 27.4.1847 and 3.8.1847; P&O/6/2, Annual Report, 8.12.1847, p. 8; *PP*, 1849, 12 (571), *Contract Packets*, q. 2337; JMA, Reel 71, Calcutta, nos 3290, 3321, 25.3.1847, 5.5.1847.

53 *PP*, 1851, 21 (605), *Steam Communication*, qq. 4056, 4157.

54 *Ibid.*, qq. 4056, 4153, 4157, 4163, 4169, 5698–5716, 5727; JMA, Reel 41, Bombay, no. 6263, 18.6.51; Reel 43, Bombay, no. 7007, 3.3.1853.

55 JSP, File 5, 16.9.1848, 17.10.1848.

56 *PP*, 1849, 12 (571), *Contract Packets*, qq. 2019, 2354, 2416.

57 *PP*, 1851, 21 (372), *Steam Communication*, q. 4169; JMA, Reel 71, Calcutta, no. 3643, 30.5.1850; JMA, A7/83, Opium Receipts, Hong Kong, 1849–55.

58 JMA, Reel 71, Calcutta, nos 3460–1, 28.2.1848, 8.3.1848; 3507, 20.10.1849; 3567, 23.2.1850; 3597, 27.3.1850; 3617, 29.4.1850. David Jardine was in Hong Kong when his cousin and namesake was in Calcutta.

59 For more on Eastern Steam and its bid to displace P&O, see ch. 4, this book.

60 *PP*, 1851, 21 (605), *Steam Communication*, qq. 4153, 5452, 5608, 5625.

61 *PP*, HoL, 1851, 10–II (187–II), *Communication to India*, pp. vii–ix; *PP*, 1851, 21 (605), *Steam Communication*, pp. vii–xi.

62 *PP*, 1852, 49 (249), *Mail Services, India and Australia*, pp. 1–4, 15.

63 JMA, Reel 43, Bombay, no. 6897, 15.1.1853.

64 *Ibid.*, Bombay, no. 7083, 2.4.1853, 4.5.1853.

65 *PP*, 1851, 21 (605), *Steam Communication*, q. 4479.

66 PRO T1/6401/A, Extracts, 1855–60.

67 So called because opium vessels out of Calcutta did not go by Galle but sailed direct for Hong Kong via Penang and Singapore.

68 P&O/1/100, 19.5.1846.

69 *PP*, 1850, 53 (693), *Correspondence*, p. 65, 22.5.1844, p. 68, 3.7.1844.
70 P&O/1/100, 27.5.1845.
71 P&O/1/101, 5.2.1847, 23.4.1847, 21.9.1847; P&O/1/102, 26.1.1849.
72 *Ibid.*, 23.4.1847, 11.6.1847, 18.4.1848; P&O1/102, 22.12.1848, 20.4.1849, 21.8.1849.
73 *Ibid.*, 23.4.1847.
74 See below pp. 118ff.
75 P&O/1/102, 14.12.1849, 21.12.1849, 1.1.1850.
76 Wright, *China's Struggle*, ch. 1 especially pp. 21–5.
77 P&O/6/2, Annual Report, 6.12.1850, p. 11.
78 *PP*, 1851, 21 (603), *Second Report*, qq. 4038–9, 4050, 4086.
79 P&O/1/101, 26.11.1851.
80 P&O/1/102, 28.1.1851, 23.5.1851, 12.8.1851, bought on the stocks, contemporary spelling.
81 P&O/1/101, 23.4.1847.
82 JMA, Reel 71, Calcutta, no. 3970, 21.1.1852.
83 JMA, Reel 42, Bombay, no. 6524, 13.2.1852.
84 *Ibid.*, 6529, 16.2.1852; Reel 72, Calcutta, no. 3975, 29.1.1852.
85 JMA, Opium Receipts, A7/83, Benares.
86 JMA, Reel 41, Bombay, no. 6159, 14.4.1851.
87 JMA, Reel 74, Calcutta, 21.5.1856.
88 JMA, Reel 72, Calcutta, no. 4057, 19.7.1852; *Overland Register and Price Current*, vol. 11, 28.10.1854.
89 *Ibid.*, Calcutta, nos 4010, 4063, 4081, 4099, 4104, 17.4.1852, 16.8.1852, 17.9.1852, 14.10.1852, 19.11.1852.
90 JMA, Reel 58, Bombay, p. 105, 15.2.1853.
91 JMA, Reel 43, Bombay, nos 6991, 7007, 20.2.1853, 3.3.1853.
92 *Ibid.*, Bombay, no. 7261, 2.7.1853.
93 *Ibid.*, Bombay, no. 7141, 30.4.1853.
94 Apparently a second steamer was ordered, but I have not been able to identify it. Better prospects for it (if built) as a transport to the Crimea might have prompted Jardines to send it there.
95 JMA, Reel 73, Calcutta, no. 4548, 2.12.1854.
96 I am indebted to Robin Craig, who kindly extracted details of these steamers from his own researches.
97 P&O/6/21/1, Annual Report, 28.5.1853, p. 8. Jardines gave P&O whatever coals the company had or were due to receive (JMA, Reel 73, Calcutta, no. 4209, 28.5.1853), but coal intended for Batavia saved the day.
98 P&O/1/103, 12.7.1853, 25.10.1853, 2.5.1854, 12.5.1854, 9.6.1854, 20.6.1854.
99 See ch. 4.
100 P&O/1/103, 25.8.1854, 3.11.1854. In 1854, P&O made 24 voyages outwards on the Bombay–China line, and 16 on the Calcutta–Hong Kong line; return voyages were 23 and 13 respectively; in 1855, 13 Bombay and 10 Calcutta outwards, and 12 and 11 returns, *PP*, 1857, Session 2, 43 (2221), *Opium Trade*, no. 26, enclosure 10, pp. 67–9.
101 JMA, Reel 74, Calcutta, no. 4605, 21.5.1856.
102 *Ibid.*, Calcutta, no. 4609, 30.6.1856.
103 *Ibid.*, Calcutta, no. 4612, 21.6.1856.
104 *Ibid.*, Calcutta, nos 4625, 4630, 23.8.1856, 24.9.1856.
105 *Ibid.*, Calcutta, nos 4630, 4638, 25.10.1856, 27.10.1856.
106 *Ibid.*, Calcutta, no. 4637, 4638, 25.10.1856, 27.10.1856.
107 *Ibid.*, Calcutta, nos 4645, 4656, 21.11.1856, 24.1.1857.
108 *Ibid.*, Calcutta, nos 4660, 4662, 24.4.1857, 30.4.1857.
109 *Ibid.*, Calcutta, no. 4662, 30.4.1857.
110 *Ibid.*, Calcutta, no. 4670, 28.8.1857.
111 JMA, Reel 73, Calcutta, no. 4145, 17.1.1853.
112 For the subsequent effect on Jardines of competition with P&O, see Harcourt, 'Black Gold'.

CHAPTER FOUR

Competition and the route to Australia, 1847–52

In the seven years since its formation, P&O had made spectacular progress on both sides of Suez. With the completion of each stage of its strategy, the company bedded itself the more surely as the sole custodian of the great Eastern trade routes. The very success of this exemplary enterprise made newcomers look enviously at what P&O had achieved and tempted them to emulate it. Though there had always been rumours of competition,[1] from 1847 P&O had to deal with rivals of real substance.

Australia and the India & Australia Mail Steam Packet Company[2]

In 1770, Captain James Cook found the east coast of Australia, and by November 1792, a ship had arrived in Sydney from North America with cargo to trade. Other ships soon followed. With the advent of steam, the Australian colonies were gripped by the possibility of having steam communication with the outside world. As early as 1837, just when Peninsular Steam had begun to operate to Lisbon and Gibraltar, 'some of the first Australian merchants in the city . . . are exceedingly anxious to have this passage established in Calcutta, intending themselves to take on the communication from Ceylon to Australia'. Even more interest was taken after P&O's service to India and China began.[3] More than one route was possible: an all-British line via the Cape of Good Hope; a Pacific route by the Isthmus of Panama or Cape Horn; or P&O's already well-tried and reliable route via Egypt and the Red Sea. All three found champions, depending on interest and geography. There was little to choose between them in terms of mileage, but the Red Sea route attracted greatest attention.

As had happened in India in the 1820s and 1830s, pressure groups in the 1840s comprised a mixture of local merchants and bankers and their British counterparts. Included in the latter constituency were some entrepreneurs who had not forgotten how P&O had pushed them aside and snatched from their hands the Mediterranean contract in 1840 and the India and China contract in 1844. P&O's expansion had not yet reached Australia; if they could set up a steam route from Australia, these men could have a second chance to operate in the East. There was also a feeling among some of the Australian steam enthusiasts that, by establishing a steam connection with Australia before P&O, the company might be prevented from spreading its tentacles to Australia at all.

In 1846, a concerted effort was made in Sydney to campaign for steam communication;[4] and in London on 17 April, a 'very large and numerously attended meeting', convened by Lieutenant Thomas Waghorn, took place at the London Tavern. In the chair was Sir George Larpent, lately chairman of P&O; other promoters included Jacob Montefiore and James MacKillop, both of whom had been directors of Curtis' defunct East Indian Steam. Waghorn, who had fallen out with P&O over the organization of the overland passage through Egypt in 1842,[5] was 'as usual "the great card" of the meeting'; a self-publicist, he hankered after 'the honour of opening [the Australian] line in [his] own person'.[6] Captain James Barber was also present; his grudge against P&O was that it would not appoint him as an MD.[7]

Among the banking fraternity at the meeting, Robert Brooks, chairman of the Union Bank of Australia and an investor in a host of other companies in the Colonies, was one of 'a veritable Who's Who' representing the Australian interest and having close family and business links with the colonists. John Abel Smith, MP, the London agent of Jardine, Matheson & Co. in China, was another banker; he had represented the mercantile community at the departmental meetings that discussed P&O's Eastern contract in 1843–44 and may have done so at this meeting.[8]

P&O was not represented at that meeting, and the MDs hoped that nothing of significance would come from it. But the urgency with which G.L. Robinson wrote to P&O about the importance of establishing steam communication with Australia, pointing out routes suitable for different seasons and 'urging a continuation [to Sydney] of the Company's existing line' from Singapore, prompted the MDs write to the Board of Trade, the Treasury and the Colonial Office arguing that there should *not* be any competition for the carriage of Australian mails now, on the grounds that Australia was so remote.[9]

Early in 1847, however, the Indian & Australia Mail Steam Packet Company (hereafter I&A) was launched. Its purpose was to connect England with Australia by the Red Sea route. Robert Montgomery

Martin, who had recently left an official post in the Hong Kong Government, was I&A's publicity agent.[10] He had a prospectus printed bearing the names of seventy merchants and bankers, persuaded *The Times* to publicize the launch, and sent a petition to the Queen from 'various Merchants and Bankers in the City of London, praying for Grant of a Charter'; a charter of incorporation was granted in June.[11]

The promoters of I&A conceived a two-pronged attack on P&O. First, they would give Australia its first steam mail service between Sydney and Singapore; that would keep P&O out of Australian waters. Then, from that base, they would make every effort to lever P&O out of its European lines. This pincer-like grip would force P&O to give I&A access to India and China. These aspirations were set out (in more diplomatic language) in I&A's prospectus which emphasized the keen interest of France and Austria in Eastern trades. Support for an Australian line would be easy enough to acquire from the London Government, and with the Board of Trade's help either the route from Australia to Singapore could be extended to England before P&O's Eastern contracts came to an end in 1853 or else, if these went to full term, the whole line from England to India and China would be 'thrown open to both companies' at I&A's command.[12] As it happened, I&A had to deal with both ends of the programme almost simultaneously, but for clarity's sake, they will be dealt with in turn.

I&A's first challenge: the Mediterranean

First, then, the Mediterranean. The initial intention was to occupy these lines in conjunction with Austrian Lloyd's (AL) but it is not certain when I&A established a link with the Austrian company. Founded in 1837 with Austrian capital, AL was a well-established concern running small steamships (built and engined in Britain) along the Adriatic and eastern Mediterranean coastlines. Waghorn, when he travelled overland from England to India in 1829 in pre-railway days, had identified Trieste–Alexandria as the shortest route to Egypt. Thereafter Trieste surfaced from time to time as a suitable mail port for the Indian mails.[13] In 1842, when P&O was about to ply east of Suez, the Austrian Ambassador in London made a formal proposal: Trieste would be considerably cheaper than Marseilles, being much closer to Alexandria, and complaints about delays in the French conveyance of Indian mails made Trieste an attractive alternative. If it was adopted, the MDs assumed that P&O would run the line, 'it being highly desirable, that no other party connected with Steam Navigation should occupy' it. AL, however, had ideas of its own: not only to run the line to Egypt but to get access to the India and China trade. Whereupon, perhaps with some prompting from P&O, the Admiralty raised several objections to Trieste, one of which was that 'where so large a capital is embarked by English merchants in Steam Navigation the employment by Contract of Vessels belonging to Foreign Merchants . . . would give serious cause for complaint to the whole body of English Ship owners'.[14]

Trieste again impinged on P&O when, as has been mentioned above, AL's steamers began to ply to Alexandria in 1845 and draw passengers away from P&O. This time, AL engaged Waghorn to prove the advantages of Trieste–Ostend over Marseilles–Calais and it was probably at this point that AL became involved in the I&A project. With the blessing of both British and Austrian governments, Waghorn's 'Experimental Journeys' took place.[15]

Waghorn's activities were carefully watched at St Mary Axe; P&O's board did not approve of what he regarded as a 'great public benefit'. To measure Marseilles against Trieste, the MDs dispatched *Ariel* from Alexandria to Marseilles at the same time as the naval vessel bound for Trieste set off with Waghorn on board. *Ariel* carried mail for 'certain leading London Journals'; one of them, *The Times*, made a feature of the contest, stating dismissively that 'it would seem that the route by Marseilles has the advantage'. P&O, 'aware of the great exertions [that] had been made of late by the Austrian Lloyds steam Company to obtain the transmission of the India mails via Trieste', offered Genoa, a rather weak alternative to Trieste that was rejected by the Admiralty.[16]

Always on the trot, Waghorn was soon involved in another 'experiment' for his continental route, this time for a railway from Trieste that would be 'altogether independent of France'. In 1845 there was talk in France about a rail line between Marseilles and Boulogne being built in about three years, and it seems that British entrepreneurs were thinking of investing in a railway through Austria and the German states to open these markets to Manchester goods. Waghorn was sent to investigate the situation. Lord Palmerston, who took more than a passing interest in Waghorn's activities, pressed Prince Metternich, the Austrian Chancellor, to take note of what his protégé said. In Palmerston's eyes, this was a good opportunity for British investment but he warned the Austrians that a 'skilful English Engineer', accustomed to railway works, was 'absolutely indispensable, because without it no British capitalists would embark in such an enterprize'. A Mr Austin, a railway engineer, accompanied Waghorn on at least one of his trips, but it is not known who the railway backers in Britain were.[17]

Waghorn's notion of where the railway should run was not at all in tune with the thinking of the interested parties in Austria. He wanted the line of rail to go westward from Trieste. From the perspective of the Austrian empire, however, Vienna was to be the point of departure, with lines radiating outwards in all directions to the provinces. The Austrian Cabinet, especially the Ministers of Finance and War, were strongly opposed to his scheme, and it was dropped at the end of 1847.[18] And Metternich made it clear to Palmerston that he was promoting AL, not a British or Australian company:

> The Austrian Lloyd's Company have been occupied with a project for the transport of the English Mail between Alexandria and Trieste, and Trieste and London, and has put itself in communication with Authorities in London . . . The Austrian Government will be ready to give to the Company all the protection & every facility that a Govt can give to a private Company . . . [It] has the right to enter in its own name into negotiation, & contract formal engagements with the *autorités Britanniques* . . .[19]

But behind these polite exchanges, the commercial and international situation was by this time changing for the worse. Very soon the whole Continent was engulfed in revolution. Shipping was disrupted and Trieste was twice blockaded, in 1848 and 1849, during the Italian war with Austria.[20]

Montgomery Martin and other I&A promoters began their campaign very soon after the London Tavern meeting, for 'various representations' were received at the Treasury before the repeal of the Corn Laws in May 1846, complaining about 'the defective state' of the line between Marseilles and Alexandria. Disarray created by the overthrow of Peel's Government postponed any new arrangements,[21] but appeals for action were answered indirectly by the setting up of a Select Committee in the House of Lords to inquire into Post Office revenue, which of course included the cost and distribution of the mail contracts.[22]

The Lords' Committee sat in June and July 1847. Sir Charles Wood, who became Chancellor of the Exchequer in July 1846 in the new Government after Peel's downfall, may have been the Select Committee's real target, for he was said to be incompetent. In any case, the drubbing the Committee gave to the contract system in general and to P&O in particular was exactly what I&A supporters had hoped for. The *Report* regretted 'the great Preponderance of Expenditure over Receipts' in the mail services:

> It is for the serious Consideration of the Government and of Parliament when these private Interests shall, on the Expiration of the existing Contract, continue to be supported at a public Cost so enormous . . . [It is expected that] a very great Reduction may be effected; and that

> a Company, deriving great Profits from the Conveyance of Goods and Passengers, may be willing to convey the Mails, receiving in no case any Remuneration . . . exceeding the Amount of Postage taken by the Government.[23]

The sum of money paid out for all contracts managed by the Admiralty had indeed risen steeply: from £155,000 in 1841 to £550,000 in 1846.[24] The Lords concluded that private owners of vessels fitted up with luxurious accommodation for which they could charge high fares should not be supported by the taxpayers; they acknowledged the worth of the fast and reliable mail service provided by contractors, but the monopolies created by the system were reprehensible.

Shortly before the Committee began its inquiry, the MDs had 'some confidential communications' with the Admiralty, most likely connected with I&A and how best to handle its – from P&O's point of view – preposterous proposals. The result of these discussions was a plan to transfer the Marseilles–Malta line from the Royal Navy to P&O. P&O's having this line would ensure that the Suez–Bombay line would pass into P&O's hands as soon as it was given up by the East India Company, and settle the question of Marseilles as the mail port, thereby silencing any further talk of Trieste.

Provided that the price was right, the Admiralty was taken with P&O's plan. Mail would go faster without transhipment at Malta, and because of improvements in marine technology, P&O would work the line more cheaply than the Royal Navy. The department was anxious 'not to lose a moment in taking steps for providing [P&O's] efficient Steam Packets to carry the overland India Mail'.[25] But enthusiasm did not lead to immediate action. Although Waghorn's railway scheme was 'terminated for the present', Prince Metternich's willingness to consider 'the adoption of some equivalent measure in future' kept open the option of Trieste as the mail port.[26]

With the publication of the House of Lords *Report*, however, the government departments concerned with mail contracts were bound to try to meet its strictures. Competition had to be encouraged, and since so much attention had been focused on P&O, savings would have to be made on the Mediterranean mail lines. By November, therefore, the mood in the Admiralty had changed. Warships were found to be needed after all: 'it should be remembered that in case of war in the Mediterranean, Naval ships would provide better defence' given the unrest in France and Italy, and diplomatic tension between Britain and Austria towards the end of 1847 was certainly a factor in the Admiralty's thinking.[27] If a contract were to be made, P&O's vessels would have to carry suitable armament and be made of wood, a risible condition in the MDs' view.[28]

As a test to see how much might be saved on the Marseilles line, the Admiralty held an informal competition, inviting P&O, I&A and Royal Mail to name a price for a contract. None came near the 'considerable savings' the Admiralty was looking for; government vessels might as well continue to work the Marseilles line and go direct to Alexandria in the fastest naval vessels.[29] This naval line was dubbed the 'Bombay Express', but its name did not alter the fact that warships could carry 'little besides the public news, in addition to one or two private letters to each mercantile firm'.[30]

As to savings, the Government decided to determine P&O's two Alexandria contracts: the 1840 contract was to end in December 1848, and the 1844 arrangement was discontinued in May 1848.[31] It was as well, in this new situation, that P&O's unsubsidized Constantinople line was available to pick up and land the 'heavy' mail from Bombay at Malta thus avoiding interruption of the service. A Southampton–Alexandria contract, however, was essential to convey the 'heavy' Calcutta mails. I&A believed that it had a strong chance to challenge P&O. Though the Admiralty had no desire to dispense with P&O as a contractor, and the Treasury merely wanted 'to ascertain whether the service could not be done at a cheaper rate', it was expected that with two companies willing to enter a contest large savings would be made on that line.[32] P&O showed its disapproval of competition on a line it had developed for eight years by tendering £27,500; this was a bid to continue the contract as if it had not been determined. I&A's bid was about £2,000 less but depended on an unacceptable term of fourteen years.[33] Neither bid was accepted.

In the hope of coming to an understanding with the Admiralty by private negotiation, the MDs claimed that P&O had a right to continue the contract because so much capital had already been put into the enterprise; besides which, the service had been performed satisfactorily and P&O's profits were moderate. To prove this last assertion, the MDs took up the suggestion of the House of Lords that 'as a general Principle in all future Contracts', contract companies should open their books to the Government and pay back a proportion of their profits if these were to go higher than a specified percentage.[34] The officers who examined P&O's books confirmed that dividends had never been as high as 10 per cent and were not likely to reach that point in the future; they reported that the subsidy paid to P&O was not 'more than it was justly entitled to receive', that the company had never been fined for any breach of contract nor shirked its commitments, and that its affairs were managed with 'economy and efficiency'. Indeed,

> considering the energetic manner in which this company had persevered in extending steam communication through new untried channels, and that it had formed extensive establishments on the faith of the continued support of the Government, and that it still contemplates an extension of its communications with the furthest southern and eastern point of the British possessions; establishing for these purposes a steam navy of considerable magnitude, at the command of the public, on any emergency – it appears to be entitled to as much consideration as is compatible with an economical administration of the duties of the Post Office.

The encomium concluded: 'Any new arrangement to be made should rather be of a permanent than of a temporary character, both to ensure confidence to the company in the conduct and extension of their concerns, and efficiency in the discharge of the service entrusted to them.' This was a proposal that the MDs could have written themselves.

Lord Auckland (First Lord of the Admiralty, 1846–49), however, was sceptical. He had no faith in profit-sharing: it would mean 'an annual inquiry [that] might lead to endless discussions and disputes and would be a source of frequent vexation to both parties', especially when it came to a definition of profit. Nor did he believe that P&O's profits were especially moderate: 'It is clear . . . that the company makes considerable profits, and I would prefer to a share in them . . . a liberal compromise by a reduction of the terms which have been proposed; and I think this reduction should be to a sum considerably lower than the £25,650 which has been tendered by the Indian and Australian Company'. In his view, P&O should not get more than £15,525, the price that the company had agreed, under pressure, for the now discontinued second Alexandria line.[35] This the MDs would not agree to, and, 'after several interviews' with the Admiralty in July 1848, the sum of £24,000, diminishing each year by £500 until January 1853, was arrived at, to the satisfaction of both parties.[36]

The MDs used the favourable Admiralty report to quash rumours of 'supposed excessive profits derived by the Company from its connexion with the Contract Mail Service'. They felt that 'the costly character of the service' was inevitable given 'the highly important national objects' that P&O's first-class steam vessels were ready to carry out at any time in any emergency.[37]

But the matter did not end there. In fairness to P&O's adversary, the Admiralty invited I&A to negotiate privately as well, anxious 'to give them every facility', though there were already doubts as to whether I&A 'could obtain capital enough for the due performance of the service they offered to undertake'. The Treasury, still insisting on a price no higher than £15,525 and 'finding that there were competing offers before them', ordered 'another opportunity for public competition'.[38] Furious at being pushed into a second contest and suspecting that I&A had a very fragile foundation, the MDs declined to fall into the trap of underbidding the opposition and reverted to their original offer of £26,500 against I&A's £18,450. The whole exercise was rapidly becoming a farce, although the Post Office, responsible for the mails, must have feared that with so little time left before the old contract expired in December, the whole Indian mail structure might collapse. The Treasury, however, bent on cutting the subsidy, ordered the contract to be awarded to I&A on condition that the company had the means to perform it.[39]

It soon transpired that I&A had no ships, no infrastructure, almost no capital and was not in a position to begin a mail service in January or at any other date.[40] I&A's pretentious programme had depended entirely on other companies which proved unable or unwilling to commit themselves to this rickety concern. As we have seen, P&O refused to cooperate; AL was a victim of revolution and war; Royal Mail may have been approached without success, possibly frightened off by P&O. Only Cunard remained and that company seems to have thought better of it at the crucial moment, unless, as the Admiralty suspected, Cunard had never had any intention of combining with I&A. John Yates, its secretary, 'could not definitely state that [I&A's] deed could be subscribed by the members of a Firm at Liverpool, largely interested in the Cunard Line, and prepared, as had been stated from the first, to supply the India & Australia Company, with the Steam Vessels, that were to enable it to compete with the P&O Stm Comy'.[41] The 'Firm at Liverpool' could only have been Charles MacIver; he had designs of his own on the Mediterranean and would surely not have got mixed up in a shaky venture. With less than two weeks of the old contract left to run, the Admiralty turned to P&O. The MDs offered £24,000, the sum they had privately settled with the Admiralty in July, and the new contract was hastily completed, to continue until January 1853 when the India and China contract would fall due.[42] To everyone's relief, there was no interruption of the India mails.

I&A's second challenge: Australia

That I&A failed in the Mediterranean was, in retrospect, not surprising: envy of the huge profits that P&O was rumoured to earn made I&A's promoters greedy and led them to imagine that they could sweep P&O away at a stroke and take both its place and its profits. In Australia too their efforts failed, though for a while they seemed set to defeat P&O because the Admiralty was urged by the Treasury to save money on contracts and I&A was ready to oblige by undercutting its more established rival.

In 1846 the MDs, determined to be the first to occupy the line to the colonies, began to look in earnest into the cost of such an enterprise. Australia's coal mines were of great interest and samples were sent to P&O's depots at Singapore and Hong Kong. A steady flow of good steam coal would have a dramatic effect on operating costs in the East; and copper deposits in the colonies promised to develop into a paying steam cargo to India.[43] Even so, in the spring of 1847, the MDs believed that 'the much talked of extension to Australia was a contingency too remote to be supported by any Government contract till the Colony [*sic*] is in a position largely to contribute towards it'. Reminding the directors of their recent correspondence – see above – with the Board of Trade and with the Treasury, however, the MDs added: 'To avoid the chance of competition [P&O] would claim the preference in tendering for such service under Government sanction . . . should it be resolved upon as a national undertaking', and proposed to run a branch from the China line at Singapore to Australia.[44] The East India Company 'threw cold water' on this offer, but P&O's board nevertheless intended to 'take the initiative' as soon as costs and tonnage were thoroughly worked out.

I&A's project moved into a higher gear in June, though there were signs of contention among the promoters. One faction wanted to give up the whole enterprise and offered to sell the charter to P&O, a move that was quickly opposed by others. Edward Moxhay, one of the London Tavern group, asked the MDs to attend a meeting as he was 'authorised to treat for the sale of the Charter of the India & Australia Royal Mail Steam Packet Co.'. Montgomery Martin told P&O that Moxhay's overture was 'wholly unauthorized', but the MDs in any case were not interested as they had their own charter.

The grant of a charter of incorporation, according to John Yates, led the I&A promoters to believe that the Admiralty would give their company an Australian contract without further ado. They also assumed that P&O would cooperate by conveying mail, passengers and cargo between Singapore and England, and the Admiralty, on behalf of I&A, pressed P&O to collaborate because 'it is obvious that [I&A] cannot carry out its intention of forming a communication between Sydney and Singapore unless it is assured that means exist for forwarding such goods and passengers as may be there landed to their ultimate destination'.[45]

The MDs, however, saw no reason why this newcomer should be helped in any way whatsoever. When Montgomery Martin asked to meet the MDs in May 1847 to discuss the subject, the reply was that 'no practical results could arise from the interview you solicit [so the directors] beg leave respectfully to decline it', and they repeated their refusal a month later. Cooperation with other companies was contrary to P&O's policy.[46]

Montgomery Martin then called on the Board of Trade. Apparently on friendly terms with J.G.L. Lefevre, assistant secretary in the department, he sought advice on how to prevent P&O from 'damaging the prospects' of I&A, and urged the Government to 'interfere' with P&O's monopoly. If I&A was not allowed to put steamers in Eastern waters, an Austrian or French company would soon appear on the Red Sea to the detriment of British trade; better I&A than foreigners. He begged Earl Clarendon (president of the Board of Trade, 1846–47), to intercede for I&A by demanding from P&O 'a final answer as to the Terms on which our Passengers and goods will be received on arrival at Singapore, or Ceylon, from Australia'; if P&O still refused (which it did), Clarendon should seek permission for I&A 'to establish the whole Line [from England to Australia] at once, so that our passengers, and the public, may obtain the immediate benefit of certain and Economical communications with England'. In short, he wanted the Government to force P&O to give in to all of I&A's demands.[47]

P&O's own plans for the Australian line were held up by uncertainties about its prospects. Captain Robert Guthrie, the company's superintendent of navigation, made an experimental voyage between Singapore and Sydney via the Torres Straits and wrote to Carleton en route on 28 January 1848 that Singapore to Sydney and back could be done in 28 days, a distance of 4,180 miles at 7.5 knots. But a committee of directors set up in May 1848 to look into the route, though able to estimate that the cost of a monthly service from Singapore to Sydney and back would be about £111,000 a year, including all outgoings, reported that it was 'utterly impossible to arrive at any accurate calculation as to what Traffic or Revenue may be expected to be created' on the route. All the same, P&O had 'a well organised Establishment in the East' that would enable the company to undertake the line 'at less hazard probably than any Company to be established for the purpose'. The only firm information would come from experimental voyages. An elaborate scheme was drawn up, involving the Admiralty and the Colonial Office and, of course, designed to make P&O the recipient of the contract at a price P&O thought reasonable, but it was ignored.[48]

Because of the need to consult with the authorities in the colonies, there was a long wait until October 1848 when tenders for a monthly service connecting Sydney to Singapore were advertised for all three routes from England. P&O and I&A tendered for the Red Sea route only; P&O's price was £60,000, much lower than its estimate derived from the experimental voyage, and I&A's was the extraordinary sum of £26,000 per year, £6,000 of which would be provided by New South Wales. The cheapness of I&A's offer was irresistible and the Government awarded the contract to I&A.[49] But this decision was taken only two weeks after I&A, unable to give 'such proofs of the existence of the Compy as an organised body . . . or of its actual command of Capital', had been deemed unfit to become a contractor, and I&A was no more able to run the Australian line than those in the Mediterranean. In a desperate last appeal to Earl Grey at the Colonial Office in April 1849, the date on which the Australian line was to begin, John Yates, I&A's secretary, blamed 'difficulties of an unexpected nature . . . at the Admiralty', 'added to which, on our making application to the P&O Co for an arrangement, by which our Passengers & traffic may be conveyed (on route to & from Australia) between Singapore and England, we are met with the decided refusal of that Company, to afford any accommodation whatever to our Trade'. The swipe at P&O was unjustified: the MDs could not have declared themselves more clearly from the outset. Nor was Earl Grey persuaded to give I&A the 'countenance & powerful support' that Yates thought might save the company.[50] Inevitably, his company was soon 'entombed in the "Winding-up Court"' without having dispatched a single steamer.[51]

This exercise in competition was a vindication of P&O as the sitting tenant. Warning signals about this competition had been sent out by the Admiralty: 4*s* 6*d* per mile was far too low to attract any 'competent party' to bid for the Alexandria line. Again, P&O's experience and past record had a value of its own and constituted 'a guarantee for further management which a newly formed Company cannot furnish'. On the other hand, I&A had a suspiciously large appetite. Without capital or experience in steam navigation, it demanded that P&O's India and China contract be 'forthwith dissolved' and handed over to I&A, although the contract had several years to run; and as if the Alexandria and Australian lines were not enough for a new company to embrace, I&A tried to grab the Peninsular service from P&O as well.[52] But important lines of communication could not be left to chance, and new companies were not all they purported to be, and that the Treasury should have been taken in by I&A's low bids is surprising. Perhaps officials were trying to prove to their masters, the Lords and Commons, what P&O knew very well, that long-distance navigation was a serious and expensive business, not suited to amateurs.

Not long after these events, another parliamentary inquiry into the contract system was held, this time in the House of Commons. Conclusions reached in this arena had a 'beneficial tendency' for P&O in that they refuted 'the sinister reports, so industriously circulated' about its contracts and activities.[53] But the Select Committee also recommended: 'the most strict and searching inquiry' into a contractor's cost and profits; 'great caution either in renewing the existing, or in forming new arrangements'; and procedures 'most likely to secure a real and true competition by responsible parties'.[54] Hard on its heels followed the next challenge to P&O.

The Eastern Steam Navigation Company

Even as I&A was about to leave the stage, a new company was waiting in the wings: the Secretary of I&A John Yates, 'in connection with other parties', formed the Eastern Steam Navigation Company in 1850 out of I&A's ashes.[55] Yates, Lieutenant John Wood, Robert Brooks and George Thomas Braine figured prominently in both companies, while the presence of two of Austrian Lloyd's directors, Joseph Edlmann and W.H. Goschen, brought that company's interest into the open. With a cohort of India and China merchants and bankers behind it, Eastern Steam looked more 'Indian' than Australian, and more solid than I&A.

A new company formed by eminent businessmen might be difficult to dispose of, and Willcox and Anderson decided to try to negotiate privately for a contract for eastern routes before Eastern Steam was formally established. They drew up a plan that would renew P&O's occupation of the India and China lines and complete the network by adding Marseilles-Alexandria, Bombay-Suez and Australia. Australia was unlikely to yield profits on its own, but as a feeder for the India and China lines, steam communication with the Colonies could be run on a relatively low subsidy.[56]

To urge P&O's case, Willcox followed Sir Charles Wood from London to his country seat and back again during October and November, because, as Chancellor of the Exchequer (1846–52), Wood had the last word in the award of mail contracts. Willcox promised that the scheme would not cost the Government 'one shilling' because of the substantial savings that would be made by replacing naval vessels east and west of Suez.[57] Willcox objected to submitting an official tender because P&O's terms were 'sure to leak out, thus arming "a priori" an antagonist or competitor', as had happened in the past. 'Send me the scheme – I will tell no one', was Wood's reply, adding that there would have to be a public tender but it would be couched 'in very loose terms' to see what routes and offers were made. In anticipation of the plan being accepted, two new screw steamers, *Singapore* and *Ganges*, were commissioned by P&O using new capital.[58]

All these efforts came to nothing, however, for the scheme was rejected in April 1851. The backing of two cabinet ministers – Wood and Lord Grey – who regarded P&O's bid as 'a most advantageous offer for the public', was insufficient to overcome the obduracy of the East India Company. As before,[59] it refused to relinquish the Bombay–Suez line because it did not want to lose the Indian Navy, and no amount of condemnation in both Houses on all sides, and in the considerable correspondence between the London and Indian governments, had any effect. The response of this beleaguered institution showed that it had long since lost its way; the stultified conservatism of the company in matters to do with shipping and communication was in stark contrast with the dynamism of P&O. Lord Ellenborough, the Governor-General of India in the 1840s, had recommended the abolition of the Indian Navy twenty years previously and regretted that he had not been able to put an end to it then. In 1850, signs that change was in the air were evident.[60]

Powerless against the East India Company's intransigence, Sir Charles Wood had to give way, becoming more caustic as the correspondence piled up. The apparent conversion to the virtues of competition by that quintessentially monopolistic institution finally made him lose patience in May 1850. He observed that

> although it may be expedient sometimes to resort to competition, with a view of imposing a check upon companies . . . my own experience of the subject has not led me to conclude that the most satisfactory arrangements for the public have been the result of open tender; and I think that on the contrary, much advantage is obtained by the Government reserving to itself the opportunity of dealing with each particular service in such a manner as careful consideration of circumstances may at the time point out.[61]

Failure to have these plans accepted was a severe blow for P&O. The board put the blame on 'much misrepresentation' of what P&O intended, and on a 'determined opposition, in quarters and among parties whose interests and views' clashed with those of P&O.[62] There was also good reason to suspect that the rejection was not due to 'difficulties of an ordinary nature' but to the promoters of the Eastern Steam Company who were pressing their own cause.[63] They had lobbied Parliament as soon as the new session opened in February 1850. Though steam communication had to make way for a number of other important matters relating to Australia – self-government for the colonies, the right to regulate their own customs duties and the future of convict transportation – once the self-government Bill was passed in May, steam communication came to the fore. Numerous petitions and memorials from Australia and by interested merchants and bankers in Britain poured in, all demanding steam communication with the colony. One petition was signed by some 12,000 of the 'most influential persons in the city of London, including the house of Rothschild'.[64]

To give credence to its ability to satisfy this demand, Eastern Steam's prospectus was suitably ambitious and wide-ranging. With a nominal capital of £1,200,000 divided into 60,000 shares of £20 each, the object of the enterprise was to supply more frequent and more efficient steam communication between 'Europe, India, and China and to establish similar communication with Australia, Java, and other parts of the East . . . in addition to the service currently undertaken by the Peninsular & Oriental Company'. Officials in the Colonial Office suspected that a second I&A was in the making, but inquiries confirmed that 'the Company now formed appears to include the names of men of some substance' who were connected with 'some of the most eminent banking firms of the metropolis, as well as the directors of the various Australian banks, and many other houses of the highest commercial character in this kingdom'.[65]

Robert Wigram Crawford was the chairman. He had been a partner for eighteen years in Remington, Crawford & Co., one the most respected houses in Bombay, and had owned a fleet of sailing ships plying to China; on retirement from India he became the senior partner in Crawford Colvin & Co. (formerly Bazett & Farquer) in London. George Thomas Braine, deputy chairman, was an India and China merchant and partner in the firm of Dent & Co., the most important mercantile house in the East next to Jardine–Matheson. There was also a west country interest: P.W.S. Miles, MP, of Bristol, was on the directorate; the company intended to use Plymouth as its port of departure and to build some of its vessels in Bristol.[66] Many of the provisional directors and shareholders, including Crawford and Braine, were involved in the opium trade.[67]

Crawford and Braine led a deputation to the Chancellor of the Exchequer, Sir Charles Wood, to explain their intentions. They sought a contract for a second service on all P&O's lines, for a single service from Singapore to Australia and for a route between Trieste and Alexandria to serve the Continent. They did not want to displace P&O but to alternate with it, thereby giving the public the advantage of competition between the two companies, with more tonnage and double the number of mails. The Trieste–Alexandria line would be provided by AL, giving access to India and China both to AL and to

Eastern Steam. The company had no vessels as yet but would buy or hire suitable vessels for the Australian line while new ones were building for the trunk lines. The promoters and their followers predicted that 'the mere existence of a rival Company . . . [would] always be the means of introducing economy into the arrangements . . . [and] would at once bring about [greater speed] . . . by the competition of rival interests'. And Yates, the new company's secretary, told Earl Grey at the Colonial Office that as P&O was the only company in a position to tender for the Singapore–Sydney line, 'a monopoly would be permanently secured to that Company, which it is the obvious interest of the public to avoid'. At least one official was not taken in by this statement, however, noting that while Yates objected to P&O's monopoly his own objective appeared to be 'to obtain the influence of the Secretary of State in placing the same monopoly in the hands of the Company he represent[ed]'.[68]

By the end of 1850, Eastern Steam had gathered enough influential support in and out of Parliament to create some unease on P&O's board. This perhaps accounted for a carefully worded paragraph in P&O's Annual Report that seemed to prepare the shareholders for the possibility that Eastern Steam would get the contract for Australia:

> It would be equally, if not more conducive to your interest if some other parties, possessing the means of ensuring its efficient developement [*sic*], could be found to undertake the [Australian] enterprise; because such an arrangement could not fail of being beneficial to this Company, by increasing the traffic on its established lines, while it would be exempted from the risk of loss, which almost invariably attends the opening of a new line of ocean steam communication.[69]

Indeed, Anderson stated, in a submission to the 1851 Select Committee, that if any other party proposed to undertake the Australian branch on better terms than P&O, the company would be willing to cooperate on condition that 'such party [had] the means and experience to ensure an efficient establishment and [could] maintain the communication'.[70] Any loss of time or a mishap would wreck the entire mail service and ruin P&O's record.

Some shareholders with a 'great stake' in P&O, however, took a different view of the situation. In a public letter, they demanded to know whether there was any foundation to the rumour that P&O was about to cooperate with Eastern Steam. If the rumour was unfounded, they asked the management to clarify its policy, should Eastern Steam become a competitor. Putting out a bold front, the MDs responded with a long recital of P&O's recent and future expansion, and ended with a curt dismissal of Eastern Steam's ambitions: 'Under what misconception . . . it is now attempted to raise a capital of £1,200,000 for a new enterprise, to carry out objects which the Peninsular and Oriental Company have already anticipated, and for which the requisite capital is already provided, the Directors need not pause to consider'.[71]

P&O still had the ability to block entry to the overland crossing at Alexandria and Suez.[72] John Yates believed that it would be easy for Eastern Steam and its associate AL to break P&O's resistance. In 1849, Lieutenant Wood – formerly of the East India Company and since 1847 AL's London representative – attempted to negotiate with P&O for access to India, but he found that P&O was as determined to make no concession to AL or Eastern Steam as it had been in 1847 to make none to I&A. And when Wood had exhausted all his arguments, Baron Rothschild called on the MDs for a 'personal conference' as a 'friend' of AL, to see what his power of persuasion could do, but he also came away empty-handed.[73]

Early in 1851, Crawford and his friends put their case to Viscount Jocelyn MP, a former secretary of the Board of Control,[74] and he in turn moved for a Select Committee on the Eastern mail services, including Australia and New Zealand.[75] There was no time to lose, because if Eastern Steam was to have any chance of sharing lines with P&O, vessels would have to be built and ready by the date (December 1852) on which P&O's contracts on either side of Suez were due to expire. The Committee's remit was to examine all three routes from England to Australia but it was P&O and the Red Sea route that 'attracted the greatest share of public attention'.

Voluminous evidence was taken. Many witnesses were critical of and hostile to P&O. Willcox, a member of the Committee, fielded questions when P&O was under attack, and Anderson, a witness, put in some vigorous rebuttals, including a classical defence of the contract system:

> The sum paid for the postal service . . . does not constitute a subsidy or bonus; terms which are frequently, but very inaccurately, applied to it. It was not a premium given to establish Steam Navigation with India, but the consideration for performing a valuable public service, stipulated for a bargain mutually agreed upon by the Government on behalf of the public on the one part, and by the Peninsular & Oriental Company on the other, each party being at perfect liberty at the time of making that bargain to reject or accept the terms proposed by the other. And the disadvantages . . . are such . . . as in a great degree to neutralize its supposed advantages.[76]

Judicious and friendly evidence for P&O was given by William Fane De Salis, recently come home after eight successful years in Australia. He had acquired land and stock in the colonies and an interest in several coal mines, including the Australasian Coal Mining Company; he was also a merchant, banker and shipowner, and had been a partner in Thacker Mason & Co., Jardine–Matheson's Australian branch. A gentleman 'of great respectability and practical knowledge', he had been 'unremitting' in his efforts to bring steam communication to Australia. De Salis had already offered himself as a candidate for P&O's directorate. With personal experience of, and strong connections with, the most important trades in the South Pacific, he would be invaluable for P&O. He was given a seat on the board in the summer of 1851, taking the place of Sir John Pirie who had died earlier in the year.[77]

Lieutenant Wood, on the other hand, was extremely hostile to P&O. Before Eastern Steam had been formed, Wood had tried on AL's behalf to get concessionary fares from P&O for Trieste passengers travelling to India. He had failed, and made much at the Select Committee of P&O's discriminatory passenger tariff. 'If I wished to go to Birmingham', he said, 'I should think it very hard if I was charged the fare to Liverpool.' Yet that was P&O's policy. The through-fare from Calcutta to Southampton, including the overland journey, was structured to penalize passengers who did not make the whole voyage in a P&O ship. Thus a merchant from Calcutta travelling to Suez would be charged the 'unvarying fare' (£127 in high season, £102 in the off season) as if he were bound for Southampton. And if he landed at Suez without a booking with P&O for Southampton, he would have to find his own way across the desert and, having arrived at Alexandria to take ship for Marseilles or Trieste, he would have to pay an extra fare – £48 from Alexandria to England via Trieste, making the total fare in the off season £150.[78] A further obstacle was P&O's rule that 'if he goes another way himself and leaves us his baggage', he would find that P&O would not take it on board one of its vessels.[79] Anderson's remark that 'we would rather have them go in our vessels than in others' was greatly resented, not least because of the proprietorial air P&O adopted towards the Egyptian crossing, which, after all, was Egyptian territory. But Anderson's justification was that the large sums paid to the overland administration by P&O gave the company 'a right to a preference',[80] to which Willcox added that 'in self defence [P&O] so arranged their tariff as to induce the passengers they brought from India to prefer going to England by that Company's vessels to Southampton, instead going away by the foreign company'.

Then there were the mercantile houses on the Continent which wished to open branches in the East and counted on keeping in touch with them by steam, but unfair rules on passenger fares and correspondingly heavy freight rates for cargo of any description, served as an effective barrier to any continental transactions.[81] Wood accused P&O

of excluding outsiders because, fearful of competition, the MDs did not think it was in the interest of the company to develop trade beyond what its own steamers could take. Denying that AL had a secret agenda to seek 'new fields' in the East, Wood said his company wanted only to promote the 'gradual development of their old lines' and 'to have a share of the passenger traffic from India'. P&O's tariff was in effect 'a prohibition'. But neither the enticements of more traffic from Europe nor the hints of competition from the Continent and the USA made the MDs change their stance.

Murray Gladstone, partner in the Calcutta house of Gillander, Arbuthnot & Co., asked by Willcox if he was surprised that P&O should so regulate its rates as to keep passengers from straying, replied that he was not surprised, 'but when the Peninsular & Oriental Company receive a very large sum for conveying the mails and for carrying on this communication with India, I consider that we should have some return . . . The steamer is a public carrying hotel, and it should treat all alike.' But Anderson stuck to his view that 'all the through passengers' should have 'a preference in booking per Desert vans over those applicants proceeding *via* Trieste or Marseilles, for whose fare we are not responsible to the Transit Comp[a]ny'.[82]

Several witnesses to the Select Committee had interests in the opium trade. Their main complaints were shortage of steam tonnage for valuable cargoes like opium and silk, the lack of choice, since P&O was the only provider of steam transport, and the high freight rates charged. One merchant complained that nothing would satisfy people in India 'unless there is competition on the line; the object is to prevent the whole of the steam communication with India centering in one company'. Others agreed with Lieutenant Wood that there was 'traffic enough on the Calcutta line to support two companies, and . . . with the subsidy paid to [P&O] divided between them, they would pay a fair dividend'.[83] Opinions like this indicate that there was little comprehension about the cost of steam shipping on long distances. And as to the practical problem of doubling the tonnage within two years, how was this to be overcome? Anderson drew attention to the surge of shipbuilding that began in 1851 with the upturn of trade: were these merchants aware that 'workmen [were] quite unmanageable on account of the abundance of work'? An engineers' strike had already put strains on the shipyards. Anderson reckoned, not unrealistically, that the fifteen vessels Eastern Steam would need for its ambitious programme would never be ready on time, even supposing that enough capital was available.[84]

Nevertheless, competition was king in the Eastern Steam camp. Crawford observed that if 'Mr Cunard . . . had not been driven by the fear of competition, he never would have had his present magnificent class of steamer; and if the Peninsular & Oriental Company had a similar stimulant in the India Seas, I think we should not now hear of such boats as the "Oriental" paraded for speed'. Lieutenant Wood too compared P&O with the Cunard company, asserting that 'where competition exists, I see that good results flow from it'. He was evidently not aware that 'competition' on the Atlantic had quickly resulted in a secret deal between Cunard and the American Collins Company. Criticism of the slow speed of P&O's ships compared to those of Cunard and Collins was answered by Anderson: speed meant higher fuel costs. Collins's expenditure on coal was very great; and 'not withstanding the very high rate of payment which they have from their Government, it is well known that they are remunerative'.[85]

Other opponents backed Lieutenant Wood, asserting that P&O had reacted to the threat of competition, and this was largely true despite Anderson's stout denials. Since 1846, passenger fares had been lowered 4 times, and 3 times after I&A came on the scene.[86] Complaints about the age and speed of P&O's vessels were also parried by Anderson: the new iron paddlers, *Singapore* and *Ganges*, both 1,200 tons and built in 1850, were at work on the Bombay–Hong Kong line in 1851. P&O was interested in the new screw engines as early as 1845 but, like other shipowners, was hesitant about the efficiency of screw propulsion for large, expensive, mercantile steamships. Competition on the Constantinople line, however, proved that screw engines were essential for profitability.[87] The company acquired its first screw steamer, *Shanghai*, in 1851 for employment in the East, and began the slow and expensive process of replacing paddlers with screws.[88] Expansion was very obviously ahead of the company's capacity to build. Yet the shortage of tonnage at this point was not P&O's doing. In October 1847, the MDs were about to apply for new capital, the first £1 million being nearly exhausted, but the financial crisis of the end of that year froze all plans for new ships or expansion, and the company was lucky to sell the three ships building for it on the stocks.[89] *Singapore* and *Ganges* were intended to begin a new programme of building, but it was not until the summer of 1850 that an additional £500,000 of capital was authorized, and only in October 1851 that the market was deemed buoyant enough for the first call on the new issue to be made so that additions to the fleet could be made in anticipation of the new 1853 contract.[90]

Crawford and his supporters envisaged 'the continuous competition of two distinct agencies'. This 'principle' assumed that the two companies would be equal. In fact, no new company could be equal to P&O. Captain J.H. Wilson, who had commanded *Hugh Lindsay* in the

1830s,[91] approved of what Eastern Steam wanted – more tonnage on the lines at lower rates in faster steamers. But with his long experience he brought some realism to the subject in his remark that 'competition is a very excellent thing but I rather think it is an abstraction; I should like to have pointed out to me any practical real *bona fide* competition going on now in anything'. He cited gas, water and omnibus companies as examples. Their managers would start by professing that they would compete with each other, 'but it lasts a very short time, and the general result is, an understanding by which the Government and the public are completely helpless, and kept at arm's length as they are now by the water companies'.

He considered that the Government paid P&O 'many thousands of pounds more than they should', but acknowledged that P&O had 'carried on the communication very well with their vessels: the only objection I should make is that the number of passengers is too great for the accommodation afforded; the only objection to the Peninsular and Oriental Company is that they are not up to the requirements of the day'.[92]

Brought on to the Committee at a late stage, Crawford was on hand to see that the *Second Report* of the proceedings put his company's case unambiguously. While acknowledging P&O's 'enterprising spirit which has been displayed . . . in the general management of the Communication which they have conducted for some years', the main thrust of the *Second Report* was to recommend that the trunk line between England and China be shared between Eastern Steam and P&O. The Committee emphasized the 'considerable inconvenience . . . the English and Indian public have at times experienced' because of shortage of tonnage and the inefficiency of some of P&O's steamers. Until the 'agitation' stirred up by Eastern Steam, P&O 'had done little towards introducing into their line those great and important improvements, as regards speed, which have . . . taken place in Ocean Steam Navigation' though the faster vessels that had been at work 'of late' were mentioned. The *Reports* from the House of Lords were generally in harmony with the Commons' conclusion, and though they shrank from recommending the Government to interfere with a private company by making rules about fares or speed – these were for the management of the company to decide – the only guarantee of improvements and greater economy was 'by the establishment of wholesome competition'.[93]

Accordingly, the official tender, advertised shortly afterwards, was drawn up exactly as the *Report* directed, except that the trunk line was divided into sections (table 4.1) so that the competitors could bid for the whole line or for one or more sections, according to their

Table 4.1 Tenders for the 1853 contracts

1	England to Alexandria, via Gibraltar and Malta, and back, and branch from Marseilles to Malta, monthly.
2	Ditto.
3	Suez to Calcutta, via Aden, Pointe de Galle (Ceylon) and Madras and back, monthly; and from Pointe de Galle to Hong Kong via Penang and Singapore in separate steamers, and back, monthly.
4	Ditto.
5	From Singapore to Sydney, via Batavia, Swan River or King George's Sound, Adelaide and Port Philip and back, every two months.

Source: *PP*, 1852, 49 (249), p. 3.

resources. For both P&O and Eastern Steam this competition marked a critical moment. If P&O's network lost even one section, its whole strategy would be in danger, while for Eastern Steam this was a once-only opportunity to establish a foothold in the India and China trades.

P&O tendered for all 5 sections for £199,600. The MDs were ready to start the two new lines (Marseilles–Malta and Sydney–Singapore) at a mileage rate forthwith if required, but in any case on 1 January 1853. The price included the addition of some 22,000 miles (Bombay–Galle and Calcutta–Hong Kong – the two main opium lines) on which a mail service would be provided free of charge. All 5 sections, together with the unsubsidized additions, amounted to 626,280 miles in the new contract, as against the 258,000 miles P&O worked in 1852. The average mileage rate for the whole contract line was about 6*s* 6*d* a mile. P&O undertook to reduce the contract price by £20,000 per annum once the railway across Egypt was completed.[94] There were 14 vessels at work and 6 building or fitting out, more than 10,000 tons in total.

Eastern Steam put in 2 tenders: one for sections 1 and 3, the other for sections 1, 3 and 5, for £110,000 (about 8*s* per mile) and £166,000 (about 10*s* per mile) respectively. These tenders included the offer of a reduction of £10,000 whenever Trieste was substituted for Marseilles as the mail port in the Mediterranean. Eastern Steam had no vessels, but intended to build either 10 or 13, depending on which tender was accepted. The earliest date that Eastern Steam could begin the contract was January 1854.[95]

No one could complain about favouritism in this contest. P&O's tender was undoubtedly the better: cheaper and able to start earlier than Eastern Steam's. A week after the tenders went in, the contract was awarded to P&O for a term of eight years.[96] Shareholders, delighted at the outcome, marked the victory with a banquet for the directors 'as a testimony of their efficient conduct of our affairs', and congratulated them for the 'well-established position' of the company. The Corporation of Southampton also held an 'entertainment' for directors and officers, by way of giving thanks for the additional work that the new contract would bring to the port.[97] Danger of competition now removed, the MDs had no objection to making amicable arrangements with Austrian Lloyd's about rates and passage money that were 'advantageous to both companies'; and the newly established French company, Messageries Nationales (soon to become Messageries Impériales after Napoleon's coup in 1852) was similarly accommodated.[98]

'Let them alone: they are too strong for us'

The challenges to P&O from I&A and from Eastern Steam demonstrate the advantages enjoyed by an entrenched contractor, for they made it virtually impossible for a new company to compete with P&O until maritime steam technology found answers to the problems of fuel economy and engine reliability. But there were other factors too. A huge investment of about £2 million was made by the Government in the Peninsular Company from 1837 and in P&O since 1840, as table 4.2 shows. In the same period, the company had put in just over £1 million of share capital as well as a substantial amount of reserved profits. Investment on such a scale could not be lightly discarded. Besides, it was clear that the Government could not find another more efficient contractor at a lower cost. This fact was appreciated by discerning shipowners like Richard Green who, as early as 1844, saw that 'it was of no use to compete with that powerful company . . . Let them alone: they are too strong for us.'[99]

Table 4.2 Mail contract money received by P&O, 1837–52

	Year	*Money (£s) received*
Peninsular line	1837–45	236,800
	1846–52	143,500
First Alexandria line (Calcutta line)	1840–52	345,000
Second Alexandria line (Bombay line)	1845–52	139,575
Calcutta–Suez, Galle–Hong Kong	1843–52	1,180,000[a]
Total	1837–52	2,101,875[a]

Note: [a] Of which the Government of India contributed £60,000 in 1843–45 and £490,000 from 1845 to 1852.

There was also the investment made by P&O in essential infrastructure. The East India Company and its acolyte Captain Henderson seized on the fact, when they were raising objections to P&O in 1844, that 'there are no dry docks in India long enough to receive either [*Hindostan* or *Bentinck*]. The Peninsular Company have no establishment or means of repairing machinery, nor are there any other means of repairing and removing such large engines and boilers with the requisite facility and despatch in Calcutta.'[100] True enough, but the MDs were well aware of the 'vast importance to this Co' of independent docking accommodation: it would 'give renewed vitality to [P&O's] operations in the Indian Seas which without it might be seriously paralyzed'. If accidents to machinery, replacement of boilers and general maintenance of hulls and engines could not be dealt with in the East, the whole enterprise would disintegrate. So, instead of wringing their hands, the MDs set about acquiring (first by leasing, later by buying) docks, repairing establishments, wharves, jetties, hulks and coal depots, as well as offices and houses for staff. No new steamship company could 'make all those great arrangements in two days',[101] nor could they breach P&O's stronghold. As Anderson remarked in 1840, P&O 'got things done'.

In the 5 years up to 1852, P&O consolidated the position it had reached in the first 7 years after its formation. I&A and Eastern Steam were P&O's most serious rivals to date, but both tried to run a race in which the champion had already reached the winning tape. Both companies had a large nominal capital written in to their prospectuses and found shareholders who were willing to put down a token deposit. But they had no ships, and, quite apart from the fact that ships take time to build, none of their shareholders – understandably enough – could be persuaded to dig deeper in his or her pockets unless a contract was signed and sealed. Eastern Steam's shareholders had paid a deposit of 2*s* a share, I&A's considerably less; P&O, at its birth, in 1840, had some £300,000 in ships and a head start of experience in steam navigation. Both I&A and Eastern Steam hoped that P&O would allow them to enter its Eastern domain, but P&O knew that on the long routes every line could sustain only one company.

The Government tried to play fair in an unfair situation, and could hardly be criticized for not putting complete trust in a new and untried company. The I&A fiasco was a warning not to do so, and even Eastern Steam's respectability was deceptive. P&O, on the other hand, was a solid and reliable operator, and, when nudged or pushed, improved its services and altered its rates while keeping the upper hand. From the vantage point of the Admiralty, far better the assurance of the sitting tenant than the hazard of strangers. Officials in this department, who were close to the actuality of early steam shipping, tended to take P&O's side; and even the Treasury could not always win the argument with the Admiralty. Together, government and company had satisfied their expectations in the dozen years since the long-distance contracts began.

With the arrival at Sydney on 3 August 1852 of *Chusan*, the first ocean-going steamship to connect Australia with Singapore for England, P&O had once again 'done what other parties had so long talked about'. In the event the service to Australia was not a success and P&O was obliged to discontinue it in 1854, not to begin again until some years later.[102] Nonetheless 'very bright prospects' were predicted as the company steamed ahead with its new commitments:[103] mail services of unique excellence had been established; the great sea lanes made secure for British trade; and Britain's distant possessions drawn closer to the metropolis.[104] P&O was proud of its own substantial contribution to these attainments. With the 1852 contract safe, P&O's strategy of expansion was all but complete and the company's position, for the time being at least, unassailable.

Notes

1 The Bombay Steam Navigation Company was building two vessels in 1845 with which it hoped to cooperate with P&O: P&O/1/100, 30.12.1845; but no more was heard of it after P&O refused to buy its vessels: P&O/1/101, 4.4.1848. In 1853, Capt. Henderson and his partners were still seeking additional compensation from the East India Company for losses he and his partners incurred when the China line was awarded to P&O: *Times*, 29.9.1853, p. 5, col. 5.

2 F. Broeze, *Mr Brooks and the Australian Trade: Imperial Business in the Nineteenth Century* (Carlton, Victoria: Melbourne University Press, 1993), chs 11–12.

3 *PP*, 1837, 6 (539), *Steam Communication with India*, q. 1040; H. Robinson, *Carrying British Mails Overseas* (London: Allen & Unwin, 1964), pp. 87–96; Maber, *North Star*, Introduction and chs 1–6; *PD*, 3rd series, vol. 113, col. 647.

4 An Australian Steam Committee asked P&O to give it an estimate of working expenses for a monthly steam vessel from Sydney to Singapore and back (P&O/1/100, 2.6.1846, P&O1/101, 16.6.1846), and a letter from Andrew Ross, hon. secretary of the Steam Navigation Committee, Sydney, New South Wales, dated 2.5.1846, wanted P&O to tender for a steam connection from Australia to Britain, but P&O replied that it would 'tender when the British Government asks it to do so'.

5 See Freda Harcourt, 'The High Road to India: P&O and the Origins of the Suez Canal', forthcoming.

6 *Morning Advertiser*, 18.4.1846; PRO, CO 201/410, no. 1772/Aus, 6.9.1847; no. 2365/Aus, 21.9.1848.

7 See above, p. 59.

8 Broeze, *Mr Brooks*, pp. 120, 244–6, states that at least nine other men who had links with Australia were present; see Greenberg, *British Trade*, pp. 188ff. for his role in the run-up to the Opium War; *PP*, HoL, 1847, 5 (225), q. 528.

9 P&O/1/100, 2.6.1846; P&O/1/101, 16.6.1846, 22.9.1846 and 22.1.1847.

10 J. Abel Smith thought that Montgomery Martin had been 'most improperly appointed', his behaviour was 'disgraceful' and 'his character otherwise very lightly spoken of': Jardine–Matheson Archive, Reel 463, fo. 79 (3), 7.6.1844; he later became known for his many books on a variety of topics.

11 *Times*, 25.8.1847.

12 BT 41/319/1831, Registrations, 22.12.1846, 28.1.1847, 7.4.1847 and prospectus.

13 *PP*, 1834, 14 (478), *SC on Steam Navigation to India*, qq. 2425ff.; T.A. Curtis's plans in 1839 included Trieste as an alternative to Marseilles as the Mediterranean mail port: *PP*, 1850, 53 (693), *Correspondence*, p. 35, 21.2.1839.

14 P&O/1/100, 29.3.1842; ADM 2/1297, fos 21–3, 20.6.1842; fos 114–6, 2.8.1842.

15 Six sea–land–sea trials were carried out with official sanction, with Waghorn in charge of mails by rail and coach between Trieste and Ostend, and fast naval vessels between Alexandria and Trieste and Ostend and England; the operation started in April 1846 and ended in February 1847: ADM 2/1302, fo. 8, 19.12.1845; fo. 111, 10.2.1846; fo. 119, 19.3.1846 fo. 151, 10.3.1846; fo. 273, 8.5.1846 and generally in ADM 2/1303.

16 P&O/1/100, 25.11.1845; P&O/1/101, 29.9.1846; *ibid.*, 27.7.1847 and 3.9.1847; *Times*, 30.10.1846, p. 5, col. 2.

17 FO 7/329, no. 14, 9.7.1846, in no. 14, 20.6.1846, (not numbered); 17.9.1846: Waghorn to Temple (Palmerston), Private, 1.11.1846; FO 7/336, no. 3, 15.1.1847, and no. 24, 19.3.1847; FO 7/334, no. 22, 8.2.1847 and no. 108, 30.6.1847.

18 FO 120/224, no. 16, 24.12.1846, and no. 24, 19.3.1847.

19 *Ibid.*, no. 100, 22.9.1847.

20 P&O/1/101, 23.6.1848; A.J.P. Taylor, *The Italian Problem in European Diplomacy 1847–1849* (Manchester: Manchester University Press, 1934), chs 1 and 2; FO 120/222, 120/224, generally; FO 590/5, 14.6.1848 and 20.3.1849.

21 FO 97/408, Mail Routes, no. 80, enclosure 1, pp. 87–91, 30.9.1847.

22 *PD*, 3rd series, vol. 93, 14.6.1847, cols 470–1, Lord Ellenborough.

23 *Ibid.*; *PP*, HoL, 1847, 5 (225), *SC into Receipts and Charges of the Post Office*, p. iii.

24 *PP*, 1850, 53 (693), *Correspondence*, Papers (C), pp. 8–9 (D), pp. 10–11.

25 ADM 2/1304, fols 258–60, 28.4.1847, and fos 275–7, 8.5.1847.

26 Waghorn's last Trieste trial took place in January 1847: ADM 2/1303, fo. 490, 29.1.1847.

27 Taylor, *Italian Problem*, chs 1 and 2.

28 ADM 2/1305, fos 513–17, 2.11.1847; this insistence on wooden vessels was an early warning about the vulnerability of iron-clad vessels in war, but iron-clad mailships were not formally prohibited by the Admiralty until 1851.

29 ADM 2/1306, fos 278–9, 7.1.1848; ADM 2/1307, fos 67–9, 7.3.1848; fos 104, 14.3.1848; fos 335–6, 5.3.1848; P&O/1/101, 29.2.1848.

30 *PD*, 3rd series, vol. 115, 27.3.51, cols 643–4, Jocelyn quoting the Bengal Chamber of Commerce.

31 ADM 2/1305, fo. 513, 2.11.1847; it was also decided to pursue the Trieste option (fo. 517) that would have made the 'considerable savings' required; ADM 2/1306, fo. 261, 6.1.1848.

32 *PP*, 1849, 12 (571), *Contract Packets*, q. 1306.

33 ADM 2/1308, fos 70–3, 8.7.1848; P&O/1/101, 25.4, 12 and 19.5.1848.

34 *PP*, HoL, 1847, 5 (225), *Post Office*, p. iv; *PP*, 1849, 12 (571), *Contract Packets*, q. 1305; *PP*, HoL, 1847–48, 16 (207), pp. iii–iv.

35 *PP*, 1849, 12 (571), *Contract Packets*, Appendix 2 (B), *Report*, pp. 214–15, Memo., Auckland, pp. 222–3.

36 ADM 2/1308, fos 152–3, 28.7.1828.

37 P&O/6/2, Annual Report, 13.12.1848, pp. 9–10.

38 ADM 2/1308, fos 242–4, 19.8.1848; fos 365–8, 1.9.1848; *PP*, 1849, 12 (571), *Contract Packets*, q. 1306.

39 ADM 2/1309, fos 50–1, 4.11.1848; fos 61–2, 8.11.1848.

40 *PP*, HoL, 1851, 10–I (187–I), *Australia*, q. 2679 (Yates admitted that the 'preliminary deposits were something like £4,000'); ADM 2/1309, fos 238–40, 16.12.1848.

41 ADM 2/1309, fos 260, 20.12.1848; fos 384–94, 16.1.1849.

42 *Ibid.*, fos 279–81, 22.12.1848; fo. 291, 27.12.1848; ADM 2/1310, fos 78–9, 6.1.1849.
43 P&O/1/101, 2.6.1846, 16.6.1846, 22.1.1847, 2.2.1847, 4.5.1847 and 13.7.1847; *PP*, 1851, 21 (372), *First Report*, q. 887.
44 P&O/1/101, 23.4.1847
45 ADM 2/1304, fos 421–2, 2.6.1847; P&O/1/101, 1.6.1847; BT 1/464/3, 668/1847, 24.6.1847.
46 P&O/1/101, 1.6.1847, 15.6.1847, 25.6.1847, 29.6.1847, 2.7.1847 and 17.12.1847.
47 BT 1/319/1831, 22.12.1846 and 28.1.1847; BT 1/464/3, 668/1847, 9.3.1847, 31.5.1847, 5.6.1847, 1.7.1847 and 9.7.1847. In return for the Board of Trade's help, Montgomery Martin introduced Lefevre to a Mr Halswell, 'a most useful committee man . . . to act as such' for Lefevre, and Montgomery Martin himself wrote to a number of MPs 'for their votes on your behalf', probably for the Select Committee on the Navigation Laws, March–July 1847: see Palmer, *Navigation Laws*, pp. 94ff.
48 P&O/3/2, Guthrie to MDs, 28.1.1848, 31.1.1848 and 15.6.1848; P&O/1/101, 7.7.1848 and 18.7.1848.
49 ADM 2/1308, fos 372, 20.9.1848; ADM 2/1309, fos 53–6, 6.11.1848, and fo. 82, 11.11.1848.
50 CO 201/420, 2866/Aus, 4.4.1849.
51 ADM 2/1309, fo. 387, 16.1.1849; ADM 2/1310, fo. 244, 20.4.1849; fo. 307, 11.5.1849; *PD*, vol. 113, col. 234, 25.7.1850. I&A asked P&O to take over its charter, deed and liabilities up to £4,000, so that shareholders could be repaid for their preliminary deposits in 1847. P&O declined: P&O/1/102, 8.5.1849.
52 ADM 2/1307, fo. 453, 1.6.1848; fos 533–7, 19.6.1848, 2/1308; fos 88–9, 13.7.1848; fos 149–51, 28.7.1848; fo. 267, 24.8.1848; fos 403–4, 26.9.1848; fos 449–40, 9.10.1848; *PP*, 1849, 12 (571): Contract Packets, qq. 2009–11.
53 P&O/6/2, Annual Report, 6.12.1849, p. 10.
54 *PP*, 1849, 12 (571): Contract Packets, *Report*, 3rd Resolution.
55 ADM 2/1310, fo. 307, 11.5.1849.
56 P&O/30/5, Anderson to Wood, October 1849 and June 1850; Willcox to Wood, 21.11.1849.
57 The annual cost of Royal Navy steamers on the Marseilles–Alexandria line (72,000 miles) was £58,000: *PP*, 1851, 51 (73): Steam Communication with India and Australia, p. 2; the Indian Navy service on the Bombay–Suez line (70,000 miles) cost more than £100,000. P&O offered to work the whole of this scheme – 332,000 miles – for £105,000: *PP*, 1850, 53 (693), *Second Report*, pp. 95–7. All three new lines would cost only £5,000 more than the current cost of the Bombay–Suez line in the Indian Navy's hands.
58 P&O/30/5, correspondence between Willcox and Wood, 15.10.1849 to 22.11.1849, 17.6.1850 and 9.1.1851; Anderson to Wood, 2.10.1850; ADM 2/1311, fo. 271, 22.10.1849; P&O/6/2, Half-Yearly Report, 30.5.1850, pp. 5–6. P&O's tender went in with an explanatory letter: P&O/30/5, 22.1.1850. There was no other bid for the Red Sea route.
59 See above, chs 1 and 2.
60 *PD*, cols 230ff., 25.7.1850; HoL, vol. 113, cols 763ff., 5.8.1850; HoC, 5.8.50, cols 763–7. According to Robert Remington, just arrived home from Bombay in the summer of 1851, all the signs were that the line would be given up to P&O very soon: *PP*, HoL, 1851, 10–I (187–I): Australia, qq. 5965–70.
61 *PP*, 1850, 53 (693), *Correspondence*, pp. 113–14, 17.5.1850.
62 P&O/6/2, Annual Report, 6.12.1850, p. 6. The plans and the official correspondence between company and government were printed for Parliament, to counter 'misrepresentations', and, for the shareholders, to show that the MDs had worked hard on their behalf: *PP*, 1851, 51 (73), *Steam Communication with India and Australia*.
63 *PP*, 1851, 21 (372), *First Report*, Appendix 1. Only one company was granted a contract in that round of tenders: the General Screw Steam Ship Company for a service to Australia via the Cape of Good Hope by auxiliary vessels. This company,

after success on the Constantinople line in the late 1840s, extended its operations to Calcutta in 1850. Serious difficulties were staved off by the Crimean War, but bankrupcy was inevitable in 1856.

64 *PD*, 3rd series, vol. 113, cols 230ff., 25.7.1850.

65 *Ibid*., col. 230, 25.7.1850; CO 201/446, 1177, 7.2.1851, and minute, 10.2.1851.

66 *PP*, 1852, 49 (249), *Mail Services (India and Australia)*, pp. 4–8.

67 *PP*, 1851, 21 (372), *First Report*, evidence of R.W. Crawford, qq. 4153 ff., and of T.G. Braine, qq. 5697ff.

68 CO 201/446, in Misc., in 1177/51, Yates to Grey, 7.2.1851, and minute of Crawford's deputation to Grey, 10.2.1851; in 1628/51, Crawford and Braine to Grey, 20.2.1851.

69 P&O/6/2, Annual Report, 6.12.1850, p. 7.

70 *PP*, HoL, 1851, 10–I (187–I), *Australia*, q. 3263, p. 425.

71 *Herapath*, 15.2.1851, pp. 175–6.

72 See Harcourt, 'The High Road to India'.

73 *PP*, 1851, 21 (605), *Second Report*, qq. 5242ff., 5296ff. and 5437ff.

74 MP (Con.) for King's Lynn, 1842–54, secretary of Board of Control, Feburary 1845–July 1846: see GEC., *Complete Peerage*, vol. 11 (London: St Catherine's Press, 1949), pp. 64–5.

75 *PD*, 3rd series, vol. 113, col. 233, 25.7.1850; vol. 115, cols 636–46, 27.3.1851. A Select Committee in the House of Lords was set up on the same subject and with much the same evidence: *PP*, 1851, HoL, 10–I (187), *Australia*; and 10–II (187–II), *India and Australia*.

76 *PP*, 1851, 21 (605), *Second Report*, Appendix 13, p. 411, 30.6.1851.

77 *Ibid*. (372), *First Report*, qq. 1ff.; Broeze, *Mr Brooks*, pp. 238, 242, 250, 251; *PD*, vol. 113, col. 234, 25.7.1850; P&O/1/102, 23.11.1849 and 24.6.1851.

78 *PP*, 1851, 21 (372), *First Report*, q. 4835; and (605), *Second Report*, qq. 4835, 5437–9.

79 *PP*, 1849, 12 (571), *Contract Packets*, q. 2047, and pp. 126–32 for detailed tables of fares; *PP*, 1851, 53 (693), *Correspondence*, Memo. of John Wood, p. 112, 16.4.1850; *PP*, 1851, 21 (605), *Second Report*, qq. 5235ff., 5323ff. and 5437.

80 *PP*, 1851, 21 (605), *Second Report*, qq. 4833–5, 5349ff., 5397ff. and 5437–40.

81 *PP*, HoL, 1851, 10–I (187–I), *Australia*, qq. 3233–9. The rate was £25 per ton according to Anderson, £40 per ton according to Murray Gladstone, partner in Gillanders, Arbuthnot & Co. of Calcutta: q. 3810.

82 *PP*, 1851, 21 (605), *Second Report*, q. 3835; q. 5351.

83 *Ibid*., qq. 5359, 5625.

84 *PP*, 1851, 21 (372), *First Report*, qq. 3308–9.

85 Hyde, *Cunard*, pp. 37–44; *PP*, HoL, 1851, 10–I (187–I), q. 3344. Collins and Cunard made secret agreements to pool their earnings from 1850 to 1855.

86 *PP*, 1851, 21 (605), *Second Report*, qq. 5509, 5515–7. Reductions (£95 instead of £143) were made for young cadets beginning their career in the Indian civil, military or medical services (no more than four to a steamer), P&O/1/100, 13.1.1846. After I&A got its charter, a 20 per cent reduction (£105) was introduced during the off season, to spread the load (P&O/1/101, 8.6.1847), together with 10 per cent for passengers returning within 12 months; and the £105 concession was extended to 5 months each way, for reserved cabins, and for women and children: *PP*, 1851, 21 (605), q. 5509.

87 P&O/1/100, 29.4.1845; P&O/1/102, 7.4.1851.

88 P&O/1/102, 12.11.1850, 14.2.1851, 1.4.1851, 7.4.1851 and 6.5.1851. *Singapore* and *Ganges* were launched in the autumn of 1850; *Madras* and *Bombay* were commissioned from Tod & M'Gregor in February 1851; and *Shanghai* was bought on the stocks from Miller & Ravenhill in May 1851. All three had screw engines.

89 See ch. 6, pp. 174f.

90 P&O/1/102, 7.5.1850 and 26.8.1851.

91 See above, p. 41.

92 *PP*, 1851, 21 (605), *Second Report*, qq. 4496–500, 4520–9 and 4627.

93 *Ibid.*, pp. iv–xi; *PP*, HoL, 1851, 10–II (187–II), *Second Report*, pp. viii–ix.

94 See Harcourt, 'The High Road to India'.

95 Eastern Steam did not give up hope of getting the Australian line. In 1854 Yates announced that the company was about to build its first steamer for the most rapid communication to Australia 'ever yet contemplated': CO 201/480/1169, Australia. However, the company was dissolved in 1858: BT 41/319/1831.

96 *PP*, 1852, 49 (249), *Mail Services (India and Australia)*, generally.

97 P&O/1/102, 9.3.1852; P&O/1/103, 19.3.1852.

98 P&O/1/103, 18.5.1852.

99 *PP*, 1849, 12 (571), *Contract Packets*, qq. 2165, 2167.

100 *PP*, 1850, 53 (693), *Correspondence*, p. 89 (nd [1844]).

101 *PP*, 1849, 12 (571), *Contract Packets*, q. 2169; *PP*, 1850, 53 (693), *Correspondence*, p. 89, (nd [1844]).

102 Almost as soon as the contract service to Australia ceased, P&O started planning its resumption. In the first instance, however, a new contract was granted not to P&O but to the European & Australian Royal Mail Company, a new concern with no experience, no ships and no infrastructure. Using chartered vessels including P&O's *Simla*, it survived from November 1856 until March 1859, but then collapsed, leaving the field to P&O once again. The case argued strongly against awarding contracts to untried newcomers. For details of one aspect of P&O's later involvement in shipping to and from Australia, see F. Harcourt, 'P&O and Orient: A Cool Partnership, 1886–1914', *The Great Circle*, 17:2 (1995).

103 *Herapath*, 11.12.1852, p. 1357.

104 *PP*, 1852–3, 95 (195), (Treasury) *Report on Contract Packets*, p. 2.

CHAPTER FIVE

Views from the boardroom, 1840–55

The boardroom

Once East Indian Steam had refused to join Bourne and Williams in creating a new concern, it was left to those two men and their close associates to make their own arrangements for the 'junction' of the Peninsular Steam and Transatlantic companies to form P&O. Both companies were ready to contribute capital in ships for the enterprise, but first and foremost a permanent settlement was needed as to the conditions under which the capital was to be put to work and by whom. It was agreed that the merger would take place on condition that each of the two original companies would be represented in the management of the new one. A meeting was then convened on 23 March 1840 at 51 St Mary Axe, Willcox & Anderson's premises in the City of London. The five men present were Bourne (in the chair), Hartley and Anderson (for Willcox & Anderson), representing Peninsular Steam, and Ewart and Carleton, representing Transatlantic. (Williams and de Zulueta had also agreed to be directors but did not attend.) At the close, those present at the meeting

> were of opinion that it would be highly desirable to limit as much as possible the issue of new shares in the amalgamated Company, as the smaller the amount of the Capital on which the profits would have to be divided, the higher the dividend would be and eventually the shares would reach a high prem[ium]. It was in consequence considered advisable not to prepare any prospectus for publication at present.

A second meeting took place on 23 April, attended by Richard and Frederick Bourne, William Fortescue, Anderson (for Willcox & Anderson) and Carleton, again representing the two companies to be merged, and with Bourne in the chair. Among the other decisions taken by the meeting, Willcox, Anderson and Carleton were 'appointed Managing Directors . . . entrusted with the general agency and management under the control of the Board', and a document specifying the privileges and obligations of P&O's three MDs and also sealing the merger was signed by all those present.

The new company's capital was fixed at £1 million in 20,000 £50 shares each; Bourne, Hartley and Willcox, the trustees of the company, to whom the shares would be handed over, would represent the property of the new company. Bourne's company, Peninsular Steam, should receive 'the value to the amount of £140,000 in shares' of *Tagus*, *Braganza*, *Royal Tar*, *'Little' Liverpool* and *Iberia* plus their goodwill because of the heavy expenses incurred by Peninsular Steam in opening the Peninsular station in 1837. Transatlantic Steam should have 'shares to the amount of £80,000 for the full value of the *Liverpool* steam ship with new machinery and other improvements and as an equivalent for their interest in the present Transatlantic Steam Company'.

The MDs were obliged to defray all the company's expenses in London (and in Southampton when it became P&O's port) 'under the heads of Clerks, Salaries, rent of Offices at 51 St Mary Axe, Taxes, Stationery, printing, postage (except foreign) and transacting Custom House business'. The cost of repairing and building ships and establishments, and all expenses in the administration of the company, were excluded, however, and were to be paid by the chairman, deputy chairman and 'ordinary' directors.[1] The MDs had full control over all servants, agents, commanders and other officers of vessels with power to suspend any of these persons, though they could not dismiss those who were not appointed or employed and paid by themselves. In return, the MDs would receive a commission of 2.5 per cent on gross earnings, and for 'the general superintendance [*sic*] and management of the concern in lieu of any other payment as Managing Directors or otherwise' 5 per cent 'on the surplus dividable profits'. Each of these commissions was to be divided equally between the three MDs. Moreover, 'in consideration . . . of the permanency of this arrangement', the MDs had the power to 'embrace all such [government] Contracts as may hereafter . . . [be made] on behalf of the Company, or during the continuance of the Company unless a new agreement should be made', and the right to a commission on any such contract. They also undertook to procure a charter of incorporation. This arrangement was one of the conditions of the 'junction' of Peninsular Steam and Transatlantic, and any directors who came on the board now or in future would be bound 'to give assent' to them.[2]

On this day, too, it was decided to appoint the 'Board of Direction'. Apart from the three MDs, Bourne immediately chose James Hartley, his partner in a number of Irish concerns who was also an insurance broker in London, becoming P&O's insurance agent in 1841. In August,

Williams offered his associate Joseph Christopher Ewart, so balancing the two sides of the company, and Pedro Juan de Zulueta, a partner of Bourne in the Peninsular Steam Company, also took a seat on the board.

There was much activity in 51 St Mary Axe between 23 April 1840 when the merger was sealed and the date of commencement of the first contract, 1 September 1840, when P&O officially began. Twenty-four meetings were held in which important decisions were taken. Many of the founders, however, were present only irregularly. Williams limited his presence to five meetings and Ewart, who like Williams lived in Liverpool, came down only in August; Pedro Juan de Zulueta was often out of the country, so much so indeed that he resigned in March 1841 to be replaced by his son Peter John de Zulueta.[3] From May to the end of November, therefore, Bourne, Hartley and the three MDs effectively ran the new company.

Capital and constitution: the early years

As soon as the royal charter was sealed on 31 December 1840, P&O began to issue some of the 20,000 £50 shares. According to the deed of settlement, the distribution of 6,092 paid-up shares was to correspond to the value of the ships that each of the group of founders had put into the merger. The actual value of those ships was £240,600, but an extra £64,000 goodwill made the total £304,600. That sum, representing the 'original' ships, was not touched until the 1850s when it diminished as ships were sold or lost, and the last of the original ships were put into general stock and depreciated like other vessels.

Schedule 1 in the deed of settlement shows how £304,600 of paid-up shares was distributed among the founders who had put money into Peninsular Steam and Transatlantic before 23 March 1840 (those with seats on P&O's board are marked*):

1 Richard Bourne*	£62,800} *Tagus* (786 tons, 286 hp)
Frederick Bourne	£26,650} *Braganza* (688 tons, 264 hp)
James Hartley*	£13,350} *Royal Tar* (308 tons, 260 hp)
Simeon Boileau	£9,500} *Liverpool* (206 tons, ?)
William Henry Fortescue	£9,500} *Santa Anna*, hulk

Value of 1: £121,800 (including £4,819 for the hulk) in 2,436 shares.

2 James Ferrier	}
Richard Williams	£80,000} *Great Liverpool* (1,150 tons, 468 hp)
James Jameson	}
James Hartley*	}

Value of 2: £80,000 in 1,600 shares.

3 Charles Wye Williams*	}	
Joseph Christopher Ewart*	£74,800}	*Oriental* (1,674 gt, 420 hp)
Francis Carleton*	}	

Value of 3: £74,800 in 1,496 shares

4 Brodie M'Ghie Willcox*	£6,100}	
Francis Carleton*	£5,750}	
Arthur Anderson*	£3,100}	
Pedro Juan de Zulueta*	£3,050}	*Iberia* (516 tons, 190 hp)
Jose Venturade Aguirre Solarte	£3,050}	
Anselmo de Arroyave	£2,600}	
Stanislaus Darthez	£1,300}	
Manoel Joaquim Soares	£3,050}	

Value of 4: £28,000 in 560 shares.

Total: **£304,600** in **6,092** paid-up shares.

About 60 people who wished to pay £25 or more of the £50 shares were recorded in schedule 2. Two well-known men in Dublin, William Potts and his son, put in the highest investment, £8,000 between them; and Dennis Sullivan, a boat builder, £100, the lowest. Under the deed, all directors had to have at least forty paid-up shares. Each director who came into P&O after 1 September 1840 – Pirie, Nairne, Thurburn, Samuel Thornton and chairman Larpent – paid the necessary £2,000 and Sir John Campbell, the deputy chairman, put in £3,250. The three MDs whose privileges and obligations had been laid out in the memorandum of agreement in April took up schedule 3; and in schedule 4 was listed a body of persons in P&O's incorporation.

For all other shareholders, or 'Proprietors' as they were known, the £50 share was split into 10 parts, and when money was required for ships, the holders would be called on to deposit £5 for one instalment. Then, when after nine more calls the tenth instalment was reached, the share was paid-up and the holder was entitled to a dividend. Votes were allotted more selectively: holders with 5–9 shares had one vote; 10–14 shares, 2 votes; 15–19 shares, 3 votes. Those with three votes 'shall have one additional vote for every additional number of five shares but so as no Proprietor shall have more than twenty votes in all' [*sic*]. To be 'qualified' and belong to the 'Body of Proprietors', shareholders had to have not less than 5 shares in the company; and the 'body' could have an AGM only if there was a quorum of not less than 30 qualified persons with 400 shares collectively.[4]

To attract a wide public, P&O printed 1,500 copies of its prospectus, but most people who responded to the first instalment on 30 January 1841 lived either in London or in Dublin and towns around that city. A dissenting minister in Woodbridge, a reverend in Ludlow, one merchant in Birmingham and another in Weymouth were the only English shareholders outside of London. Irish investors were so keen to put their money in 'their' company that the first ordinary 3,241 shares had to be allotted to English and Irish persons in almost equal numbers. 'Indians' (British men who lived in India, later referred to as 'Anglo-Indians') were allotted 2,017 shares, but 'those highly respectable and influencial [*sic*] parties' in or connected with India were lukewarm in promoting what P&O described as this 'great national undertaking'. Until early 1847, when there were about 900 shareholders, nearly three-quarters of the capital of the company was held in Ireland; and although the remainder of the shares were set apart for 'Indians', barely half were applied for, and of those who did apply most did not take any shares.[5]

P&O chose Messrs Williams, Deacon, Labouchere, Thornton & Co. to be its bankers in London; and in Dublin, Labouchere & Stafford and Richard Williams & Sons (Richard Williams was Charles's brother), and James Harvey in Limerick. Bankruptcy ruined Richard Williams & Sons in 1847–48, and presumably the other Irish bankers were wiped out as well, for from 1848 onwards the Royal Bank of Ireland took their place, and Messrs Williams, Deacon & Co. remained P&O's bankers until 1970.

Every Wednesday for the first five years of the company's existence, the directors had a meeting in the boardroom. If the chairman or his deputy was absent, the fourth director to enter the room would take the chair. New directors were elected by the board which was to number no fewer than 10 and no more than 16 including the MDs. Ordinary directors earned 1 guinea for each weekly attendance (two meetings a week from 1846); they collected their guineas at the end of the half-year.

Accounts for directors' attendance, 1 September 1840–31 March 1841:

Directors	*No. in attendance*	*Amount*
Captain R Bourne	10	£10 10*s*
Sir John Campbell	28	£29 8*s*
J.C. Ewart	2	£22 0
J. Hartley	60	£63 0
Captain S Thornton	38	£39 18*s*
C. Wye Williams	6	£6 6*s*
P. de Zulueta	4	£4 4*s*

At least one MD had to attend each meeting, but their attendance was unpaid.

At the half-year meeting, in late May or early June, a dividend for the first six months was declared but no accounts were seen or discussed; at the annual general meeting (AGM), at the end of November or early December, all items relevant to the company could be raised, and the other half of the dividend was declared. At the first AGM, in November 1841, the distribution of ordinary shares was shown as:

6,092 paid-up shares and invested in the company	£304,603
New shares taken in Britain and Ireland, two instalments paid	£31,505
732 new shares in Calcutta}	
583 new shares in Madras} . . . instalments paid	£21,135
10,648 £50 shares each, amounting to	£357,243

At the end of 1842, subscribed capital and instalments not yet called for stood at:

9,385 shares, issued in England and Ireland, amounting to	£469,250[a]
2,108 shares, issued in Calcutta and Madras	£105,400
11,493 shares	£574,650
Total amount invested and paid up	£432,838
Instalments not yet called for	£141,812

([a] Included the founders' paid-up shares.)

No more scrips were issued until the MDs knew that P&O would have a mail contract for India and China.[6]

The power struggle, 1841–47

The board meetings of the 1840s and early 1850s were witness to various disputes in which the MDs came under attack. This was due in part to a personal power struggle over a period of years between Anderson and Sir John Campbell, in part because by the end of the decade shareholders had become a more important, because more numerous, constituency and their questions about the running of the company could not be overlooked. The recurrence of certain issues – how far should the power of the MDs be constrained and how important were political connections to the company's success? – point up some of the important lines along which P&O was developing in these years.

While P&O was extending its field of operations and opening up new trades for Britain, a struggle for power was going on in its boardroom. No doubt the original eight directors who were all friends – Bourne, Hartley, Willcox, Anderson, Carleton and de Zulueta, with Williams and Ewart calling in from time to time – would have been happy to continue to work on their own. But, with a view to bringing some Eastern Steam directors on board, the deed of settlement had required that the board have at least 10 (but no more than 16) members. Towards the end of the year, Anderson offered T.A. Curtis the office of deputy chairman and a seat for one or two of his friends,[7] and promised the chairmanship to George Gerrard de Hochepied Larpent.[8] But Curtis was still smarting from his failure to snatch the mail contract from P&O. The concessions he demanded from P&O were not forthcoming, and his 'jarring views' stopped the negotiations. All Anderson's arrangements were undone and Larpent was told to wait for a better time.[9]

Meanwhile, Samuel Thornton, an 'outsider' – that is, not a member of the original eight – who had offered himself in August as a provisional director, was confirmed on P&O's board. His family included high-ranking aristocrats, a director of the Bank of England and several MPs. His career began as a boy in the Royal Navy in 1811; his service ranged from Europe, the Pacific, South America to the first Burma War in 1824–25 – he was known in naval circles for hoisting the British flag after the capture of Rangoon – and retired in 1827 a post-captain on half pay.[10] His cousin, the Hon. John Thornton Leslie Melville, became one of P&O's first two auditors. Both had links with Williams, Deacon & Co., P&O's bankers.[11] Another 'outsider', Sir John Campbell, was then invited to join, apparently for no particular reason other than that one more director was needed.[12] He had mercantile connections in India, and perhaps his knighthood (even if his honour came from the Hanover side of the royal family) could be useful to the new company. Conscientious and courteous, though apparently unacquainted with large steam-shipping concerns and their management, he took the board meetings seriously, and in February 1841 he was elected deputy chairman.[13] From that point onwards, he saw himself growing into the chairman's seat, certain that he would soon be upon it.

Thornton and Campbell, together with the three further 'outsiders' who crossed over to P&O – Nairne, Pirie and Thurburn – when Curtis's company was dissolved in March 1841, put a different hue on the board, especially as Williams, Ewart and Pedro Juan de Zulueta attended rarely.

True to Anderson's offer, Larpent became P&O's first chairman in May 1841. Though he was a figure-head with no interest in the working of the company – after attending one board meeting he dashed off to canvass for a seat in Parliament – he was one of the type the MDs wanted: returned as MP for Nottingham in the July election and made a baronet,[14] he might prove useful. Campbell was hurt that he was not chosen for the chair, the more so because a clause in the deed stated that the company 'shall appoint the Chairman out of their number' of directors. As Anderson wrote the deed, however, he could waive a clause if it suited him to do so.[15]

All these developments took place without Anderson's attendance, for in December 1840 he went on tour in the Mediterranean on company business.[16] There was little time for him and Campbell to size each other up before he sailed away, but the two men must have taken a dislike to each other instantly, and when Campbell was appointed deputy chairman in February he seized this early opportunity to show it; and Anderson's long absence allowed Campbell, with the support of the other 'outsiders', to have the influence he wished for.

Before Anderson left for the Mediterranean in December (and before Campbell had entered P&O), the board specified the objects he should aim for on his mission. Two were particularly important: he was to go to Egypt, 'political affairs permitting', to 'open a negociation [*sic*] on behalf of the Company if opportunity offers with the Pacha' about the transit across his territory; and 'to collect such information relative to the traffick [*sic*] in passengers and goods in the Mediterranean and Levant ... on the lines proposed to be established under Contract with the Government, as will enable the Directors to decide' whether it was expedient to go further. Anderson was 'empowered to act on his own judgement in matters ... [that] require[d] immediate decision, reporting his proceeding thereon'. This minute was copied for Anderson's guidance. Very soon after he had set sail, the Admiralty told P&O that its proposal of a contract line to Constantinople would not be taken up. The directors sent this news to Gibraltar via *Oriental* for Anderson, telling him his 'proceeding to Constantinople' was 'premature'. Instead, he should make inquiries at Malta about eastward traffic 'with secrecy and caution'.[17]

From the perspective of 51 St Mary Axe, Anderson free-wheeled around the Mediterranean in a manner that astonished even his closest colleagues. The board sent him several letters, expressing concern and ordering him to come back at once, but he ignored the summons and, on his return in October, he found that two resolutions relating to him had been passed unanimously. The first was about the use of the company's funds, Anderson having spent an unknown amount on his travels: henceforth no money was to be taken by an MD from company funds without ratification from the ordinary directors and the other two MDs. On top of that, while travelling about in the eastern Mediterranean, he had announced that a mail contract line connecting England, the Black Sea and the Levant was shortly to be opened, forgetting – wilfully or not – that no such line had been sanctioned by the Government. Directors were horrified to see that news of this fiction had been spread as far as Bombay. Thus the second resolution ensured that a single MD could not act on proposals for new or extended lines on his own. In addition, a committee composed of Larpent, Campbell, Nairne and Thurburn was set up to inspect the documents Anderson brought back.[18] At his second appearance at the board, no minutes were taken. This was unprecedented, and we may assume that the language exchanged at that meeting was too hot to be recorded. In any case, his colleagues were severe with him, refusing to pay his expenses.

Was Anderson merely thoughtless or were his activities meant to show his power? Whatever the directors made of it, they were angry and fearful. Anderson had given P&O a high profile throughout the Mediterranean and beyond, although the board had warned him to be circumspect; the company was in its infancy and its enemies would readily smear its reputation. The board was also anxious about the way he had behaved in Egypt. Sent out to negotiate with the pasha for the company's business, Anderson acted as if he was the British Government's envoy. The documents he came home with showed that it was, in the board's view, 'very imprudent on the part of the Company to engage hastily' with the pasha, without the consent of the British Government or the board. The final embarrassment in Egypt was his intrusion in two conflicting projects that were jostling for the pasha's attention – a British railway and a French ship canal. Anderson immediately put all his energy into promoting a ship canal, writing to ambassadors and cabinet ministers, urging them to invest in it and publishing a pamphlet on the subject. But projects like these were matters for high politics between Britain and France and, to avoid any more of Anderson's off-the-shelf ideas, the board banned any publication touching the company for which it had not given permission.[19] Eighteen months passed before he 'explained his proceedings' in the Mediterranean to the satisfaction of the board. He was then given £630 for his expenses.[20]

Unkind 'rumours' dogged P&O for some time afterwards. In 1842, *Herapath's Railway & Commercial Journal* (hereafter *Herapath*) picked up 'some curious reports abroad' connected with the company's involvement with the Egyptian transit to the effect that P&O had 'a want of confidence in its management or stability, or both', and in 1843 *Herapath* got wind of a pamphlet about Anderson's time in Egypt which was 'Not Printed for Sale'.[21] *Herapath* wanted to know what the company was hiding: 'No offence . . . but we like to know how public companies particularly those drawing large sums annually from our Treasury go on'. Indeed *Herapath* was so virulent that P&O threatened to take its owner and editor, John Herapath, to court.[22]

Ill-feeling between Anderson and Campbell was fuelled by the *Herapath* episode but it was the issue of the MDs' relationship to the board – Campbell's opinion was that the MDs had far too much power – that caused a rift between them. The deed of settlement seemed almost wilfully ambiguous on the subject, clause 21 for example stating that 'the Company shall be governed and managed by the Board of Directors, subject to the powers given to the Managing Directors': while the first half of the sentence was very much to Campbell's taste, he could not swallow the qualification contained in the second. In May 1842 Larpent suddenly resigned as director, chairman and MP, taking the Chiltern Hundreds after the opposition alleged that he lodged a sum – £5,000, £10,000 or even £20,000 – as a bribe for 2,000 voters to make sure of winning his constituency. John Arthur Roebuck, MP for Bath, told the House of Commons that 'Sir Somebody Something Larpent' tried to hide behind 'ill-health' to avoid an inquiry on his 'sins', and after a long debate on the writ, the vote was a resounding majority of ninety-five against Larpent.[23] Campbell expected to be chosen as chairman in Larpent's stead, but the call did not come. Angry words between him and Anderson flew back and forth: the deed stated that a new chairman should be chosen 'with all convenient speed' and that the board 'shall appoint the Chairman out of their number',[24] but Anderson would not hear of Campbell taking that office. At the AGM in 1843, 'more than usually numerous' shareholders were present because the rift between them had come out in the open. A General Briggs asked why the company did not have a chairman, and many other shareholders were surprised that Campbell was not elected. 'The directors' (probably Hartley and de Zulueta) 'entrusted' a shareholder 'to move a resolution . . . that they should have a Gentleman at their head', and that head was Campbell. He 'had intelligence and prudence . . . On every occasion he had employed . . . singularly business-like habits, gentlemanly demeanour, and inflexible integrity, united to an uncommon share of that uncommon quality – common sense'. Presumably, however, the motion did not have a seconder, as there was no vote on it; if there was more to it, it was not recorded. Still mere deputy chairman but in the chair for the meeting, Campbell had to pronounce to the meeting the humiliating words that he did not have 'that political influence and high character which would give weight and stability to the Company'.[25]

The company was still without a chairman when a spat in a board meeting early in 1845 led to Campbell's resignation as deputy. It had been agreed in 1841 that questions brought to the board should always be postponed for fourteen days to allow more thought on an issue, and time for the distant directors to attend, and also to stop a proposal from being rushed through when there were only a few directors present. At the meeting in question a resolution was passed that 'the principle of recording Protests from individual members against the decision of the majority of the Board, would lead to great inconvenience'. Campbell, together with Hartley and de Zulueta, dissented and Campbell resigned. Although there is no record of why he was so angry, there is strong evidence that Campbell would have thrown up his office only if the subject of the resolution was the next chairman. His resignation was made at a very inconvenient time, and he knew it. P&O had just started the mail contract for India and China, and the share market would be upset if this senior officer left in a huff. So colleagues were able to persuade him to withdraw his resignation. After all, there seemed to be no one in sight who fitted Anderson's requirements,[26] so there was still a chance for the chair.

But on the quiet, Anderson did find the right man, and at the end of the year P&O's second chairman, Patrick Maxwell Stewart, MP for Renfewshire, was presented to the AGM. The MDs justified their choice because it was 'highly essential to the Company's interest that one, at least, of the Directors should have a seat in Parliament'. Shareholders who were friends of Campbell must have disagreed, for there was an ugly scuffle outside the boardroom. *Herapath*'s reporter was refused entry 'under peculiar circumstances', and one shareholder, according to that journal, was warned as he went into the boardroom to hold his tongue or be thrown down the stairs. Stewart was said to be a man of 'well-known talents and honourable character, and suavity of manners' with many business interests, including the Royal Mail Company. Son of a baronet and brother-in-law of the Duke of Somerset, his social attributes were excellent, and his political persuasion – free trader – was that of the MDs themselves. His only weakness was his health; he died within the year, in October 1846.[27]

Now, surely, Campbell could not be passed over again. But Anderson deliberately kept the office open once more, waiting for the candidate of his choice. Meanwhile, at the end of 1846, James Allan was suddenly spirited away from his post as secretary to the board which he had held since 1840. He was thanked for his services and given £500. His retirement did not last long, however, for he came back the next week as an assistant manager. The MDs recognized that Allan was management material, and wanted to train him so that he could take the place of one or other of the two older MDs when they retired or died. This was a prudent measure, for Willcox was in his sixty-first year and Anderson in his fifty-fourth. Carleton, aged 47, would (or so it was thought) be able to carry the flag with Allan, who was in his thirties. Campbell had no objection to Allan's promotion but he was insulted by the boorish way in which Anderson had taken away his secretary, for he was not given time to find a new one during a very busy period, now that meetings were held twice a week. Campbell found an assistant secretary in Charles Wellington Howell; he entered P&O in the managing department, was then sent to the secretariat to help, and finally, after a year's trial, became secretary to the board, a post he filled until 1872.[28]

Another altercation was stirred up between Campbell and Willcox and Anderson when the latter two canvassed for seats in the June 1847 general election and won: Willcox for Southampton (1847–62), Anderson for Orkney and Shetland (1847–52). As a mail contractor, the connection with government was important to P&O at any time and especially when competition was emerging, but Campbell asserted that as MPs they would not be able to give the company their full attention. This was a fair comment, and he was so persistent about it that in July, Willcox and Anderson offered 'certain proposals respecting their own situation in the Company'. It was a plan for them to withdraw from their managing duties in stages. To deal with a development of such gravity, Campbell convened a committee, chaired by himself, with Pirie, Hartley, Nairne and Ewart, with powers to confer with counsel and solicitors, the MDs having their own legal advisers.[29] Months passed without a consensus between the two groups, however, and the issue was pushed aside by more urgent business.

By 1847 a whole year had passed since Stewart's death but P&O had not yet found a new chairman, and shareholders were getting restive. Campbell maintained his opinion that he 'never *did* and never [*could*] concur' with Anderson, Willcox and some other directors who regarded it as essential to have an MP in that post. P&O ought to keep out of politics: 'no commercial man whatever his position – his rank – or his wealth – [would] give one extra passenger or one extra bale of goods' to P&O's ships, whoever the chairman was, and he thought it was dangerous to identify the company with any political party. But the opposite view was held by the MDs, some of the ordinary directors and many shareholders: a close link with Parliament was indispensable. Nevertheless, Campbell and several directors 'kindly expressed a hope that [the MDs] would not let [him] be passed over' for the office. Later that day, however, their 'conversations' with

Campbell were interrupted by Willcox and Carleton. These two called Campbell to their office 'to consult with [him] on an important point'. He was then (in his own words)

> for the first time told that overtures had already been made by Sir John Pirie to Mr Baring, and that Mr Willcox had seen Mr A[bel] Smith who had recommended Mr James Matheson MP to be our Chairman and this had been done without any reference or communication with myself, clandestinely and in a discourteous manner and in one which I do not consider the past devotion of my time and attention to the interests of the Company in any way merited.[30]

Matheson accepted the offer, and Campbell left the office of deputy chairman at once and for good. A few days later, as if nothing had happened, his colleagues 'cordially' invited him to take the chair at the 1847 AGM 'as on former occasions', but he did not allow himself to be trampled on again. Pirie was given the deputy's office and held it until his death in 1851, after which there was no deputy for the next ten years.[31]

Though Campbell had resigned his seat on the board, he was still a shareholder, and his last public appearance was at the 1848 AGM. Once again the mood was hostile as many shareholders were inclined to blame the MDs for the depression, and this gave Campbell a chance to pour out his grievances and differences with Anderson.[32] His long speech – calculated to annoy Willcox and Anderson – showed, however, that his ideas of running a large incorporated shipping company in a competitive environment were out of touch. The MDs (now only two, Carleton having died in October) had, he complained, acquired 'more numerous' ships than the company needed instead of putting the funds in good government securities. Anderson's response to 'the question of investing the reserved funds in available public securities' was biting:

> If we do this, we shall . . . have to call up some fresh capital, for we have been using those reserved funds for which we had not any immediate necessity, in carrying on the operations for the company. To give an exemplification of this, we have received from the proprietors only £976,000 of capital in shares, but we show you, by our balance-sheets, that we have bought ships for you to the value of £1,200,000 or upwards. There you have your capital profitably employed, instead of being lodged at a bankers.

In a second question about investment Campbell turned to insurance. Annual insurance premiums in the open market pressed heavily on profits: 'the average of losses [had] not exceeded in a long series of years, 3 per cent, whilst the premium chargeable by Insurance establishments [was] rarely under an average of *six* per cent per annum'. An insurance fund was set up in 1842. In 1848, the time had come to move forward. As Anderson said in reply to Campbell,

> Let me ask what the company has this insurance fund for? It is to meet some extraordinary casualties. Suppose that we lost a ship worth £50,000 or £60,000; if we had our money lying at a bank or in some public securities, how, in such case, should we proceed to replace the ship? We must contract with the shipbuilders and engineers, and pay out of money thus placed in securities, and we get our ship, perhaps in about eighteen months or two years; where we have laid out the money already in the building of the ships, and we have besides a fund ready to repair any losses that may be sustained. I consider that to be a more advantageous method of investing money than paying it into Consols or any other securities.

Great Liverpool, P&O's first loss, was a good example. In February 1846, the vessel was wrecked on rocks off Cape Finisterre. It had been insured outside for £30,000, had a considerable amount in its 'depreciation account', and a portion of the insurance inside the company. Out of these three accounts the company had a new vessel 'without trenching in any way whatever, even to the extent of a single shilling, on the original capital of the Company'. Moreover, *Ripon*, the replacement, was complete in seven months. A much better ship, she had an iron hull and the best engines of the day, and her steam pressure was *9lbs* per square inch, high for the period. All losses were handled in this way.[33]

For his part, Willcox answered Campbell by telling the shareholders how to become self-insurers. At first, he said, P&O went to underwriters who asked for 6 per cent. Much too high. So, through James Hartley – he was a broker and had a small insurance concern of his own – all the directors and their friends subscribed 'very large sums on each policy at five per cent', so the underwriters gave way. 'This', Willcox went on, 'led to my becoming for the first time in my life an underwriter. I took a line of £500 upon every one of the company's ships from its commencement to the present. Consequently . . . I find myself at the present moment £991.12s.3d in pocket . . . I always thought it was somewhat *infra dig* for this company to have insured at all.' Both Anderson and Willcox had several 'Hear! Hear!' calls.

With such bitterness between himself and Anderson, why did Campbell stay on so long? He was ambitious, and in another type of business might have made a good chairman. But Anderson could surely have found a way to get rid of Campbell sooner had he wanted to, and the fact that he did not provides an important part of the reason for Campbell's long innings on P&O's board. Through the autocratic way in which the MDs, and in particular Anderson, conducted themselves, they made enemies among both directors and among the increasingly important constituency of ordinary shareholders. Campbell became a focus for these dissenting points of view, and could not have been removed earlier without harming the company.

Proprietors v. directors

Towards the end of the 1840s, there were usually many more gentlemen, merchants, men of the cloth, soldiers and sailors in attendance at the two annual shareholders' meetings than there had been early in the decade, and as the list of shareholders grew their voice grew correspondingly in importance. Some proprietors fawned on the MDs and directors who worked 'so nobly, so assiduously . . . and so disinterestedly' for their dividends, like Mr Penney, an original shareholder who called himself a 'very good accountant'.[34] Others, however, were not so docile.

One complaint that came up in meeting after meeting was that shareholders wanted to know more about P&O's finances than was given in its six-monthly reports. In 1846 William Dent[35] took up the campaign that had begun a few years earlier to have the accounts published and circulated *before* the meetings. Why not publish like railway companies or the Royal Mail Company? The current situation was unsatisfactory: the shareholders were 'called upon to vote [on the accounts] somewhat in the dark of the real state of their affairs'.[36] One director made the feeble excuse that the meetings would not get a quorum because proprietors would not bother to come if they could read the report at home. Williams, on one of his rare visits to London, reminded the meeting that P&O was not only a mail contractor but also a mercantile company; it would be foolish to reveal its financial secrets to the world. Royal Mail was no example to follow: *that* company showed accounts only as a way of covering its financial problems.[37]

After the 1848 AGM, however, when there was a very strong objection against not publishing the accounts, the rule was that they were to be laid on the table for seven days prior to the AGM. Shareholders could also see the accounts at other times by appointment. For the 900 or so shareholders, of whom a large proportion lived in Ireland, that chink of light was useless. But the directors evidently thought that they had given away too much, because in 1851 there was another change with the effect that the accounts could be seen only by appointment 'except under such circumstances and on such occasions as may be consistent with the interests and welfare of the Company', whatever that might mean. This made Dent and his friends even more inquisitive. Dent took a professional accountant with him to inspect the accounts and was rebuked for allowing someone who was not a shareholder to see them. However, as his accountant could find nothing amiss, the episode did not make any difference. Later still, the accounts were laid on the table for two weeks prior to meetings; and *Herapath* continued to publish the précis with the report twice a year.[38]

Another contentious issue was the retirement of the MDs, the appointment of their successors and, underlying it, the whole question of the balance of power between MDs and ordinary directors. On this, too, the MDs were forced to make concessions which they later substantially withdrew. The issue takes us back to July 1847 and the 'proposals' Willcox and Anderson made to the board on becoming MPs.[39] Willcox and Anderson agreed that they would retire in turn but only under conditions that Campbell's committee would not entertain. The two MDs intended to keep all the privileges of an MD under the deed, whether they were in work or not, until death. Campbell argued that because they were not fully engaged in the company's work on account of their parliamentary activities, they were not looking after the company and should reduce their commissions. The MDs demurred: they had two assistants in the managing department – James Allan, who in practice had to take the brunt of the work, and a Mr Andrew – and claimed that they had help enough even when they were busy in Parliament. The MDs also wished to reserve the right of nominating their successors, although the deed empowered the board to select new MDs 'from its own body'. The MDs would not budge on this point whatever was written in the deed. Their object was to preserve 'intact . . . a System of Management under which the Company's affairs have attained a degree of prosperity unparralleled [*sic*] by any similar enterprize'. But they promised, when they retired, 'a very large pecuniary concession' from their commissions.[40]

As rumours leaked out about this boardroom strife, Anderson could not avoid referring to the issue at the 1847 AGM. He told the meeting that the MDs' aim was to find a way of preserving 'a continuance of efficient management' to ensure P&O's future prosperity. Some joint-stock companies had numerous managers, he said, but he 'felt certain that when the executive of a Steam Navigation Company was handed over to such a board, the sun of its prosperity would set'. Aiming at Campbell and 'without intending the slightest disrespect' for the board, he rejected the opinion held 'out of doors' that the ordinary directors had no power over the MDs. With tongue in cheek, he said that the directors were 'omnipotent': it was they who had control of the company. He ended with a fable, however, that was easily interpreted: a serpent with twelve heads and one tail could not get anything done, but a monster with one head and twelve tails could do wonders. Few shareholders would have disagreed that Anderson was the monster.[41]

The papers that had been put aside in July 1847 were looked at again in January of the following year, but there was no agreement despite the fact that Campbell was no longer on the board. However, in May 1848, 'concessions volunteered by the Managing Directors' were deemed to be in the interest of the company, and the board accepted their final proposals. These were that Willcox would retire on 30 September 1850, Anderson a year later, and that from those dates both would reduce their commissions.

In the end, however, the MDs had to concede rather less than this. Carleton, who believed that he would be around for some years, took little part in the above transactions, but made it clear that he would stay at his post after his two colleagues had gone. He promised to reduce his current commission by half, starting on 1 October 1851, and to give up all the commission (2.5 per cent) on the £500,000 of capital that would soon be issued for the company's further expansion.[42] But five months later, on 22 October 1848, Carleton died suddenly of 'gastric fever' at the age of 48. This unforeseen death overturned the arrangements that Willcox and Anderson had agreed, and this had the effect of further concentrating power in their hands. At the AGM in December it was now 'contemplated' that Willcox would retire at the end of 3 years, and Anderson in 4. Anderson's announcement that he 'still retained his intention of retirement, provided circumstances should render it expedient', was vague; he added that 'he would never quit the helm, till he saw who was to steer the ship', a strong hint that he did not mean to retire at all.[43]

A third contentious subject was that of the MDs' earnings; once again Anderson came under attack but emerged with his position confirmed. At the generally nervy and aggressive 1847 AGM – General Briggs picked on the annual report at length on the grounds that he had never come upon 'a more meagre production . . . nor one more unsatisfactory'; Carleton wondered how Briggs had managed to take up such a lot of time if the report was so thin – William Dent made the MDs disclose the amount of commission they earned by asking for clause 78 in the deed to be read. Thus for the first time shareholders had an idea of the amount of commission the three MDs earned. Emoluments were small during the whole of the first 5 years of P&O's existence – £1,800 a piece – but in 1846, the sum rose to £2,857, 'a handsome allowance . . . but not too much' considering all the obligations the MDs had to meet, and the great risk they took in 1840, when Willcox and Anderson discarded their thriving shipbroking concern and Carleton left a secure appointment in Liverpool. It was thanks to the MDs that the company was doing so well. So well for themselves too: the MDs and their personal friends 'held 4,000 shares in the Company', proof that they had a deep interest in its success.[44]

At the 1848 AGM the subject resurfaced, raised once again by William Dent who proposed a new 'system' of P&O's management. He and other shareholders disliked the way Willcox and Anderson were able to pay themselves whatever they wanted in secret; it would give 'great confidence in the company if a committee was to go into the accounts', and Dent suggested that such a committee would promote economy in the management. His friend Malcolm Morris went further: he thought that 'the present system of Managing Directors was a perfect incubus on the Company' and was sure that if the proprietors would 'agitate the question . . . they might put an end to it'. Pirie, in the chair, would not have such criticism thrown at the MDs. He warned the meeting that Dent's 'committee to go into the company's accounts' would be 'neither more nor less than a vote of censure upon the management . . . I should retire from the direction at once'. And when Anderson rose to reply, he told Dent that 'the only possible mode of getting rid of the managing directors was by dissolving the company itself'. 'I have no wish to do that', said Dent.[45] Nor did the others. There was instability enough from outside, with Europe in flames and riots and 'political excitement' in England. Some of it touched the company: P&O's clerks were sworn in as special constables 'to act in suppression of any disturbances that might take place in consequence of the Chartist Meeting' on 10 April.[46] The company had to show stability, for any sign of a crack in P&O's fabric would be pounced on by its enemies and the share price would plummet. At the next AGM, in 1849, when shareholders heard that Anderson had been through a gruelling inquiry in a Select Committee on Contract Packets[47] and come out well for the company, the dissenters toed the line. General Briggs, after seeing accounts laid out on the table, said 'nothing could be more satisfactory'; and Patrick Douglas Hadow, now a director, maintained that it was 'only by the cordial co-operation of all parties that the affairs of this Company could prosper', and showed himself quite ready to believe – however unrealistically – that 'there was every disposition' on the part of the MDs 'to concede to the general body of Directors that control which the deed of settlement accorded to them'.[48] Crude and showy though he might be, Anderson was the man to hold the tiller in a turbulent sea.

At home in 122 Leadenhall Street

The year 1848 marked many changes in the company. Since 1840, P&O had worked rent-free in the offices of Willcox & Anderson, but when business east of Suez increased in 1846 the company needed much more space. It was the MDs' obligation to provide suitable premises, and when in November 1845 the King's Arms Inn & Hotel, just around the corner from 51 St Mary Axe, came up for sale, they bought the whole estate freehold for the company for £7,250. Plans were drawn by an architect, Mr Beachcroft, and the cost of necessary new building was £8,000. In March 1848, P&O moved into 122 Leadenhall Street, which remained its home for more than a century. The MDs 'volunteered' to pay a rent of £1,000 per annum for its use out of their commissions. Six years later, the MDs tried unsuccessfully to buy no. 121 but were able to take a lease from the charity which held it in trust; and from the trustees of St Thomas's Hospital they bought leases of eighty years on each of nos 123, 124 and 125. All these houses were demolished to give a frontage to no. 122. The new construction provided much more office space, some of it for rent, and a spacious entry to the courtyard. P&O also bought ground next to the new dock in Southampton on which it built offices and shop space. By 1858 the company was the freeholder or lessee of over £60,000 in property.[49]

Apart from Carleton, all P&O's founder directors worked in their pristine building for a few years, but several fell away in the course of the next decade. Pirie died in February 1851. In October of the same year, Richard Bourne's death in his eighty-first year marked the end of a long and successful career. He was the real 'father' of P&O (an honour that Willcox liked to attach to himself).[50] There was no successor waiting in the wings in Bourne's large family, nor perhaps would Anderson (who had no children) and Willcox (who had one son, Brodie Augustus, and a daughter married to Pedro Juan de Zulueta) have allowed it. The other founding father, Williams, resigned in 1854. He had been 'a sort of honorary director' in P&O for some time, and in his mid-seventies he wished to be 'actively occupied' with his City of Dublin Company. He died in 1866 at the age of 86.[51] Two more of the founders died at sea: James Hartley in 1857, on the way back to London in one of P&O's ships after a visit to India where he had 'an important agency';[52] and Rear-Admiral Samuel Thornton, drowned falling overboard from *Ripon* near Malta in 1859.

The new directors who gradually replaced them had varied backgrounds. Patrick Douglas Hadow, a barrister, came from a family of merchants in Bombay who were involved in the opium trade, and he promised to direct his attention 'to this branch of the Company's affairs in a special manner' when he was elected to the board in 1849. Because of his legal knowledge, he was attached to the managing department in 1854 and, in 1861, his appointment as deputy chairman revived that office, vacant since Pirie's death.[53] After all the upheaval with Campbell, a more compliant person, Joshua Carter, was chosen to replace him on the board in 1848. Carter had spent twenty-three years in India in the Civil Service, working in several important offices there. This experience, and the fact that he was an early shareholder, made him 'well entitled' to sit on the board. However, ill-health and frequent absences brought him to resign four years later.[54] Another East India Company graduate also had a brief life on the board. Charles Hood Chicheley Plowden was a member of a large family of high-ranking officers in that company. In 1844, he was the secretary of the commission set up to revise P&O's plans for the eastern lines. On retirement in 1862, he joined the board, but died in 1866.[55] William Fane De Salis, by contrast, became a director in 1851 and did not retire until the end of 1895, one year before his death. He was P&O's first director who had lived and worked in Australia. In his eight years in New South Wales he became a flock-holder, owned coal mines and was 'extensively engaged' in business as a merchant and shipowner in Sydney.[56]

After Williams gave up his seat on the board, Irish shareholders called for another director but they had to wait until 1856 for a vacancy when John George, a barrister, director on the board of the City of Dublin Company and, in 1859, MP for Limerick, was elected. Ten years later, he resigned as MP and director to take up an appointment as judge of the Queen's Bench in Ireland. His successor, in 1866, was George Carleton L'Estrange, 'an Irishman at birth [who] possessed in a peculiar degree the confidence of the Irish Proprietors, who form[ed] so important a body' in P&O. He died in 1881.[57] Thomas Mathias Weguelin, MP, a governor of the Bank of England (1855–57), was a partner in the important merchant bank of Robarts, Lubbock & Co. and 'a man of great commercial knowledge'. His interests were in St Petersburg, but by winning one of the Southampton seats in Parliament, which he held from 1857 to 1859,[58] he was no stranger to P&O's business. He became a director in 1858 but left ten years later to attend to his other enterprises.[59]

Most directors in the first generation were steeped in the sea in one way or another but few of their replacements had much, if any, detailed knowledge of steam navigation, perhaps because the technology, especially screw propulsion, had undergone so many improvements since 1840 that, for short voyages at least, it had become commonplace. Captain William Hutcheon Hall (1800–78), RN, CB (KCB, 1867, rear-admiral, 1875), who took Samuel Thornton's seat in 1856 and held it until his death in 1878, was the only new board member with naval experience, having served in the first Opium War in China and in the Crimean conflict. A practical man, he invented a type of anchor and iron bilge tanks. He was also the author of *Sailors' Homes*[60] and *Our National Defences*.[61] After Nairne died in 1866, he was succeeded by another author, Hadow's friend Edward Parry Thornton, CB (no relation of Samuel). E.P. Thornton's career in the Indian Civil Service lasted for thirty years (1830–60) during which he wrote the *History of the British Empire in India* in six volumes (1841–45; second edition, 1858) and a *Gazetteer of the East India Company* in four (1854). He remained on the board until 1888.[62]

James Allan stepped into Carleton's place in the managing department and after the six-month trial period became an MD. Most of his life was 'exclusively engaged in the business of steam' and he had 'thorough knowledge of every detail of its management'; his qualifications for the post of MD had been recently enhanced by his tour of Eastern ports. As an MD, Allan was given by Willcox and Anderson the same commissions as Carleton: one-third of the MDs' 2.5 per cent commission on gross revenue and 5 per cent from profits. But if that payment was less than £1,500 per annum, Anderson would make it up, and if it was more than £2,500, Allan would have to give it back to the company. In 1855, the lower limit of Allan's salary was raised to £2,000 and the upper limit to £3,000.[63]

The only other new face on the board in this period was that of James Matheson, MP (soon to be a Baronet), P&O's third chairman. He took up the appointment in January 1849, having possessed 'the qualifications requisite' for filling the vacancy.[64] The senior partner in the prosperous firm of Jardine, Matheson & Co. in China and India, he retired in 1843 at the age of 47 for a more pleasant life in England and Scotland. He held the Ashburn constituency for four years, and in the 1847 election moved to the Ross and Cromarty seat that was nearer to his estate at Stornoway. In 1848, he took over the merchant bank of Magniac, Smith & Co. (Jardine, Matheson & Co.'s bankers) to save it from bankruptcy, and built it up into one of the most respected houses in the City. An ideal figure-head, he was wealthy, well known, an MP, and most unlikely to interfere in P&O's business. In his first speech to the proprietors, he told them their company had conferred 'inestimable benefits on the nation at large' by accelerating 'the communication with our magnificent empire in the East, bringing it . . . to our very doors' – an uplifting start. However, his attendance was irregular at the twice-weekly meetings and he was often unable to preside at the AGMs. His heart was in Scotland, and he bowed out in February 1858. There was no difficulty in electing a new chairman this time. Before the month was out, Willcox was elected *nem. con.*

Proprietors v. directors (again)

In the early 1850s there were further disputes between MDs and shareholders, but these led to the consolidation of Anderson's power in the company. Having won the 1853 mail contract, the MDs found themselves involved in a serious controversy with the Admiralty, and manipulated the AGMs in 1853 and 1854 so that shareholders blamed the Government, not themselves, for the company's difficulties. The MDs had taken a risk when they priced their tender very low in the belief that the pasha would abolish or at least reduce the duty on cargo across Egypt. There was a sudden and unforeseen disappearance of coal in the East, however, and the MDs appealed for the suspension of some Eastern parts of the contract.[65] The Admiralty's answer was that though the rise in the rate of freight had been considerable, that was no reason for terms of 'a contract so recently entered' to be modified; it would be 'a most dangerous and improper proceeding to release a public contract from an agreement for no other reason than that it had turned out to be unfavourable to [the contractor]'.[66] Only a penalty of £35,000 would allow the suspension, and the MDs refused to pay (they were short of cash). Shareholders were alarmed by the possibility that the Government would re-open the whole contract and 'make better terms for the public than those to which they are at present bound for a period of eight years'.[67] That would be 'entirely unacceptable' and 'almost fatal to the interests of the Company'. But 'fatal' too for the Government if P&O stopped the 'essentially necessary' mail service. As long as the Government and the company remained locked in this difficulty, the directors had to reduce the half-yearly dividend to 3 per cent instead of the 4 per cent then expected by shareholders. This was 'more or less unpalatable' to some, but Wyndham Goold, MP for Limerick (1850–54), praised the MDs for 'the manly straightforward way' they had handled the problem. He had never heard of such a 'monstrous doctrine' as that of the Government; it wanted 'to screw [the company] down as much as [it] possibly could'. Meanwhile Colonel Bagnold advised P&O to throw up the contract and trade on freight and passengers because 'public spirit and patriotism' did not sit well in commercial matters; and John George (later to become a director) was of the opinion that the MDs had 'not mere honesty, but great moral courage and firmness' in announcing the lower dividend.[68] He might not have showered such hearty praise on them if he'd known that they raided the repairing and insurance funds for £28,000 to make up 3 per cent for the second half of the year.

Then, in June 1854, proprietors were shocked to learn that there would be no dividend at all in the first half-year. Anderson worked hard to persuade proprietors 'not to be frightened into rushing into the market with their shares' because this difficulty was 'a passing cloud'. P&O had 'attained to a magnitude and public importance unprecedented in the annals of private maritime enterprize'; there was no cause for alarm. He should know, he said, for he was, 'if not the largest, one of the largest shareholders in the Company' himself, and he had not parted with a single share.[69] But some shareholders parted with theirs very quickly. The £50 shares, which once stood at £85, or 70 per cent premium, fell to par, wiping £1 million off 30,000 shares. *Herapath* noted the 'misery' for those who were 'accustomed to the receipt of good dividends, [when] all at once they are reduced to a state of destitution', and advised the shareholders to 'fast and pray'.[70]

Fortunately for P&O, France and Britain went to war in March 1854 to help Turkey keep Russia out of Constantinople. Anderson 'lamented' war, yet 'he had turned it over in his mind and looked at it in all sides with reference to the financial interest of the Company, and could see no harm in it'. Every ship taken up by the Admiralty for the Crimea made things more difficult for P&O, because mails to India and China could on no account be interrupted. But exactly for that reason, the MDs had better leverage to negotiate with the Government. The suspension of the contract was granted in November with a small penalty and some concessions from P&O. Financially, the company did well in the war because its ships were bigger and better than many other hired vessels. The MDs insisted on the highest price (50*s* per month per ton) and government warrants always came promptly. Shareholders congratulated the company for its 'zeal', 'patriotism and gallantry', for the ships 'had come under fire at Sebastopol': P&O's 'good old flag . . . would float at the main until all opposition had been overcome, and the power of the despot was crushed'.[71]

Anderson faced the battle with the Admiralty with relish, but Willcox felt deeply ashamed at having misjudged the cost of the contract and deprived the shareholders – some of them widows and orphans – of their dividends. He was

> apprehensive that a time was approaching when he could no longer expect to possess those powers of endurance which were absolutely necessary in one who had to carry out the arduous duties of the management. So long as the Company remained prosperous he naturally

Table 5.1 Total 5 per cent commissions from profits for MDs, 1841–66

Year	£	*Year*	£	*Year*	£
1841–42	3,417	1850–51	7,792	1859–60	12,195
1842–43	2,755	1851–52	6,977	1860–61	5,000
1843–44	1,500	1852–53	5,434	1861–62	5,004
1844–45	7,173	1853–54	9,000	1862–63	6,710
1845–46	?	1854–55	15,843	1863–64	6,039
1846–47	6,648	1855–56	15,390	1864–65	5,347
1847–48	6,952	1856–57	20,350	1865–66	3,199
1848–49*	10,552	1857–58	14,649		
1849–50	7,434	1858–59	16,594		

Source: P&O/6/52.

> hesitated to withdraw; but when a cloud came over the Company last year . . . his mind was at once made up.[72]

Willcox resigned his managing directorship on 30 September 1854, though he remained on the board as a director. To make amends to the shareholders and honour the promise he made in 1848, Willcox gave up the whole of his 2.5 per cent commission from gross earnings, but kept his third of the 5 per cent commission from profit.

Willcox's donations to the company, about £8,000 in 1854, rose each year to £14,000 in 1862, the year of his death, yet he was still able to leave £126,000 for his family. He wanted his money to go to pay employees in the form of bonuses, for it was absurd to 'expect to retain talent without paying for it'; and he hoped that those 'lads fresh from school', now grown men, many of them talented, would be kept on in the company. On the same day, Anderson announced that he intended to stay an MD 'for a year or two more, should health and strength be spared to him', but meanwhile, he would set up a fund – the 'Provident and Good Service Fund' – – by putting in it one-third of his portion of the 2.5 per cent commission of gross earnings (about £1,500 per annum). His object was to attract 'persons of superior qualification and conduct' to enter the company, and his fund would provide permanent allowances to employees who deserved them for their 'long and faithful service' or 'extraordinary exertions'. Like Willcox, Anderson retained his third of the 5 per cent per annum commission.[73]

The timing of these announcements was perfect. Dejected and alarmed at news of the dividend, shareholders had their minds turned to a remarkable and admirable action from the two MDs. John George was 'taken quite by surprise by [their] noble and munificent generosity'. Several members suggested that a testimonial should be arranged for them, so William Dent formed a committee and in March 1855, a special meeting was held to present to each of them 'a magnificent service of plate', suitably engraved: *Herapath*'s reporter thought it 'on the whole . . . very chaste and beautiful'. For Dent it was 'scarcely credible' that anyone 'in modern times' would voluntarily relinquish 'such emoluments, particularly in this every-day, money-making City of London, and in these times, when wealth is so much coveted'.[74] *Plus ça change* . . . With Willcox out of the managing department and the modest Allan as usual in the background and working hard, Anderson had total power in the company.[75]

Notes

1 Deed of settlement (National Maritime Museum, MS 92/031), clauses 74 and 75.
2 P&O/2/1, generally; P&O/1/100, 16.12.1840; *Herapath*, 11.12.1847, p. 1372.
3 P&O/2/2, 17.3.1841.
4 Deed of settlement, clauses 10, 11, 22.
5 *Herapath*, 29.5.1847, p. 645.
6 P&O/6/1, Reports, 30.11.1841, p. 6; 30.11.1842, p. 7.
7 P&O/20/5, nos 87–91; P&O/51/2.
8 See ch. 1, p. 59.
9 P&O/15/2, 4.11.1840, 18.11.1840, 25.11.1840, 26.11.1840, 26.1.1841 and 30.1.1841; P&O/1/100, 17.11.1840.
10 O'Byrne, *Naval Biographical Dictionary*, p. 1178; P&O/2/1, 5.8.1840; P&O/1/100, 19.11.1840.
11 Deed of settlement, clauses 5 and 6.
12 I have not been able to find anything about his background.
13 P&O/1/100, 19.11.1840, 26.11.1840 and 27.2.1841.
14 P&O/1/100, 4.4.1841, 5.5.1841 and 11.5.1841; in meetings without a chairman or deputy, the fourth director to enter the boardroom would take the chair.
15 Deed of settlement, clause 64.
16 P&O/1/100, 6.11.1840. He left a day or two after 16.12.40: see ch. 2, p. 000.
17 *Ibid.*, 23.12.1840.
18 *Ibid.*, 18.5.1841, 15.6.1841, 29.6.1841, 13.7.1841, 7.9.1841, 12.10.1841, 19.10.1841, 26.10.1841 and 23.11.1841.
19 *Communications with India, China, &c.: Observations on the Practicability and Utility of Opening a Communication between the Red Sea and the Mediterranean by a Ship Canal, Through the Isthmus of Suez* (hereafter *Observations*) (London, 1843).
20 P&O/1/100, 2.5.1843, 16.5.1843 and 23.5.1843.
21 *Communications with India, China, &c. via Egypt. The Political Position of Their Transit Through Egypt* (1843); P&O/1/100, 7.11.1843.
22 *Herapath*, 29.11.1842, pp. 1215–6; 2.6.1843, pp. 559, 664; 29.11.1843, p. 1236; P&O/1/100, 12.9.1843 and 2.7.1844.
23 *PD*, 3rd series, 63, 10.5.1842, cols 338–42; 10.6.1842, cols 1429–50.
24 Deed of settlement, clause 46.
25 *Herapath*, 29.11.1843, pp. 1236–7.
26 P&O/1/100, 4.2.1845, 11.2.1845, 18.2.1845 and 25.2.1845.
27 P&O/1/101, 9.12.1845 and 22.10.1846; *Herapath*, 8.12.1845, p. 2665, and 12.12.1846, p. 1561.

28 P&O/1/101, 18.12.1846, 22.12.1846, 29.12.1846 and 3.12.1847.
29 *Ibid.*, 27.7.1847.
30 P&O/1/101, 23.11.1847, 26.11.1847 and 21.12.1847.
31 *Ibid.*, 3.12.1847, 7.12.1847 and 21.12.1847.
32 *Shipping & Mercantile Gazette*, 12.12.1848, p. 2.
33 P&O/6/1, Report, 29.5.1846, pp. 4–5; *Shipping & Mercantile Gazette*, 16.12.1848, col. 4; this Report is covered over five columns in very small font.
34 *Herapath*, 10.12.1859, p. 1245.
35 Dent & Co. was second in importance to Jardine, Matheson & Co. on the China coast.
36 *Herapath*, 10.12.1859, p. 1245.
37 *Ibid.*, 12.12.1846, pp. 1561–2.
38 *Ibid.*, 8.12.1849, p. 1228; 13.12.1856, p. 1274; P&O/1/103, 5.12.1851; P&O/1/104, 7.12.1855 and 11.11.1856.
39 See above, p. 154.
40 P&O/1/101, 27.7.1847.
41 *Ibid.*, 11.12.1847, p. 1374.
42 *Ibid.*, 23.5.1848, 26.5.1848 with 21.7.1847, 14.9.1847, 13.10.1847 and 15.1.1848.
43 *Herapath*, 16.12.1848, p. 1293.
44 Voting at the AGMs was regulated by clause 22 of the deed: holders of 5 shares were qualified, thus 5–9 shares = 1 vote; 10–14 = 2 votes; 15–19 = 3 votes. At 20 shares or over, shareholders could have an extra vote for every 5 additional shares up to 20 votes, but no more. Campbell had 265 paid-up shares, though the MDs could easily round up a few of shareholders each with 20 votes. But it did not go that far in meetings.
45 *Herapath*, 16.12.1848, p. 1293.
46 P&O/1/101, 7.4.1848.
47 *PP*, 1849, 12 (560), *SC on Contract Packets*.
48 *Herapath*, 8.12.1849, p. 1230.
49 *Ibid.*, 3.6.1848, pp. 585–6; P&O/1/104, 26.8.1856, 5.9.1856, 11.10.1856, 24.4.1857, 10.7.1857, 4.9.1857, 11.9.1857, 25.9.1857, 27.11.1857, 15.4.1858, 20.4.1858 and 25.5.1858.
50 P&O/1/101, 22.1.1847, 16.2.1847, 13.4.1847, 7.9.1847 and 10.9.1847; P&O/1/102, 15.12.1848, 19.12.1848, 22.12.1848 and 29.10.1850; P&O/1/105, 5.2.1861; *ILN*, 1.11.1851, p. 539; P&O/6/1, 4.12.1851.
51 P&O/1/103, 15.9.1854; died 2.4.1866.
52 *Hampshire Advertiser*, 18.4.1857, p. 5, col. 6; he also possessed 'a valuable coffee estate' in Ceylon which he had bought with Francis Carleton.
53 *Herapath*, 31.5.1849, p. 552, 6.12.1849, p. 1230; P&O/1/103, 8.12.1854; P&O/1/105, 15.1.1861.
54 *Herapath*, 16.12.1848, p. 1291; P&O/1/102, 30.1.1852.
55 *PP*, HoL, 1847, 5 (225): SC on the Post Office, and see ch. 1, this book; P&O/1/106, 14.11.1862; P&O/1/107, 24.7.1866.
56 P&O/1/102, 24.6.1851; *PP*, 1851, 21 (372), q. 1; P&O/1/118, 1.11.1895; he died 3.8.1896.
57 *Herapath*, 13.12.1856, p. 1276. L'Estrange (apparently not related to the late Francis Carleton) died 19.9.1881: P&O/1/107, 9.12.1866.
58 He then sat for Wolverhampton, 1861–80.
59 *Herapath*, 5.6.1858, p. 579; Boase, *Modern English Biography*, vol. 3, pp. 1255–6.
60 *Sailors' Homes, Destitute Sailors' Asylums, and Asylums for Aged Seamen, Their Origin and Progress* (?London, 1852).
61 Published London 1876.
62 P&O/1/103, 24.10.1856; P&O/1/110, 25.6.1878; Boase, *Modern English Biography*, vol. 1, pp. 1291–2. Thornton died 10.12.1893: *Times*, 12.12.1893, p. 10.
63 P&O/1/102, 22.6.1849; P&O/1/104, 4.3.1856; P&O/6/52, 1849–60. All three MDs paid £500 per annum to Carleton's widow until 1850, an obligation in the deed; and Willcox and Anderson gave back to the company one-third of the 2 per cent

commission that Carleton would have had each year until 1860, a sum just under £110,000.

64 *Shipping Gazette*, 16.12.1848, p. 2.

65 *Ibid.*, 4.6.1853, p. 588.

66 *Herepath*, 10.12.1853, pp. 1299–1300.

67 *Ibid.*, p. 1300.

68 *Ibid.*, pp. 1300–1.

69 *Herapath*, 17.6.1854, p. 596.

70 *Ibid.*, p. 608.

71 *Herapath*, 9.12.1854, p. 1253.

72 *Ibid.*, 17.6.1854, p. 596.

73 *Ibid.*, pp. 596–7; *ibid.*, 8.12.1855, p. 1236; P&O/6/3, 31.3.1855.

74 *Herapath*, 10.12.1859; P&O/1/105, 12.6.1860.

74 P&O/1/102, 14.11.1851–24.2.1852; P&O/1/103, 11.1.1853–7.6.1853, 24.1.1854–26.5.1854; P&O/1/105, 19.4.1859; see also Harcourt, 'The High Road to India'.

75 Allan was brought very reluctantly to the fore when Mr R. Penney told the meeting that he would like 'to see something to grace [Allan's] sideboard' for his 'devoted assiduities [*sic*]'. It was the clerks and other employees in the company who subscribed for the present of plate, not the shareholders. Allan was very embarrassed when he heard what they were doing. He earned much more than they, and had he known about it before, he would have stopped them. This tribute was indeed 'a token of regard': *Herapath*, 10.12.1859; P&O/1/105, 12.6.1860.

CHAPTER SIX

Nuts, bolts and money, 1843–65

Highs and lows in the market, 1845–48

After *Bentinck*'s launch in June 1843, no more ships were built until the MDs were certain that the company would get the mail contract for India and China. When in July 1844 they knew that the India and China contract was theirs, they set about increasing the fleet. George Bayley,[1] principal surveyor for Lloyd's Register of Shipping, was engaged for three years to give P&O 'the aid of first-rate professional talent' and to superintend each new vessel. This mail contract was so important a landmark for P&O that Richard Bourne, in his seventies, seized the chance to make another mark by 'strongly advocating upright stems and stern posts instead of raking ones adopted in new iron vessels'. His proposal was passed to George Bayley, but he advised the board to leave things as they were to avoid delays.[2]

Shipbuilders all over the country were invited to tender for the new vessels, but the MDs preferred London or south-of-England shipyards. Money, Wigram & Sons and Ditchburn & Mare, both of Blackwall, William Pitcher of Northfleet, William Fairbairn & Sons of Millwall, and Thomas & Robert White of Cowes on the Isle of Wight were contracted for building hulls; while Miller, Ravenhill & Co. of Blackwall, Maudslay, Son & Field of Lambeth and John Penn of Greenwich constructed the engines in or near London, though Liverpool (the engineers Vernon, Curtis, Kennedy & Co. and Fawcett & Preston) and Scotland (Tod & M'Gregor of Partick and Caird & Co of Greenock) were not overlooked. Although the mail contract had to start in January 1845, no vessel could be complete before 1846 however much the MDs, Bayley and Andrew Lamb tried to make the shipbuilders and engineers work faster. Sometimes the delay occurred because the hull was built a long way from the engines: the hull built in Caird's yard in Greenock had to be taken to Fawcett & Preston's workshop in Liverpool to have its engine fitted. Miller & Ravenhill caused a delay of at least three months because they forgot to give *Madrid*'s plans to Fairbairn, who was to build the hull. But Caird's tardiness was the worst of all: *Malta* was a whole year late and P&O's solicitors were told to stop his money.[3]

Nevertheless, the directors were able to tell the shareholders that their investments were doing well. The company had 'attained its . . . independent position', and its success was attributed to confidence in the regularity of its vessels. As for the 'pecuniary interests of Proprietors', 'the only prudent course to pursue', said the board, 'is that of providing out of the annual profits the means required'

> 1st. To maintain the Vessels in the highest state of working efficiency; and for that object, to keep always in hand a sufficient sum to cover the repairs of the vessels.
>
> 2nd. To proceed as your Directors have hitherto done, in establishing and maintaining a sufficient Insurance Fund to meet casualties, the minimum of which, as relates to their Company, should not be less than £100,000, to be invested in approved and available securities.
>
> 3rd. To maintain a Fund to meet the depreciation of the Vessels, out of which, new Vessels shall be provided to supply the place of Hulls and Machinery worn out in the service.[4]

The MDs went on to say:

> They are adopting the surest means to protect, permanently, the interests of their Proprietors, by maintaining and perpetuating, at its original value, the floating property of the Company. They have well-grounded expectations, that the income of the Company will enable them to carry out these measures satisfactorily, and at the same time to provide a remunerative Dividend to the Proprietors, on their capital embarked in the undertaking.[5]

However, as we shall see, ways and means of meeting these objectives were to become problematical as the fleet increased.

In the summer of 1846, the MDs expected to see 22 sea-going vessels by 1847 (11 older vessels and 11 new ones), to be distributed across the various stations as follows:

Southampton–Alexandria	2
Southampton–Constantinople	3
Southampton–Peninsular	3
Southampton–Italian coast	2
Alexandria–Marseilles	1
Suez–Calcutta	3
Bombay–China	3
Hong Kong	1
Spares	4

Four spare vessels were barely sufficient to cover all lines, however, as any one or more of the eighteen were under repair at any given time and casualties and losses could happen anywhere.[6] The MDs told the board that 'there should not be less on average than four vessels in course of construction every year' for extending operations, since this was 'absolutely necessary to protect the interest' of the company; and in the company's accounts, provision was made under three heads, and charged to each year's trading profits: 5 per cent for vessels gradually wearing out (the depreciation account); 5 per cent on floating capital (the Insurance Fund), and 10 per cent on floating capital (repairs). Discord between the managing department and the board over the number of ships required led to 'a full discussion' in October and in consequence a financial committee consisting of the MDs, Campbell, Pirie and de Zulueta was set up to see if there was need for 'any further expenditure for New Vessels'. The MDs evidently won the others over, for the committee laid an estimate of cost for 14 new ships before the board on 24 November 1846:

Cost of 14 steamers launched, under construction and contracted for, including the purchase of *Achilles*	£602,973
Less for *Ripon* to replace *Great Liverpool* which has been provided for out of the Insurance and Depreciation accounts	(£62,000)
Extent of engagements	£540,973
Deduct amount in cash paid on accounts above	(£275,183)
Amount due at this date	£265,790
Amount of capital yet to be received to meet above:	
Four instalments on 6,452 shares	£129,040
Instalments due on previous calls, U K and India	£12,330
1,800 reserved shares unissued	£90,000
Amount of capital receivable	£231,370
Deficit	£34,813

There would, it was said, be 'sufficient funds to meet all engagements' for the present. Additional vessels, however, would be required to meet 'the further extension of the operations of the Company', and more capital would have to be raised in due course. Profits up to the financial year 30 September 1846 were £128,000, so £40,000 was added to the Depreciation Account and two more vessels were ordered.[7]

The financial committee examined 'the present and prospective state' of the company's engagements again in March 1847. P&O's shares had a premium of £30, so the company kept 1,810 paid-up shares

(£144,800) as reserves, to be sold only with 'express approval' of the board. On the new vessels, £290,000 remained to be liquidated and would be paid for by the funds of the company together with those shares, if needed, over two years: £160,000 in 1847 and £137,480 in 1848. Based on the results in 1845 and 1846, the committee estimated that a 'moderate calculation of undivided profits (after payment of dividends) for the ensuing twelve months may be safely . . . about £100,000'. And,

> to protect the Company's interests and to meet the urgent demand which exists for extending its operations in order to guard those interests, it is essential that several new ships should be put in hands, and contracts entered into, for the completion of the same in all 1848 [*sic*]; and that this Company must either adopt this course or anticipate the possibility of other capitalists entering the field as competitors. At the present moment the Managing Directors report that the state of the negociation they have in hands with Her Majesty's Government for the extension of the Company's mail contracts in the Mediterranean, renders it very likely that three to four steam vessels, in addition to the present fleet will be required if the Company undertakes the service alluded to.

When the first £1 million of share capital was all paid up, the company would petition the Treasury for permission to raise a further £500,000 in the form of 10,000 new £50 shares. The reserved shares would be offered to the shareholders at par in proportion to their holdings; and when the new shares were issued there would be a 'considerable bonus to the Proprietors in the premium on [them]', a move which 'the prosperous state of the Concern fully warrants'.[8]

In this rosy environment, the committee made a detailed plan that would cover 'auxiliaries to their existing lines, or [new lines] when called upon by Government to extend their operations for the public service'. The company should not let Italy and the Black Sea go to competitors; and east of Suez there were choice lines – Calcutta–Singapore, Hong Kong–Shanghai, and Bombay–Suez – waiting to be taken up by P&O, because 'it appears probable Government may be compelled to open [them] under contract for mail service'. A 'Summary of additional Ships required' was laid out to show where 11 proposed new vessels, at a total building cost of £328,000, would be employed, and in the spring of 1847 there seemed to be nothing on the horizon that would stop the company from carrying the plan out. It was P&O's

> duty strongly to urge the importance of the principle of occupying lines now requiring the benefit of steam navigation not solely in the expectation of realising large profits, but in order to prevent those lines being taken up by other influencial parties who could not be limited in their

> operations and who might hereafter become powerful rivals to the P&O Company on their existing lines.[9]

The financial years 1845–46 and 1846–47 were so good for P&O that at the end of 1846 the MDs raised the annual 7 per cent dividend to 8 per cent. Moreover they believed that the company's profits in the financial year 1847–48 would be as good as those in the previous two years, for P&O had a sound economy and a 'judicious development of traffic', and at the half-yearly meeting in June 1847, the directors announced that the new £500,000 capital would shortly be distributed at par.

However, shareholders who assembled for the December 1847 AGM were in the lowest of spirits. Since October, a severe depression had been hanging over every business, and the money market was certainly 'not favourable'. The directors admitted that the results of 1845 and 1846 'exceeded their expectations' and had they been 'rash enough to act upon that short experience', they might have recommended 'a somewhat larger division of profits' to the shareholders. But capital in building had increased, and in January 1847 the fare to and from India had been reduced by 10 per cent, lessening the income from that quarter by several thousands of pounds. Building engagements for new ships were stopped where possible – six of the new vessels were already employed, and others were still building – and the new capital was not required after all, even though as a mail contractor P&O had to work as usual on contract lines, and the MDs bought *Jupiter* to keep the Peninsular line open, while *Achilles* was sent to China. The directors thought it incumbent on them to tell the assembly that they did not have a lot of money to throw about:

> Some parties, indeed, who appear only to have looked on one side of the account, have even gone so far as to assert, that the receipts arising from the conveyance of goods and passengers might be sufficient, together with the amount of postage, to meet the remuneration for such service; but those, who have such an opinion, must evidently labour under a very erroneous impression of the expensive nature of the service and the numerous heavy demands from the various causes referred to, which the maintenance of such a fleet in the Eastern seas requires . . . [On the subject of profits, the shareholders] should be satisfied with a well secured moderate Dividend, after due provision has been made to meet the depreciation of the Property, and that all insurable are fully covered.[10]

With Europe growing more rebellious by the day, trade had come to a stop, and it looked as if the three wooden paddlers building for P&O when the crisis broke would be difficult to employ or sell.

Unexpectedly, however, rebels who organized the Sicilian insurrection paid £60,000 for 2 of them, *Vectis* and *Bombay*, through various, mostly British, middlemen. This rising did not last long and the Neapolitan Government bought *Ganges*, the third ship, for £65,000 and snatched *Vectis* and *Bombay* before the rebels could put their hands on them. But *Bombay* and *Vectis* had been sold to a party intent on going to war with a lawful sovereign friendly to Britain, and under the Foreign Enlistment Act this was a criminal act. C.W. Howell, P&O's secretary, represented the company at the Central Criminal Court in July 1849 and thanks to Sir Fitzroy Kelly, QC, the verdict was 'Not Guilty'. He rested P&O's defence with verbal criticism: the plaintiff did not know 'the distinction between "fitting-up" and "fitting-out": A lady was "fitted-up" by having her ears bored, not "fitted-out" till the earrings were actually in their ornamental situation; so here the vessel was "fitted-up", perhaps, but no guns or other munitions were aboard; so she was not "fitted-out" in the words of the forbidding law . . .'.[11]

With this 'casual and incidental profit' in hand – the money from the first two sales was safe in P&O's coffers with the proceeds of the third yet to come – the MDs distributed bonuses among the shareholders of £1 per share to make up the 8 per cent dividend for 1848, and some of the money went towards £93,550 'on account of the new ships during the last eight months for which no Capital has been provided'. And having sold those 3 ships, the MDs were able to order 2 new ones, *Ganges* (2) and *Singapore*, new paddlers which were faster and had iron hulls. This was an example of how quickly steam navigation was improving, especially in machinery.[12]

Stagnation in 1848 and early 1849 gave the MDs time to reflect on the way they had managed the company since 1845. While they struggled to carry on their commercial lines in the Mediterranean and the Levant, they did not then have the measure of what they were undertaking in the East. Operations in the Eastern seas, it was thought, would consist 'merely' of two trunk lines, one between Suez and Calcutta and the other connecting Bombay with China via Point de Galle in Ceylon; and 'it was supposed' that the amount of capital required would be about £400,000. Once the enterprise was launched, however, it was clear that the public would demand facilities 'and the other expensive branches of a marine establishment, such as docks, warehouses, machinery, sea stores, coal depots &c' in India and China, at a distance of 8,000 to 10,000 miles from head quarters, requiring a much more expensive staff and a 'considerably increased amount of capital' for the necessary number of vessels. Moreover, there were no steamers to hire in Eastern seas in the event of any casualty. The company had to depend entirely upon its own resources, and, although Indian opium was carried safely from Bombay to China in P&O's steamers, the ships could not bring very much silk home because it was produced mostly in the districts around Shanghai, and the company then lacked the tonnage for the China coast.

It was at this point that the board raised the subject of a partnership between P&O and the Government. Perhaps they felt the company had simply taken on too much. More likely, they hoped that, in such a partnership, the Government would always shield P&O from competition and also keep the dividends stable. After all, the public purse maintained the ships, and the steamships were at hand in time of war:

> Under such circumstances, in any future contract, it might readily be conceded, that, should the surplus profits in any one year exceed a fair and moderate Dividend to the Shareholders, after due allowance being made for a sinking fund, the payment from the Government for such service and for such period should be reduced by a repayment to the full extent of whatever that excess might be, giving to the Lords of the Treasury the necessary facilities to enable them to ascertain the correctness of the accounts.[13]

So, in 1848, while P&O opened its books for an inspection by Admiralty officers, the MDs put the idea of a partnership to them. But the Earl of Auckland, First Lord, would have none of it,[14] and the proposal fell out of sight until 1867, when it was revived in very different circumstances.

Screw propulsion

For the first ten years of its life, P&O's sea-going vessels were propelled with paddle-wheels. These were awkward and inefficient, their engines took up a lot of space in a ship and steam pressure was not in general more than 5–7*lbs* for fear of explosion of the boilers. After his experiments in 1837 Francis Pettit Smith found that screw propulsion was more efficient than paddles. In 1843, HMS *Rattler* was the first to be equipped with a screw, and Brunel's *Great Britain* crossed the Atlantic with a screw in 1845.

Captain Bourne had a keen interest in this new invention. In 1846, he urged the MDs 'to collect every information in their power from the Admiralty and private individuals regarding the advantages and disadvantages attending the adoption of the Archimedean Screw propeller'.[15] At the end of 1846, Bourne set up a committee to see if the company ought to order ships with this new engine: 'As a preliminary step, it is highly desirable that accurate information be obtained from the different parties who at the present moment are connected with Steam Vessels propelled by the Screw, in order that the board may consider whether or not, it is advisable to adopt that propelling power in lieu of the ordinary Paddle Wheel.'

Whatever information was gleaned, however, the subject was dropped.[16] The MDs were still treading very cautiously in January 1850, and the two new ships they ordered from Tod & M'Gregor (*Ganges* (2) and *Singapore*) were both paddlers, though other companies in the Mediterranean were fitting their vessels with screws. But P&O could not remain competitive without increased tonnage or screw propulsion. In September, screws were talked about again, and the MDs inspected three naval ships fitted with screws that the Admiralty wanted to sell, but P&O declined to purchase such unadaptable vessels.[17] P&O was not too friendly with the Admiralty because from June that year it would only approve hulls for contract ships if they were made of wood, iron being considered too thin. P&O objected strongly, and gave £500 to the English Association which was testing 'the comparative merits of Wood and Iron Ships for warlike purposes',[18] though it was to be the Crimean War that settled the argument.

The state of P&O's fleet showed that something had to be done 'to meet the competition on the Constantinople line and the increasing requirements of that trade'. For improving and extending the company's operations, more ships were needed, and for competing in the Black Sea two screw-propelled vessels, *Madras* and *Bombay* (2), were ordered. With other costs, £220,000 would be ample. However, P&O knew it would have to wait for at least a year before these new ships would be ready for sea. Moreover the Treasury had received from Bombay a memorial signed by a large number of inhabitants and merchants, asking to extend the steam mail service to Shanghai and other ports on the coast, and paddlers were not suitable for China's sea;[19] indeed even if the Government did not extend the mail service from Hong Kong to Shanghai, the MDs knew that the company had to monopolize that coast. So, as screw vessels were becoming quite widespread, it would be prudent to purchase one or two.

But with bad years now out of mind, business flourished, and though Tod & M'Gregor offered a large screw ship to the company for sale, it was bought by other persons while the MDs were trying to make up their minds. However, Tod & M'Gregor would be glad to build a 1,600–1,800-ton screw ship on its own terms, to be completed in 12 months. The board sent James Allan to Glasgow to see if any other shipyard could do better. No chance: every shipbuilding firm in Glasgow was 'very full of work', so P&O had to accept Tod & M'Gregor's terms.[20]

Then James Hartley stepped in. He and 'others' had arranged with Miller & Ravenhill to construct 2 screws of 700–800 gt but found that they did not want them any more. Could the engineers take over and finish them to P&O's liking? Indeed they could. The MDs purchased *Shanghai* for £18,000 and *Chusan* for £19,000. The first ship, sent to the China coast, had a new steering apparatus to regulate the screw; and Captain James Brown, who supervised *Shanghai*'s outfit and had much experience of screw ships, was appointed its commander.[21] A third screw vessel, *Formosa*, was purchased from Smith & Rodger of Govan, Glasgow. On 15 May 1852, *Chusan* left Southampton for Australia, arriving at Sydney on 4 August; and on 7 August *Formosa* went to the same destination. Like *Chusan*, the ship took just short of three months, to the amazement of Sydney's residents. They had never received their letters from home so quickly.[22]

After this taste of the new technology, P&O ordered or purchased many screw vessels, and two paddle steamers, *Sultan* built in 1847 and *Malta* built in 1848, were converted to screw in the 1850s. By May 1855, P&O had a fleet of 41 ships of which 21 were screws; and by 1867 out of a fleet of 50 ships (including 4 under repair and one fitting out), 42 were screws. The new engines covered less space in the hull, allowed more cargo to be carried, and with higher steam pressure – a big jump from 9 to 25*lbs* or more in 6 double-ended tubular boilers – achieved higher speeds. This invention was a significant advance in the history of steam navigation. In 1855, P&O donated £100 to the committee formed by all the leading engineering firms to raise a testimonial to Pettit Smith.[23]

Highs, lows and wars, 1851–60

Apart from the 3 purchased screw ships, *Bombay* (2) and *Madras* were the only new ships in 1851–52; they were also the first 2 screw-propelled ships constructed for the company. The MDs had in mind a series of large vessels to follow, and they had £500,000 share capital to pay for them. However, having won the 1853 mail contract for India and China, the MDs were taking on half as much mileage again as under the 1845 contract, as tables 6.1 and 6.2 show.

It did not take long to realize that £500,000 would not be enough to pay for 14 new ships. Share capital of £200,000 had already been issued in October 1852, and although £300,000 remained as yet unissued the MDs proposed instead to take up the £100,000 debentures which had been authorized in 1847. After some discussion, the board decided to borrow from the Treasury up to a limit of £500,000. In the memorial to the Treasury, the company stated that P&O's

Table 6.1 Mileage in P&O's 1845 mail contract

Station	*Miles per voyage*	*Total Miles*
1 Southampton to Vigo, Oporto, Lisbon, Cadiz and Gibraltar	3 × 2,400	86,400
2 Southampton to Malta and Alexandria, monthly, on the 20th of the month	6,084	73,008
3 Southampton to Malta and Alexandria, monthly, on the 3rd of the month	6,084	73,008
4 Calcutta to Madras, Point de Galle, Aden and Suez, and Point de Galle to Penang, Singapore and Hong Kong, once a month	15,590	187,080
Total	34,958	419,496

Source: *PP*, 1849, 12 (571), *Contract Packets*, Appendix 1, p. 217.

Table 6.2 Mileage in P&O's 1853 mail contract

Lines	*Voyages*	*Mileage*
Southampton to Alexandria	2,951 × 2 × 24	141,648
Suez to Calcutta	4,757 × 2 × 24	228,336
Point de Galle to Hong Kong	3,031 × 2 × 24	72,744
Calcutta to Hong Kong	3,104 × 2 × 6	74,496
Singapore to Sydney	4,630 × 2 × 12	55,560
Marseilles to Malta	659 × 2 × 24	31,632
Bombay to Point de Galle	911 × 2	21,864
Total Mileage		626,280

Source: *PP*, 1852, 49 (249), *Mail Services (India and Australia)*, p. 2.

existing property was valued at £1.2 million, that the company had no debts or liabilities and that, with the addition of 14 ships and 21,000 tons, the value of the property would be £2 million.[24] The financial committee estimated that £800,000 would be needed for new ships and for maintenance of the extended service about to be undertaken; of this sum, £250,000 had already been paid, leaving net liabilities of £550,000. It was possible to raid the Guarantee Insurance Fund which was standing at about £210,000, but the directors thought that that money should not be appropriated to the outlay above because

Table 6.3 The new services, 1853

1	A bi-monthly communication between Southampton and Calcutta direct
2	A bi-monthly communication between Marseilles and Malta, to meet the direct steamers between Southampton and Alexandria
3	A monthly communication between Bombay, Ceylon, Singapore, and China, as at present
4	A monthly communication between Calcutta, Singapore, and China, which, with the Bombay and Ceylon service, will provide a bi-monthly communication between England, India and China
5	A communication once every two months between Singapore and Australia, taking the western route to Sydney, via King George's Sound, Adelaide and Melbourne

Source: P&O/6/1, Report, 29.5.52, p. 4.

it was 'highly expedient . . . to preserve intact the present rate of Dividend to the shareholders and to take advantage of the present favourable state of the money market for raising money on debentures'.[25] The debentures were sold in bonds of £1,000, in terms of 3 and 5 years and at the rate of interest of 3.75 per cent. They were quickly taken up. Within days of the New Year, £166,000 went to shareholders, and Williams, Deacon & Co. 'wished to take £150,000–£200,000 for their friends'. A few more days and the applications rose to £271,000, from which P&O cleared the bankers' loan of £228,000, just before the due date (26 January). By August 1853, the loan was complete, but for the last £117,000 for 3 years the rate was 4 per cent.[26]

Up to the end of 1852, P&O could find satisfaction in what it had done and in what it was about to do under the new mail contract. The directors were eagerly looking forward to having five new lines, shown in table 6.3, in their hands.

However, the fact that P&O had cleared one large loan from the bankers by another large loan showed that the company was short of available cash, as is confirmed by a snapshot of the company's means in November 1852:[27]

Cash at the Bankers.	£11,000
Investment in Egyptian Bonds	£99,000
Bills receivable	£83,365
Deduct Bills payable	(£25,000)
	£168,365
Royal Bank of Ireland	£1,510
Total	£169,875

Moreover there were signs of an economic downturn at the turn of the year while the Great Powers were bickering and lining up against each other in the Black Sea. As soon as the new mail contract started on 1 January 1853, P&O faced a dilemma that was not resolved for nearly two years: either fulfil the terms of the mail contract agreed in March 1852 or pay a penalty of £35,000.[28]

While the directors argued with Admiralty, the MDs were desperately trying to scratch together some money for the 1853 dividend. For P&O, many negatives – the rise in the price of coal and all other necessaries for navigation, the very low tender for the mail contract, passenger fares that had been reduced and now could not be changed, heavy losses on the Australian line – all came at once. With little available money, the MDs hoped that debentures would replace capital. In November 1853, when accounts were closed for the previous financial year (October 1852–September 1853), the usual 10 per cent for repairs and 5 per cent for the Insurance Fund were reduced to 7.5 per cent and 4 per cent respectively, and the dividend dropped from 8 per cent to 6 per cent.[29] Worse, in 1853–54, there was no dividend at all at the half-year meeting, a shock that caused shares to fall to par from the high £70s.[30] The MDs were afraid to pass a dividend at the AGM, but behind closed doors, after a frenzied hunt, they found bits and pieces of paper at the back of drawers in the office, just enough to cover themselves and give the shareholders 7 per cent. Two secret documents, from 30 September 1854, show how the MDs created a dividend. One stated 'the value of ships for calculation of Insurance, Wear and Tear and Depreciation, has been taken at the sum of £1,250,000.' The other, a 'Memorandum of P&O Company's Shares disposed of on the Company's behalf', told how money for a 5 per cent dividend was made up:

Cost of shares transferred by R Williams & Sons, also residue of new shares unallotted and held for the Company with instalments paid thereon, during 1846–1854	£66,000
Received for proceed of above shares, disposed of at at various times from 1848 to the closing of the Account by sale of 19 shares on 1 July 1854	£93,822
Profit resulting from the investment and sale	£27,716

The version of the dividend the MDs conveyed to the shareholders was that they 'were compelled to take from the debts a large number of the Company's shares . . . disposed of, from time to time, as opportunities offered to do so with advantage'. And on top of this happy result, a bonus came from the directors: they added to £27,716 the sum of £2,284, making £30,000 so that shareholders could have £1 per share. Thus a 7 per cent dividend emerged: 5 per cent from £66,000 and 2 per cent from £30,000 from the sale of the shares.[31]

As table 6.4 shows, from 1858, 7 per cent was the core dividend and bonuses, called 'payments', were made up of any extra money, not necessarily from profits, but often from underwriting and the Willcox & Anderson's Good Service Fund (W&A). In early years, the MDs deemed 'it right to record their conviction, that without making such provision previously to the division of any profits, no steam navigation enterprize can be said to be placed in a sound financial position, and that to do otherwise would be tantamount to paying a Dividend out of Capital'.[32]

New ships were needed more than ever when the Crimean War began, and the large vessels that were building for the new mail contract were instead taken up at once by the Admiralty: *Simla*, *Nubia*, *Candia*, *Alma*, *Manilla* and *Colombo*. Other vessels – *Valetta*, *Malta*, *Pottinger* and *Precursor* – were taken up at various times, and two vessels were bought by the Government: *Tartar*, a very small wooden paddle collier of 300 gt, and the giant *Himalaya*, with an iron hull and screw engines, of 3,438 gt.

Himalaya, conceived in the autumn of 1851 as a great ship (perhaps to outdo Brunel's *Great Britain* in Bristol) and destined to be the flagship of the company, was intended to lead a series of large vessels. But as the building of *Himalaya* took such a long time, *Bengal*, not quite so grand and intended to be second in the series, was completed first and was for a short time the largest steamship in the world. *Himalaya*'s hull was built by C.J. Mare and its paddle-wheels constructed by John Penn & Son; but with that done, Penn and P&O's superintendent engineer, Andrew Lamb, thought that a screw propeller would be 'highly desirable', so an ordinary three-bladed propeller was fitted. That one was not suitable. A two-bladed screw was tried. That did not suit the ship either, so the right one had to be found. *Himalaya* was ready to launch in April 1852, but waited for the shaft and screw to be fitted on the slipways of the Thames; and in October 1853 rough weather stopped the ship from being removed from moorings at Blackwall to Deptford to receive its boilers. But in December, *Himalaya* was registered and in January 1854, at last, made its maiden voyage. She was indeed of 'national interest': the largest steamship in the world with the most elegant fittings and decorations. The directors had 'every confidence' in saying that she would have 'a higher rate of speed than had hitherto been attained by a large ocean-going steamer'. True, but there was a price to pay. When that voyage was over, *Himalaya* became

Table 6.4 Share capital and dividends, 1841–67

Year	*Share capital issued (£)*	*Core dividend (%)*	*Dividend paid*
1841	357,240	7	21,994
1842	433,230	7	25,520
1843	433,230	7	31,81
1844	453,230	7	35,670
1845	489,530	7	44,559
1846	489,530	8	52,570
1847	885,000	8	73,511
1848	977,050	8	78,008
1849	990,054	8	78,731 + bonus of £4,319 (£1 per share), for becoming underwriters (U)
1850	1,000,000	8	80,000
1851	1,068,711	8	82,000
1852	1,169,610	8	89,955
1853	1,169,610	6	74,186; 2% (repair) + 1% (insurance) funds deducted
1854	1,447,405	5	37,500: ditto; £66,250 + £27,716 from various P&O shares = 7%
1855	1,635,100	7	109,904:100,000 in suspense; bonus 2% (£37,500) = 9%
1856	1,641,610	7	114,912 + 3% (£32,832 from U a/c) = £147,744 + bonus 2% = 12%
1857	1,700,000	7	119,500 + 3.5% (bonus: £59,500) + 1% (£17,000 from U a/c) + 2% (£34,000) from W&A = 13.5%
1858	1,700,000	7	153,000 + 2% payment (£34,000) + 2% (from U a/c) + 11%
1859	1,800,000	7	124,000 + 3% payment (£35,750) = 10%
1860	2,000,000	5.5	102,000 + 1% (£19,500 from U a/c) 2% (£34,100 from W&A) = 8.5%
1861	2,100,000	7	143,500 + 3% (£61,500 from U a/c) = 10%
1862	2,100,000	7	147,000 + 4% (£84,000 from U a/c) = 11%
1863	2,100,000	7	147,000 + 3% (£73,500 from U a/c) + 2% payment (£42,000 = 12%)
1864	2,100,000	7	147,000 + 3% payment (£73,500) = 10%
1865	2,200,000	7	152,250 + 3% (£66,000 from U a/c) = 10%
1866	2,334,605	6.5	144,500 + 2.5% (£55,667 from U a/c) = 9%
1867	2,579,835	nil	– 177,047

Sources: P&O/6/52, P&O/3/25–30.

a white elephant: it consumed 71 tons of coal each day and no commercial steamship company, even with a subsidy, could sustain that level of fuel consumption at the time. Luckily for P&O, Britain was about to declare war on Russia. The Admiralty wanted troopships and *Himalaya* had room for 3,000 troops. First chartered, then purchased by the Government, she was sold for £130,000, 'a reasonable price', but P&O might have lost money on her all the same.[33]

When the rate of interest on debentures reached 5 per cent in 1855, £220,000 debentures were paid off, and the second supplemental charter having been granted in April, £1 million of new share capital began to be issued. But instead of the usual £5 a call, shareholders had to put down £10 per call at par, so the directors had plenty of money for the new ships. 13,796 of the £50 shares were taken up very promptly. About 100 shares were put aside for the few proprietors residing in India, and a sprinkling of rajahs and Indian merchants. The rest remained 'in the hands of the Directors . . . for the general benefit of the Company', with a promise to offer them in two years' time. After two bad years, it was difficult for P&O *not* to look rich in those years of warfare. The company was not only 'in a highly prosperous state, but . . . had attained a stability' of a high character; and as long as money was cheap, it was better to borrow than raising it on shares. True to their promise, the directors distributed the last of the new million. They put a premium of £3 on the remaining unissued 5,764 shares and set up a little fund which gave 'every individual of the Proprietary a due proportion of the benefit arising' from those shares. The Report tells the story in more detail:

> The residue of these shares, on the 1st January last, was 5,764; and the option of taking them up with £10 paid, at £3 premium, was freely responded to by the Shareholders, the total amount applied for on those terms being 10,420. The available number was therefore apportioned rateably among the applicants, and a fraction of only 96 now remains, dependent on the replies of Proprietors in India. A fund of about £17,000 having thus been realised, the Directors propose to add thereto a sufficient amount from the general earnings of the half-year to admit of the payment of fifteen shillings on every paid-up or £50 share, and three shillings on every new or £10 share, in addition to the dividend hereafter recommended; this course will give every individual of the Proprietary a due proportion of the benefit arising from the disposal of the 5,764 shares referred to, while the Company are placed in the advantageous position of having the whole 20,000 new shares duly entered on the share register, with £10 paid.[34]

Large incomes flowed into P&O's accounts when the war started in earnest and when it was over, the MDs put £100,000 in suspense for

Table 6.5 Values and reserves, 1850–51 to 1859–60 (£s)

Year	*Values*	*Reserves*
1850–51	1,176,814	465,665
1851–52	1,304,168	461,680
1852–53	1,976,558	476,679
1853–54	2,206,433	448,839
1854–55	2,246,026	460,768
1855–56	2,170,395	485,451 + 98,854 in suspense
1856–57	2,370,040	812,944 (profit from 1855,1856&1857)
1857–58	1,886,176	323,775
1858–59	2,111,921	299,494
1859–60	2,228,100	294,186

Sources: P&O/6/52, P&O/3/25–27.

the huge repairs that were left behind. Profits from the war stood at £813,944 in 1857, so the MDs were able write off 7.5 per cent depreciation instead of the usual 5 per cent, and £70,000 was shared between the Insurance Fund and the Proprietors' Underwriting Account, 'thereby maintaining the principle that the actual value of the Company's property should be fully equal to the amount of capital contributed by the Shareholders'.[35] Such profits did not last, however, as table 6.5 shows.

P&O emerged from the war into a different climate. Steamers made good transports in wartime and as P&O was more efficient than others, the Admiralty demanded more from its vessels. Then, with hardly a year gone by for repairs, there was a call for transports for the Persian Expedition at the end of 1856, then for the suppression of the Indian Mutiny in 1857. A 'severe financial crisis which agitated the commercial world' at the end of 1857 did 'not [pass] away without its disturbing effect on the Company's business'. Indeed, P&O had little time to see what was happening outside its own domain. Shipowners who had employed their ships in the Crimea were now looking for work in eastern and other seas. P&O had to keep in front of these interlopers, but it was not easy. Only nine new ships (two of them paddlers) were built for the company in 1857–60, partly because money was tight again in and after the 1857 crisis, and the MDs took to buying second-hand vessels. Anderson sold his small *Union* to the company for £7,000: he needed bigger vessels for his Union company to which the Government had granted a subsidy for the South Africa line. Hartley also had a small fleet and his *Azof*, larger and more useful, was bought by P&O for £27,500. *Ottawa*, built in 1854, was bought in February 1857 for £21,000 and *Malabar* was bought on the stocks from William Denny & Bros of Dumbarton, for £30,000. A job lot of four ships costing more than £255,000 in all was purchased from John Laird, Birkenhead: *Behar*, *Orissa*, *Ellora* and *China*, all built in 1855–56 and added to P&O's fleet in January 1859. *Columbian*, built by W Simons & Co, Glasgow, in 1855, was sold to P&O at the end of the year for £28,000, though she was found to be 'notoriously' slow.[36] P. Rolt, of the Thames Iron Co, offered *Nepaul* for £31,000; *Granada* was bought 'for not more than £24,000' from Summers & Day of Northam; and *Emeu* (built by Robert Napier, Govan, Glasgow), which after a short life with Australian Pacific Mail was sold to Cunard who chartered her to the European & Australian Royal Mail Co., finally landed in P&O's fleet at a price of £33,000.[37] All purchased vessels were modified or added to in some way or other when they came into P&O's hands, and a cheap ship would have become quite expensive by the time it was ready for sea; sometimes also the transaction would have to be cancelled because of the Admiralty's stringency. The list at the end of 1860 had 43 ships working, one ship building, 2 'under orders for India' and 7 on troop services in the China Expedition.[38]

Coals and new tonnage, 1859–65

P&O could not get back to its prime, but without a clear strategy it could not go forward either. The company, like Anderson, was tired. But passengers, whether mercantile or civil, complained about the 'vexatious slowness of the ships', exorbitant fares and freight rates. Clamorous voices damned P&O's monopoly, and Anglo-Indian newspapers and the Chamber of Commerce in Calcutta were never short of criticisms to fling at the company.[39] It was 'unsound in policy, injurious to commerce, and especially unjust to the Anglo-Indian community', and there were calls for 'the earliest opportunity' to arrange 'for the conveyance of the additional Mails, with an association entirely independent of the Peninsular and Oriental Steam Navigation Company'.

P&O was inured to hostile remarks, but 'the great rise in the cost of coal on all stations took away what little profit had been earned', and profits were also hit by a general rise in the cost of 'almost every article consumed in the outfit, repair, and navigation of the steamers' when in 1859 another war broke out between Italy and Austria, with France on Italy's side. As an indirect result of the war, which fortunately began in the spring and was over by November, P&O was given a one-year mail contract for £14,000 to carry mails between

Table 6.6 Share capital and debentures (£s) 1840–41 to 1855–56

Year	*Issued share capital*	*Debentures*
1840–41	357,240	nil
1841–42	433,230	nil
1842–43	433,230	20,000
1843–44	453,230	nil
1844–45	489,530	nil
1845–46	489,530	nil
1846–47	885,000	nil
1847–48	885,000	nil
1848–49	990,054	nil
1849–50	1,000,000	nil
1850–51	1,068,711	nil
1851–52	1,169,610	nil
1852–53	1,169,610	496,000
1853–54	1,447,405	500,000
1854–55	1,635,100	400,000
1855–56	1,641,610	290,200
1856–57	1,700,000	280,000
1857–58	1,700,000	280,200
1858–59	1,800,000	407,000
1859–60	2,000,000	458,000
1860–61	2,100,000	500,000
1861–62	2,100,000	434,200
1862–63	2,100,000	500,000
1863–64	2,100,000	498,000
1864–65	2,200,000	642,500
1865–66	2,334,605	626,500
1866–67	2,579,835	726,600
1867–68	2,700,000	800,000
1868–69	2,700,000	799,000

Malta and the British Ionian Islands. But share capital had now reached its £2,000,000 limit and the company had to have recourse again to debentures even though the rate of interest had reached 5 per cent, as table 6.6 shows.

Coals were always the largest item in P&O's running expenditure. The super-heating system, said to be economical on fuel, was in use in the late 1850s, and so as far as it had been tried, it was 'very satisfactory'.[40] P&O tried it out in 1859. Practice being 'worth all the theory in the world', Willcox told the shareholders that *Ceylon*, fitted with the new apparatus, had saved 500 tons of coal in a round voyage on the Southampton–Alexandria line, and 5 sets of the apparatus were sent out to be fitted in India.[41] At the same time, the MDs decided to try a new type of engine that would also save a considerable amount of coal. Engineers had been testing various methods, but it was John Elder, of Randolph & Elder, the Clyde engineers, who in 1854 found that expanding steam with two-cylinder engines would consume less coal, and to prove it, he sent a sea-going vessel across the Atlantic. His compound engines sustained higher steam pressure and fuel consumption was lower. Little notice was taken in Britain at first of his invention, though it was used by American companies on the Pacific side where coal was sparse. However, C.J. Mare, the Blackwall shipbuilder, was very interested in these engines, and as he was about to become insolvent at the end of 1855 he asked the MDs 'not to pass him by' should the company decide to build a ship 'for the engines constructed by Messrs Humphrys', engineers of Deptford.[42] Mare's yard was taken over by a new company, Thames Iron Works, in 1857, and the MDs did not start bargaining with Humphrys, Tennant & Co until December 1858. Mr Humphrys spoke to the MDs about 'the advantages of two cylinders per engine' and left a memo:

> The double cylinder is the most simple machine. To obtain the benefits of expansion, steam jackets and large cylinders must be employed in connection with either a separate expansion valve or an additional cylinder. The latter would be of the greatest practical value. Our engine has made 60 m revs without any apparent wear, we doubt the possibility of making any separate expansions valve do duty equal to this.[43]

Humphrys, Tennant promised to construct screw engines with a guarantee that they would not consume more than 3*lbs* of coal per ihp per hour. P&O's average consumption was about 4.5*lbs* per ihp per hour, and Andrew Lamb, now the superintendent in Southampton, thought it was worth a trial. In January 1859, the directors ordered the construction of 'a pair of engines on a new principle of such power as would best test the economy promised'.[44] The engines would be ready to be fitted in the hull, built by Thames Iron Works, in January 1860 and the engineers expressed a 'strong desire that engines be put into a ship of about 310 ft in length and 40 ft beam'. However, the length was 348 feet and after the launch in October 1860, *Mooltan* had a bumpy ride. The vessel started with difficulty in attaining 12 knots in the trials in April, and was not cleared by the surveyor until July 1861. Though allowed to make its maiden voyage, *Mooltan* had a 'derangement of machinery' when near Gibraltar that had to be repaired; and on its return to Southampton, a number of defects had to be put right. As the engineers promised, its engine consumed only half the fuel an ordinary engine would have done, and *Mooltan* was meant to be P&O's new flagship. It was 'fitted up with a solidity and splendour which had not been seen, in the finest vessel in this company'.[45] However, furniture with 'magnificent mahogany and teak' did not help the ship's unreliable engines. *Mooltan* broke down frequently and its 'great length-to-beam produced severe rolling in a cross sea'; its lifting screw (the first in P&O's fleet), steam-steering gear and hydraulic capstans were also unsatisfactory.

Records in P&O's archive say *Mooltan* 'was never a successful ship',[46] but that was a long time afterwards. In December 1861, the MDs were so glad that these new engines consumed less coal that they went ahead to order three pairs at a discount from Humphrys, Tennant for *Poonah*, *Rangoon* and *Baroda*; *Golconda* and *Carnatic* were added,[47] and all five were registered in 1863–64. Miller, Ravenhill and Salkeld (now in Newcastle) constructed engines of the same type for *Tanjore* and *Delhi*, and these were ready for sea in 1865. Of all these eight ships, *Tanjore* proved to be the most economical with a steam pressure of 25*lbs* ihp, and that shows that the technology used in its engines had improved significantly in a very short time. For the others, their machinery was 'too advanced for its time'.[48] Having spent nearly £1 million on these 8 ships, the MDs ordered 2 paddlers and one ordinary screw steamer for the company, and purchased 11 further vessels, 5 of which came from William Denny & Bros of Dumbarton, Scotland.

Notes

1 To my knowledge no relation of Henry Bayley, the MD.
2 P&O/1/101, 18.12.1846, 29.12.1846 and 5.1.1847.
3 P&O/61, Report, 5.12.45, pp. 7–8.
4 For more on the depreciation account and on P&O's accounting methods generally, see C. Napier, 'Fixed Asset Accounting in the Shipping Industry: P&O 1840–1914', *Accounting, Business and Financial History*, 1:1 (1990).
5 P&O/1/100, 19.5.1846.
6 P&O/1/101, 13.10.1846, 24.11.1846, 1.12.1846.
7 *Ibid.*, 22.3.1847. *Achilles* (992 grt, built in 1839 by Robert Steele of Greenock) was purchased in September, 1845 for Iberia, and in 1846 made the first P&O voyage in the Black Sea: P&O/65/28; P&O/6/1, Report, p. 6. *Jupiter* (610 grt, built in 1835 by Scott of Greenock) was chartered in 1847 and purchased in January 1848, for Iberian service.
8 P&O/1/101, 23.4.1847.
9 *Ibid.*, 18.5.1847, 28.5.1847.
10 P&O/6/1, Report, 8.12.1847, pp. 6–7.
11 *Ibid.*, Report, 13.12.1848, pp. 15–16; *The Annual Register*, 5.7.1849, *Chronicle*, pp. 70–2; P&O/1/102, 16.3.1849. A further prosecution was heard in the Court of Chancery (King of the Two Sicilies *v.* Willcox and Others).
12 *Shipping & Mercantile Gazette*, 16.12.1848.
13 P&O/6/1, Report, 8.12.1847, pp. 4–8; Wright, *China's Struggle for Tariff Autonomy*, pp. 50–2.

14 *PP*, 1849, 12 (571), *SC on Contract Packets*, Appendix 2 (B), pp. 214–17, 222–23.
15 In fact P&O had built a prefabricated twin-screw tug, *Atfeh*, in 1842 for service on the Mahmoudieh Canal in Egypt, but this was a specialized situation not necessarily to be taken as a precedent for deep-sea operations. I am indebted for this information to Stephen Rabson.
16 P&O/1/100, 29.4.1845; P&O/1/101, 1.12.1846.
17 P&O/1/102, 11.1.1850, 13.8.1850, 20.9.1850.
18 *Ibid.*, 24.1.1851, 31.1.1851 and 4.3.1851.
19 *Ibid.*, 14.2.1851.
20 *Ibid.*, 1.4.1851, 25.4.1851, 9.5.1851 and 16.5.1851.
21 *Ibid.*, 29.4.1851, 23.5.1851, 8.8.1851, 12.8.1851 and 30.9.1851.
22 *Ibid.*, 23.5.1851, 8.8.1851, 12.8.1851, 16.9.1851 and 30.9.1851; Miller & Ravenhill left London for Newcastle-on-Tyne between P&O's receiving *Shanghai* and *Chusan*, and set up as Miller, Ravenhill & Salkeld in a yard at Low Walker: P&O/65/102.
23 P&O/1/103, 9.3.1855.
24 *Ibid.*, 5.10.1852, 8.10.1852 and 15.10.1852; £100,000 was sanctioned in 1847 but not used; and in 1852, £400,000 was added to the £100,000 debentures to make £500,000.
25 *Ibid.*, 23.11.1852.
26 *Ibid.*, 30.11.52, 11.1.1853 and 21.1.1853.
27 *Ibid.*, 3, 23.11.1852.
28 *Ibid.*, 5.10.1852; *Herapath*, 10.12.1853, p. 1300.
29 *Ibid.*, 25.11.1853.
30 *Herapath*, 17.6.1854, p. 607.
31 P&O/6/52, Memoranda; P&O/6/1, *Report*, 6.12.1854.
32 P&O/6/1, 31.5.1855, p. 7.
33 *Ibid.*, Report, 1.12.1851, p. 6; P&O/1/102, 5.9.1851; P&O/1/103, 30.4.1852, 29.3.1853, 2.12.1853 and 17.1.1854; P&O/65/154; *ILN*, vol. 24, 21.1.1854, 27.6.1854; and vol. 25, 7.7.1854, 14.7.1854.
34 P&O/6/3, Reports, 31.5.1855, pp. 8–9, 3.6.1857, pp. 5–6.
35 *Ibid.*, Report, 5.12.1857, pp. 6–7.
36 P&O/6/1, 30.5.1859, p. 6; *Times*, 20.12.1860.
37 P&O/1/104, 13.2.1858 and 1.10.1858.
38 From 1841, every Report had a fleet list with ships' tonnage and horsepower, and, from 1843 until 1876, details of the lines on which each was employed.
39 T1 6401/A, Bengal Chamber of Commerce, 31.10.1857, pp. 4–5 ff.
40 *Herapath*, 4.6.1859, p. 564; 9.6.1860, p. 563; 8.6.1861, p. 572.
41 *Ibid.*, 9.6.1860, p. 563.
42 P&O/1/104, 1.12.1855.
43 P&O/20/5, Memo, nd (December 1858).
44 P&O/1/105, 24.12.1858, 28.1.1859.
45 *Ibid.*, 5.4.1861, 30.4.1861, 19.7.1861, 30.7.1861, 2.9.1861, 3.9.1861 and 15.10.1861; *ILN*, vol. 39, 3.8.1861.
46 P&O/65/222.
47 Five hulls of this group were built by Thames Iron Works, two by J. Samuda of Poplar, and the last by Money, Wigram, all in London.
48 P&O/65/115.

CHAPTER SEVEN

Crisis and rescue, 1853–67

As we saw in chapter 5, Anderson weathered the storm in 1854 and emerged with his position in the company enhanced. But the financial difficulties P&O faced from 1853 on give rise to the question whether the company was by this stage being well run.

Gentlemen and large sums

The 1853 contract for India and China doubled the amount of business in the company, and new vessels were always building. One might have expected to see some new senior employees about the place, especially as Anderson had taken to spending several months of each year in Egypt. Sometimes he needed to negotiate with the Pasha, and in 1859 he established a stock farm for animals and vegetables to provide fresh food for passengers, but his main reason was to escape the British winter.[1] Indeed even when he was in England, Anderson did not spend all his time on P&O, and he was chided by Dent for taking so much time with the Crystal Palace Company of which he was chairman. Anderson would have none of it: the Crystal Palace was 'a national undertaking' and it was an honour to be its chairman.[2] In fact the largest of his outside interests was the Union Steam Collier Company that he had formed in 1852. It traded in the Mediterranean with 5 small steamers on a capital of £60,000. They did well as transports during the Crimean War, and in 1856 the company was registered as the Union Steam Ship Company Ltd. After failing to break into Brazil (he and Willcox had sent their sailing vessels there in the 1830s), Anderson was granted a mail contract by the Admiralty of £30,000 per annum for 5 years to call at the Cape of Good Hope with passengers and cargo. Union Steam's board consisted of Anderson, Patrick Hadow, Thomas Hill (a merchant, agent for P&O in Southampton and Anderson's brother-in-law), and Henry Faudel, a merchant in the City. Anderson remained the chairman until his death in 1868.[3]

Anderson's outside interests disturbed P&O's shareholders, and they urged the board to elect a third MD, alongside Anderson and Allan, because Anderson was 'advancing in riches and years'. But Willcox – officially retired but who still 'attended at the office every day, [thinking] the time had not yet arrived for an alteration' – defended him: two were 'quite sufficient at present . . . There was plenty of work in Anderson.' Even if it was necessary to have another MD, the present MDs, not the board, would select him; in any case, the company's affairs 'were now well managed'.

Were they? It is difficult to say, because hard on the end of the Crimean War P&O received a succession of imperial demands from the British and Indian governments. These seemed lucrative but they distorted the company's trading. In an overview of the accounts between 1853 and 1867 (table 7.1), we see that operating expenditure was expanding faster than operating income, and from 1860 up to and including the critical year 1866–67 subsidies were being diminished.

As can be seen from column A of the table, receipts earned from trade were always less than outlays except for four years: 1856–57, 1862–63, 1863–64 and 1865–66. During the Mutiny (1856–57), transport of troops was taken as trade and receipts were £26,000 above outlays. In the other three years (1862–63, 1863–64 and 1865–66), although specie was carried in huge amounts, the surpluses were very small in proportion to the great outlays. Expenditure consisted of the cost of navigation, food for crew and passengers, ships' repairs, insurance, depreciation, and payment to the pasha for the overland transit and administration. Column D shows the size of subsidies that the Government granted; they cover outlays every year. But the dividend, the coal and facilities like coal depots, docks and repair establishments all over the East had to be paid for out of profits. The company was in a dire situation in 1853–54, 1854–55 and 1855–56; even the money from transports for the Crimean War hardly helped because in 1857–58, transports for the Mutiny and the commercial downturn brought the margin to a much lower level. Column E shows how much more the Government would have had to grant for the subsidies to cover the deficits in column C. The last year on the table speaks for itself: by 1867–68, the company badly needed to be shored up.

Dips in the market were beyond P&O's control, but businessmen at the half-year meetings also believed that the MDs were wasteful. Mr Gliddon, a shareholder and himself auditor at a 'large establishment', was amazed that P&O did not put a veto on unnecessary expenditure. In 1859, after probing the MDs, he declared that 'there

Table 7.1 Operating income and expenditure net of and including subsidies, 1846–47 to 1867–68 (£000s)

Year	*A* *Receipts*	*B* *Outlays*	*C* *A–B*	*D* *Subsidy*	*E* *C +/– D*
1846–47	302	443	–141	225	84
1847–48	491	540	–49	220	171
1848–49	490	517	–27	206	179
1849–50	493	522	–24	204	180
1850–51	592	576	–47	204	157
1851–52	577	597	–20	203	183
1852–53	716	766	–50	216	166
1853–54	1,005	1,095	–90	220	130
1854–55	1,096	1,217	–121	226	105
1855–56	1,211	1,294	–83	226	143
1856–57	1,484	1,458	+26	227	253
1857–58	1,377	1,535	–158	273	115
1858–59	1,721	1,773	–052	399	347
1859–60	1,883	2,015	–132	468	336
1860–61	1,863	1,935	–072	425	353
1861–62	1,802	1,888	–086	414	328
1862–63	1,862	1,851	+011	413	424
1863–64	1,917	1,908	+009	413	422
1864–65	1,732	1,750	–018	404	386
1865–66	1,866	1,864	+002	377	379
1866–67	1,730	2,004	–274	351	77
1867–68	1,778	2,061	–283	534	251

Source: Accounts.

must be a want of economy somewhere . . . I know that gentlemen have large sums entrusted to their care, and they go on year after year without any inquiry into the manner in which they conduct their affairs . . . Insensibly, and without any dishonourable intention at all, they are apt to sink into extravagant habits.' This home truth made Anderson very annoyed. The proprietors got a bonus with their dividend from the emoluments he and Willcox had given up, he snapped, and Gliddon 'ought not to say anything about extravagance'; and an astonished John Sylvester Godfrey said 'God bless me what are the Directors for, if the auditors are to have a veto . . . It would be simply absurd.'[4] But Gliddon might well have been on the right track for extravagance, for in November 1859, the directors resolved to start a savings drive. Nothing was done, however, until August 1861 and only in June 1862 was there movement: from 1 July all clerks were to be appointed and paid by the board rather than by the MDs. Evidently the MDs were not in a hurry.[5]

As for the MDs giving attention to expenditure, Allan had the heavy charge of machinery and navigation. Anderson, however, went on 'special missions' for the company, and due to 'occasional reasons of health' was required to be absent 'as hitherto'. As a result, Anderson restored the office of deputy chairman (filled by Hadow) in 1861, and appointed three assistants in the management department. The first was J.A. Olding, brought back from Hong Kong where he had spent several years as P&O's agent. Olding was given a long list of 'most of the detailed work' by Anderson who praised him for his 'diligence and ability'. But as Anderson was frequently away, he could not know what was going on in the department. Indeed in 1861, he confessed that since 1856 he had been 'too burdened' by duties of 'an important general nature' to be concerned with matters of detail. The second assistant was Henry Bayley; he entered P&O in 1848 as a clerk at £70 per annum, worked his way up into the management department in 1854 to reach this senior appointment – a fitting example of Willcox's image of 'a young lad, grown to young man' in the company. Anderson told the board that the directors would have to pay Olding and Bayley directly, although he would top up their salaries from his commissions if need be.[6] The third assistant was John Ritchie of the coal and stores department: his salary was £120 per annum when he first came to P&O in 1844, and he was sent out later to India where, in due course, he became superintendent at Bombay. Before joining Olding and Bayley, Ritchie was sent East again to make a hasty inspection, to see where savings could be found in the company's agencies.[7]

An observant young man, Franklin Richard Kendall, stationed in Singapore in 1861, sensed that headquarters had been doing 'some odd things lately'. Anderson was supposed to be trying to make savings in the company, but he seemed to be 'getting rather in a clique, and if you keep well with [him] all right, but if not, look out for squalls. Mr Olding is, I believe, the man nowadays.' Ritchie might be 'a great man in a great place' in 122 Leadenhall Street; his Eastern inspection showed that, although he could wield 'the pruning knife', he took 'a narrow view of things'; he did not listen to anyone or 'add anything to the company's interest or to its popularity'.[8] But Anderson thought Ritchie was 'eminently qualified for a prominent part in the management'. When Ritchie took up his appointment, Anderson put the three assistants on the same footing as the MDs in their relations with the board, 'except that they [would] not be Directors'; Olding and Ritchie were senior to Bayley.[9] As he did not want the company to bear any extra cost, he gave up his commission on the company's mail contracts, a donation which, he said, would identify his 'private interests entirely with the interests of the Shareholders at large'. By giving up huge commissions for the MDs, Anderson started to break down the wall that had divided the MDs and the board since 1840. Another sign was the discontinuance of the £1,000 paid annually by the MDs to the company as 'tenants' in no. 122.

Both Kendall and the young Thomas Sutherland, an assistant in Hong Kong, disapproved of Anderson's 'new men with high salaries', and their attitude was vindicated by the appointment in 1859 of J.C. Loch as travelling inspector in the East and superintendent in Hong Kong. Loch arrived at the time of the China Expedition when his brother, Sir Henry Loch, Governor of Hong Kong, accompanied Lord Elgin up the coast to Peking (Beijing). J.C. Loch was Remittance Man: in Kendall's words, 'an Eton boy, very well connected, vastly superior to P&O's men', someone who could stay with Lord Elphinstone at Government House in Bombay, an 'aristocrat' who moved in the 'best society'. He lacked 'the tenacity of a businessman', but he was very adept at spending money while Sutherland did all the work. When this was noticed at headquarters, Loch was sent to Madras, a minor port for P&O with not much money to play with. He soon departed, leaving a shortfall of over £1,000 in the accounts.[10]

Loch's performance notwithstanding, Anderson was confident that the 'expediency of making such preliminary arrangements' as the appointment of the three assistants would ensure 'a future efficient executive management of the Company's business upon which its continued success will so materially depend', since 'circumstances . . . at no distant period' would 'compel' him to give up the post he held. He had 'much satisfaction in knowing that there [was] an amount of practical experience, energy, and talent in the Company's establishments', and declared that P&O was 'better organized and performed more efficiently at the present time [1861] than at any former period of its progress'.[11] Observers like Gliddon might have had a different view.

Willcox's sudden death in November 1862 (he was struck by falling timber while workmen were felling a tree at Roydon Lodge, his estate in Hertfordshire, and died the following day) should have been Anderson's cue to leave the management to younger men. But Anderson believed that he was indispensable and instead saw it as his chance to become chairman, thereby adding another burden to the management department: he held the reins yet could not see what was happening in the company. Allan was overstretched, and soon Bayley was the only assistant in the management department: Olding, after 'a failure of health for a considerable time', died in September

1865, and in October Ritchie's 'unfortunate state' (he had lost his mind) barred him from working again. In this crisis, William Alexander Bethune, a Scot who had worked at P&O since 1848 and had been sent to the agency in Malta and thence to Egypt, was called back to London to work under Bayley when Bayley was made 'senior assistant'.[12] Two men from other departments were also brought in to help. But it was an illusion to think that the company was as efficient or as well-organized as Anderson believed. Though he was still a past master in negotiating a contract, his judgement was erratic.

Postal payments and non-postal services

At the end of 1860 Anderson 'had great hopes' that P&O would acquire 'an additional money subsidy'. The 1853 contract for India and China was about to end, and negotiations between the company and the Government were pending. To win the 1853 contract, P&O had reduced its favoured average monthly rate of 6*s* 2*d* to 4*s* 6*d*, but the company would not be able to sustain this rate much longer. The Government might want a competition but Anderson did not think there was much to fear on that score. No other company had as many vessels, docks and plant in the East as P&O, and there would be 'no great encouragement for any new Company to enter into a competition'. As for P&O's 'much vituperated monopoly', the company had 'attained to a position which rendered [P&O] practically secure against any attempt at a competition'. How had P&O attained it? 'Not by the favour of any government, but by their own skill and enterprise and nothing else.' Contracts were 'public benefits which entitled the Company to some consideration at the hands of the government'. Anderson would prefer a terminable arrangement of twelve months rather than a long fixed term contract, because it was impossible to say how P&O might be affected by prices in the future.[13] His statement was presumptuous. P&O's monopoly was safe as he spoke, but if prices could shift so could the safety of P&O's position.

Parliament had been debating the subsidy system in 1860 and big changes were on the table. One change was the hand-over in April of responsibility for overseas mail from the Admiralty to the Post Office, a department that was expected to be business-like and economical. Moreover, the Report of the Select Committee on Packet and Telegraphic Contracts stated that

> the responsibility of the Treasury should be complete and effective . . . The decision on Post Office contracts is not a mere Post Office question, but frequently involves considerations of an imperial character affecting our political relations, our colonial empire, the efficiency

> of our army and navy, and the spread of our commerce . . . As the management of the packet contracts is now vested in the Post Office subject to the Treasury, arrangements should be made securing to the Treasury sufficient knowledge of what is done.

Among the recommendations, new contracts 'as a general rule should be put up to open competition' and for the renewal of existing contracts, 'it is hard to reconcile the two important considerations of economy and efficiency . . . but we are of opinion that the practice of renewing contracts to existing holders has been carried to an extent which should no longer be sanctioned'.[14] Anderson went in and out of the Post Office (it was round the corner), trying to find out what was going to happen.

The MDs knew that if they did not find a way to consolidate the seven contracts they had worked so hard for – Southampton–Gibraltar/Lisbon, Southampton–Alexandria (× 2), Suez–Calcutta (× 2), Suez–Bombay, Bombay–Shanghai, Suez–Australia – the company would be broken up. Although Anderson's health was poor, he put all his energy – aided by Hadow as deputy chair and by Olding, Bayley and Ritchie in the management department – into his mission to obtain one comprehensive contract.

Having decided that the company would not take on another contract if the Government offered a similar or lower subsidy when the 1853 contract came to an end in December 1859, Anderson made it known that after that date P&O would carry on with the postal services but would not bind itself for more than twelve months. He was concerned for the future, and learnt from Frederick Hill – an assistant at the Post Office, brother of Rowland Hill of the 'one penny stamp' and secretary to Lord Stanley of Alderley, the Postmaster-General (PMG) – that the PMG intended to review the whole service. On 13 July 1860, the company received a letter from the PMG which began with the Peninsular line: it had a subsidy of £21,000 for three calls a month between Southampton and Gibraltar or Lisbon. The PMG wanted it to stop, and also a general reduction in subsidized mileage from that specified in the 1853 contract.

Anderson would not hear of it. His answer on 19 July to the PMG was: P&O had seven different contracts that the company had acquired over the years; some of the lines had not received any remuneration; the time had come for all services to be included in one contract; and a proposal of terms on which P&O would be prepared to carry on was laid out, including the Peninsular line.[15] No bending of the knee here.

Four months elapsed without a response so, frustrated and afraid that the Post Office would follow the Select Committee's Report and put the carriage of mails out to tender, Anderson decided to sharpen his knives.

Anderson had an important bargaining counter thanks to the situation that had developed in China. The largest and most long-lasting of various rebellions in China was the *Taiping*, which took its name from a military–religious society and continued from 1852 to 1864. Taipings took very little, if any, notice of the 'barbarians', and Westerners in China repaid the compliment. But they too had plans to do more than sit quietly in the same place. The five ports opened for foreigners after the first Opium War were not enough: America had started to open Japan to the West in 1854 (see below) and Britain wanted access to more ports and to China's interior. In 1856, an allegation about a Chinese owner's vessel, *Arrow*, and a British consul, and the execution of a French missionary, gave both the British and the French Government an excuse for reprisals and in March 1857 warships and troopships were set to head for China. 'As the service was of a pressing nature', P&O's agencies got supplies of coals for the Expedition. Towards the end of the year, P&O's *Ava* carried Lord Elgin (now a Special Commissioner) and his retinue up the coast while early in 1858 British and French troops captured Canton and threatened the coastal areas.[16] Elgin, the French Commissioner and American and Russian plenipotentiaries forced the Chinese authorities to sign the Tientsin Treaty in which eleven more ports were to be opened, opium legalized, Kowloon Peninsula opposite Hong Kong secured for Britain, and the emperor forced to accept the concept of international equality in trade and diplomatic relations. In Peking (Beijing), however, the Emperor refused to end China's ancient traditions, and in 1860, Elgin and his retinue went back to Peking with an enormous Expedition to kill, loot, burn the Summer Palace, and open the Yangtze River to foreign shipping. The British employed 41 warships, 143 troop transports (of which 7 were from P&O), 10,500 troops and another 2,500 in a coolie corps; the French had 60 vessels and 6,300 troops.[17]

The Expedition and the four-year run-up to it were of great public importance for Europe and the East. As there was always little travelling out of season, the single-contract China line had been quite enough for a dozen or so ordinary passengers, a handful of letters and poor cargo. But with personages like Lord Elgin and government passengers going and coming, the MDs saw a commercial opportunity, and in March 1857 set up a second service on the same line so that two calls a month were made, giving news to the public and to the Government as early as possible. The second service was 'voluntary', i.e. had no subsidy, but like the contract line it carried mails, government passengers and their baggage. So in 1860, with the Government's business in China still unfinished, P&O was still running the voluntary line and making monthly contract calls between Bombay and Shanghai, marking a contrast with the terms of the 1853 contract (twice-monthly calls between Galle and Hong Kong) of which the MDs did not wish to remind the Admiralty.

On 21 November, Anderson gave notice to the Post Office that the second (voluntary) Bombay–Shanghai line would stop on 31 December. The Government had strong reasons to fear this happening. The China Expedition had started in October and George Charles Gordon had not finished with his hostilities in Peking. Then, on 22 November, to make clear why P&O was going to discontinue that line, Anderson sent the PMG an angry letter, rubbing in the message that P&O had not received 'any remuneration whatever for that Service' and that Stanley had not given the slightest attention to a very important matter – P&O's future. A number of complaints had been laid out in Anderson's 19 July letter. The cost of coal was 'greatly enhanced' with no prospect of its reduction. The company, therefore, had to raise the rates of passage money and freight on the contract Bombay–Shanghai line (with effect from 1 January 1861), so the shareholders 'naturally look to some proportionate augmentation of the payment for the postal Service for the same object'. Extra consumption of coal to keep up the contract rate of speed and numerous other expenses attendant on fulfilling the contract increased the cost of the service while diminishing the company's capacity to earn revenues from commercial traffic:

> The tonnage and passenger accommodation taken for Mail Rooms, Sorting Rooms, Post Office parcels, Cabins for Post Officers and Admiralty Agents, their Assistants and Servants, with their provisions, the reduction of passage money on the recently greatly increased number of passengers sent by Government orders, and the extra quantities of Baggage allowed to them, the extra risk of navigation, and wear and tear of the Ships, caused by the necessity of keeping the Contract time ... spare Ships in readiness to prevent accidental interruption of the postal Service, the prevention of Economical arrangements in working the lines of Communication in the manner best adapted for developing the Commercial traffic in freight and passage money, which ... forms upwards of nine tenths of the Income of the Company, are such that the Company would suffer no financial loss by the immediate abandonment of the Postal Service.
>
> The Directors ... feel that they cannot consistently with the duty which they owe to the proprietary of the extensive enterprise with whose interests they are entrusted, subject that body to indefinite continuance of an unremunerative Service.

Anderson's letter created great trepidation and there was much running about with notes and 'verbal directions' between 122 Leadenhall Street, the Post Office and the Treasury. Anderson more than hinted that the company could easily forsake the postal services, and this idea came out in the open at the AGM in December 1861 as the question of 'whether the Company could not better carry on its ordinary business at moderate speeds without the postal subsidy than with it, supposing the Government to be so unreasonable as to refuse to give a proper amount of remuneration for the services rendered'.[18] Lord Stanley immediately gave Frederick Hill 'verbal directions' to ask P&O to withdraw the notice of discontinuation and go on working the second (voluntary) line 'in the event' that it was needed 'in the present state of affairs in China'. Next, Anderson was told that the 'new complete Contract' he had proposed was not on offer, but the PMG proposed instead that P&O should go on as at present, with the Post Office paying £2,000 for each round voyage on the non-contract China line for 6 months, and also £5,000 per round voyage for one of the 4 Southampton–Alexandria lines. P&O's reply was that the non-contract China line had formed part of Anderson's proposal in the letter of 19 July; however, to prevent any inconvenience to the public, the second set of regular monthly calls would be made as usual but only temporarily.

The Post Office then put three options to the company for a new contract for India and China, hoping the company would take up one of them; they were all thrown back. However, 'to meet the views' of the PMG as far as possible, the MDs said they would perform as before for an annual payment of £220,000 for the contract lines to India and China, and go on temporarily with the Bombay–Shanghai voluntary line at £2,000 for every complete voyage. The Post Office tried again: what reduction from £220,000 if the Government gave P&O a three-year contract? None: under existing circumstances, the directors declined to bind themselves in anything not terminable at twelve months, and all the conditions in the 19 July letter remained intact. At this point, the Post Office had nothing more to say except to advertise for tenders and a competition.[19]

For nearly two weeks, there was a flurry in the Post Office. Having taken the Admiralty's place on 1 April 1860, the Post Office did not have any experience of competitions. Frederick Hill had 'conversations' with Sir Samuel Cunard to try to learn from him. Cunard knew all about new companies: it would not be less than two years from the acceptance of tenders to the time a new company was ready to start. Building ships would take 15–18 months (he himself was having 4 ships built at that moment), then there were 3 months of trials and lastly, the time needed to get the ships on station. Cunard thought that a company that wanted 'effectually to compete for the India and China service' would require a capital of £4 million. That sum could be raised quite easily if the contractor had an 'established reputation', but Cunard was wise enough to keep out of P&O's way, even though he had that reputation himself.[20]

Back in the Post Office on 24 December, Frederick Hill, who seemed to be the most eager of the officials to have a competition, asked the Treasury for its authority to do so. The Treasury thought differently: the only way to break the deadlock was to make both sides give way *temporarily*. Though the Post Office had 'no prospect of being in a better position than at present for putting up this service to public competition', many reasons had been laid out for *not* putting the mail services out to tender. So the Treasury sanctioned the existing arrangement: the present £220,000 subsidy for India and China plus £2,000 for each round voyage on the non-contract China line and £5,000 per round voyage for one of the Southampton–Alexandria lines, though the MDs made it clear that the non-contract China line was temporary and that they would perform only for the next six months.[21]

Accordingly in April 1861, P&O and the Post Office agreed that on 30 June that year, the non-contract line would stop. However, in May a small bomb exploded. Robert Longfield, QC, MP, a Liberal–Conservative Irishman, put a question to the House about the China line, after which the news of its imminent discontinuation spread widely. Ten days later, Samuel Gregson, MP, chairman of the East India and China Association, wrote to Gladstone, the Chancellor of the Exchequer, telling him that the committee of his Association had learnt of the proposed discontinuation with great surprise and regret:

> They beg to impress upon you, the great inconvenience and annoyance such an alteration would impose upon the Mercantile Community, especially at a time when our Relations with China have become more intimate, and there is every prospect of an increasing Trade – and consequently enlarged correspondence with that Country. The Committee . . . trust that you may be induced to reconsider the matter before sanctioning such an inconvenient alteration, and they hope that you will not allow the question of the small subsidy to weigh against the favorable [*sic*] consideration of such an important object.

Gregson's members were merchants and shippers. The Expedition had made China bow to the West and his Association was looking forward to an Eldorado in the interior of China. Gladstone wanted to know how much of a fuss Gregson was really making over the China line. W.A. Stephenson told his master that he had 'heard the subject discussed on several occasions' and that people were blaming the

Government for discontinuing the Hong Kong–Shanghai line, for the second service was of great use,

> large numbers of Government Passengers having been carried by the vessels of the [P&O] Company, and no doubt political as well as military advantages secured thereby. In a Military point of view of course the same importance can no longer attach to a frequent communication with China – but politically and commercially it may be as much wanted now, perhaps as before: and it certainly appears to me doubtful policy to discontinue a service which had proved very valuable, and to which the mercantile communities in the Country and in China have become habituated at the moment when the results of our recent policy in China are about to develop themselves, [and] are watched with much anxiety. Might it not also produce a bad impression amongst the Chinese themselves?
>
> As a *mere postal Service* I apprehend it might be dispensed with, but on other, and especially political grounds, I should think it worth while to retain it for at least a time.[22]

Gladstone's only comment, however, was: 'I have some jealousy, especially after what has happened, of postal payments for non postal services.' In a letter written to the PMG in June, his views were made clear:

> I am desired by my Lords to state, for your Lordship's information, that they have caused a letter to be addressed to the [East India and China] Association stating that, having given the subject their attentive consideration, and feeling every disposition to attach due weight to the opinion of the Association, my Lords could find no sufficient reason to justify the continuance of the second mail at the cost of the State, beyond the time for which notice had been already given.[23]

But the 'no postal payments for non postal services' dictum was hastily quashed. The number of persons interested in China trades was increasing, deputations from the provinces and in Glasgow called on the Treasury, *The Times* had something to say about Australia's connection with China and two memorials were presented to the Chancellor, remonstrating against the discontinuation of P&O's second service. The Post Office was left to resolve the problem. On 9 July 1861, Sir Rowland Hill suggested that 'the expense attending the continuance . . . might be met by levying an encreased [*sic*] rate of postage' because China postage rates did not pay the cost of the packets, and 'the mode of meeting the urgent appeals of the merchants and others interested in the trades of China, Japan and Singapore appears to me to be a very proper one'. Postage of all letters sent to and received from places beyond Ceylon was doubled – letters that had cost *6d* for half of an ounce of weight now cost 1*s*, and so on for higher weights. Lord Stanley had been wanting to raise the price of postage in the East anyway, and this was now 'a fair opportunity' for doing it; and, to be even-handed, he included Australia and New Zealand too. In August, Sir Rowland Hill had huge posters printed so that the public could see the new rates of postage.[24]

P&O remained on the outside while the Treasury and Post Office were 're-establishing' the second line and was surprised when, at the end of July, the government agreed to 'the sudden resumption of the double service', the terms being £24,000 for 12 voyages per annum. There is no evidence to show that the company and Gregson's Association worked together, but P&O was sufficiently well-known to the people whose business was affected by communication to and from China for the Association to have taken up their cause without the company's prompting. Gladstone did not like to be beaten by Gregson, but he was glad that the £24,000 per annum for P&O's second line was to be paid for by the public, not by the Government. But P&O had nonetheless won that round.

However, three young officials talking in private on 16 November 1860 – W.A. Stephenson of the Treasury, W. William Page, assistant to the secretary in the Post Office, and Clifton from the Admiralty – had recognized P&O's importance before all the sparring of December that year broke out. Stephenson believed that if a competition were held, any newcomer who won a parallel line to P&O's would face an uphill struggle. P&O would not allow any part of its domain to be given to another company. A steamer needing to anchor at night at Suez could not do so because the light-ship was P&O's private property; the company 'held almost the only available space for coaling in the harbour of Pointe de Galle', and it had facilities at Aden and Singapore 'which no other Company could enjoy except at enormous expense'.[25] The Government would therefore certainly 'fail in the attempts [to reduce the cost of mails] and be obliged . . . to place the Service again in the hands of [P&O] on any terms they choose to dictate'. So after the Treasury had agreed to P&O's proposal of £220,000 plus remuneration for Southampton–Alexandria and the non-contract China line, at the end of a long document about P&O and the contracts the PMG added the words of Page, Stephenson and Clifton at William Page's request:

> I must not conceal from your Lordships the serious apprehension which I entertain that no Tenders may be received either from the Peninsular and Oriental Company, or from other responsible persons able to commence the service on the expiration of the present Contracts, and that the Department may be driven at the eleventh hour into making terms

> with the present Contractors [P&O] in order to prevent a total interruption of the service. But this is a difficulty which must, sooner or later, be overcome, unless the perpetual monopoly of the Indian Service be given to the Peninsular & Oriental Company, and it appears to me that the Department had better encounter it on the present occasion, rather than consent to pay what, in reality, would be a higher subsidy for a smaller service, without in any way improving its position for throwing open the service to general competition.[26]

These were serious words, but no one took the 'present occasion' to confront the problem because the Government did not know how to approach this gargantuan task. The fundamental questions affecting P&O's future remained unanswered.

A slippery slope

As clouds were gathering on the horizon for P&O, huge amounts of specie, both gold and silver, were being shipped by the company to Egypt, India and China. This was not a new cargo for P&O, but demand for this cargo increased thanks, indirectly, to the American Civil War, peaking in 1864 and then running down rapidly thereafter. Because of the Civil War (1861–65), the accustomed exports to Britain of raw cotton from the southern states were blocked by the north. While Lancaster's mills were shut and workers starving, cotton regions in Egypt and India suddenly came to life. Egypt's bales fetched 'fabulous' prices,[27] as did Indian cotton taken round South Africa, while Bombay cotton was the first bulk cargo to be taken on the overland route from India because the price was high enough to make it worthwhile. Specie was sent out to pay for the precious staple, and as the price of cotton soared, new banks and companies sprang up like mushrooms. Bombay became the busiest port in the East. A sea of shares swirled about, with frenzied speculators pushing up prices, even though many, like the notorious Back Bay reclaiming project, turned out to be worthless paper.

The profit expected at 122 Leadenhall Street from the carriage of specie was diminished from 1862 by the Compagnie des Services Maritimes des Messageries Impériales (MI). Hitherto, French vessels carrying specie as far as Alexandria would hand it over to P&O to be transhipped eastwards. Now, MI, using the Egyptian railway which was open to all, began to ply east of Suez itself with a twenty-four year contract with the French Government and an enviably large subsidy. Although the two companies were on good terms on the surface, P&O was afraid of this interloper, for MI broke the monopoly on P&O's China line, and the two companies competed both for specie outward and for silk home. It was inevitable that the newcomer would try to poach passengers from P&O and to compete for specie from Marseilles by charging a lower rate of freight. (The MDs used to have one rate for both Southampton and Marseilles, and when they took off 0.5 per cent at the French port to match MI, Rothschild and other merchants objected and said they would send all their specie via France, so P&O had to revert to the usual rate for both ports.[28]) P&O still had advantages over the French: MI made 12 round voyages a year to China, whereas P&O made 24, and the French did not touch Bombay at all. MI, however, made return voyages in a shorter time because its ships went straight to Suez, and this enabled French cargoes of silk to corner the market in Lyons. Moreover, French steamers were new and much larger than the vessels P&O sent to the China Seas, and the difference showed.

The trend in table 7.2 shows that in the shipment of specie the French company was catching up with P&O at Marseilles because of MI's lower rate of freight.

Rumours in 1864 about peace in the USA made speculators jittery, and when the war ended in February, mayhem broke out in Bombay. Shares of all sorts became useless overnight; and, as quickly, banks, firms and individuals found themselves bankrupt. Francis Lidderdale, senior partner in Jardine, Matheson & Co. (this concern was unscathed because its partners kept out of the speculation) tracked the crash in Bombay: on 22 April, 'we shall have a very serious crisis here'; a week

Table 7.2 P&O and MI, value (£000s) of specie outward, by port, 1861–70

	P&O		*MI*	
	Southampton	*Mediterranean*	*Marseilles*	*Total: all ports*
1861	762	?	?	10,288
1862	11,855	?	?	18,168
1863	11,386	6,231	3,837	21,454
1864	8,217	8,330	7,770	24,317
1865	4,177	4,588	5,167	13,932
1866	2,853	3,798	3,379	10,030
1867	902	1,711	1,043	3,656
1868	3,214	4,475	2,499	10,188
1869	3,860	4,965	1,126	9,051
1870	3,195	938	371	4,504

Source: India Office Archive, V/17/1, *Annual Statement*, no. 18, *Total Value of Gold and Silver from Southampton and Marseilles, through the Mediterranean to the East.*

later, the market 'has been quite upset by the state of panic and general distrust'; in the middle of May, 'the monetary crisis has since increased in a very serious extent'; and in June, 'it is impossible for me to describe the state of panic & stoppage of business . . . I do not see what is to become of Bombay unless confidence is in some measure restored'. The Back Bay shares went down from Rs45,000 to Rs2,500, 'absolutely unsaleable' with all the others.[29]

Britain was not immune to the effects of the American war, nor was P&O. Both abroad and at home, inflation was soaring. Prices of naval stores and coal rose, and there were demands from all directions for higher wages. In Bombay and the main ports in the East, and in London and Southampton too, there were demands for higher wages. The company had to bend to them or lose trained employees. Moreover, whether bought on the stocks or built for the company, ships had to be paid for. At the same time money was held back and trading stopped. Long before the peace, P&O was in a very vulnerable situation. Anderson blamed the Post Office (since 1861 in charge of all mail contracts), saying that mail contracts debarred P&O from working in more economical ways. True, but that was the nature of mail contracts. Shareholders were not satisfied. The 1863 AGM was 'most tiresomely extended' by proprietors who wanted 'to know too much'. Mr J. Jones argued heatedly with Anderson about diversification, asserting that P&O would be ruined if it did not change its first-class-only passenger policy. Mr Gliddon chimed in, claiming that there were hundreds of second-class people knocking at the doors of other companies which were making a profit out of them, whereas P&O had made 'no progress of business for the last five years'; capital had increased by more than £300,000, while the value of the ships stood still. Anderson's answer was that 'it would be disagreeable for the higher class of folks to be elbowed by such vulgar people'. In fact, there were berths for servants, artisans and a few 'respectable' people who had run out of money, but these were never advertised and were a very small proportion of the first-class passengers. Anyway, Anderson did not like to be told what to do: he had been a MD since 1840 and he knew 'how to manage the affairs of the company as well as [Gliddon] and with tolerable success'.[30]

By 1865 the situation was much worse. P&O was 'badly affected by stagnant business' in India and China, silk freights were falling off, there was 'almost total cessation of specie shipped outward' and the company was unable to reduce its expenditure to match. On top of this blow came the Government's decision to transport regiments to and from India in its own vessels, which, when they were built, would take some government passengers from P&O's berths. Anderson, who was usually in good spirits at meetings, adverted to the 'extraordinary mortality' in the company that year: 31 men had died, from Olding in the management department to 5 stewards at sea; and to round off the 'melancholy' Report, *Corea* disappeared in a typhoon in Chinese waters with 103 persons on board, by far P&O's biggest loss for the whole period from 1840 to 1914.[31] Gliddon's eagle eye spotted the £66,000 that directors found 'to prop up the dividend' of 9 per cent. He said they 'were doing an unwise thing' and he warned the proprietors that 'it was their duty to watch the judgment with which the Directors conducted their affairs'. Gliddon accused the board of trusting, like Dickens's Mr Micawber, 'that something would turn up'; but, 'unless there was some greater energy put forth, something would "turn up" greatly to their disadvantage'. But nothing was done. That 'greater energy' of the 1840s and 1850s was not there any more.[32] Then in May 1866, shock waves spread all over the country when Overend Gurney, one of the most respected firms in London, collapsed. This was followed in June by 'Black Friday', the steepest fall in the stock market since 1825. Many firms were brought down and by the end of the year it was clear that this was 'a commercial crisis of unprecedented severity and duration', not only in this country, but throughout the East. Ordinary business ceased and P&O felt 'great stagnation of trade'. Having risen to a short-term high of £81 during the American Civil War, the company's share price fell. Another ship – *Jeddo* – was lost near Bombay, two directors – Nairne and Plowden – died and a third – George – left for his post in Ireland. One might have thought that the company was indeed about to collapse, though Bayley's appointment as MD gave Allan the help he badly needed and George Carleton l'Estrange and Edward Thornton came on to the board.[33]

As share prices went down, debentures went up. The MDs went to the Treasury to try to ease the situation, and on 7 February 1867 they were granted the fourth supplemental charter for a new £1 million of share capital, while £300,000 debentures were added to the previous £500,000. Again, debentures were taken up very quickly to the new limit of £800,000. With Anderson ill again in June 1867, Hadow had to acquaint the shaken proprietors at the half-year meeting with the damage P&O had sustained and to try to stop them from throwing their shares into the market. There would be no dividend declared in that meeting, and there was little hope of a dividend in December. Sweetening the bad news as much as he could, he cobbled together a list of half-true statements. There was no need for anxiety: the current expenditure on repair and maintenance was 'unusual', he said (as if it had suddenly risen to £439,400, the highest ever), but he knew very well that it had been mounting up for years. As for the state of the fleet, his version was that the ships were 'as good as new in many respects', but in fact there were too many old and out-of-date vessels that were responsible for much of the expenditure. There was the depreciation too; no money could be set aside for it this year, but no matter, the fleet was 'in a perfect state of efficiency'. Moving away from these combustible matters, he thought that although P&O's position 'might not perhaps look so bright as upon some former occasions' and the dividends could not be as good as at other times, the company was 'sound and satisfactory'! Anderson sent a message to the meeting from his sick-bed: he was holding on to his 800 shares and urged them not to sell their shares because 'the history of such commercial vicissitudes' were usually cyclical; to no avail, however, as we can see in table 7.3. Loyalty was fragile: the shares dropped sharply from £60 in June to £50 in December on average. *Herapath* stated that shares that stood at £70 in January 1867 fell to £40 in June.[34]

'Important national interests' v. the bottom line

Anderson's refusal in 1860 to get locked once again into a contract for several years unless a more advantageous way of working the contract could be found was a stroke of foresight, and the extraordinary amount of specie carried in the early 1860s allowed P&O to bump along under the short-term arrangements agreed with the Treasury. But by 1866 time and money were running out. P&O 'gave private notice [to the Post Office] that the company could not go on losing money as they

Table 7.3 Average prices (£s) of P&O paid-up £50 shares, 1861–70

Year	*June*	*December*
1861	64.76	69.64
1862	69.75	73.80
1863	76.08	81.88
1864	81.12	80.69
1865	81.64	74.93
1866	70.42	63.43
1867	60.22	50.76
1868	57.14	53.26
1869	48.63	46.15
1870	43.80	44.70

Source: *Economist*, 1860–1914. *Economist* started a weekly share list in October 1860.

were doing'; if the Government did not give notice for determination of the twelve months' arrangement, P&O 'must give notice to the Government' so that the company could bargain for a much better subsidy.[35]

Anderson tried to persuade the then Postmaster-General, the Duke of Montrose, 'to arrange the terms for carrying out [a new contract] by private negociation', but the reply was short and negative: His Grace was debarred by the Commons from negotiating with Anderson without a competition even if he thought it expedient. So Anderson gathered what energy he had for important interviews while a small group consisting of Hadow, Allan, Howell and Bayley set out to save their company.[36] Fearing that P&O might be wound up in the new year, Howell published a *Statement of the Position and Operation of the Company from its Incorporation to the Present Time*, a history of more than seventy pages full of P&O's exploits and achievements. It was circulated in time for the 1866 AGM to mark the company's twenty-fifth anniversary (in 1865), but really to make known what P&O had done since 1840 and what the public would be deprived of if the Government refused to bail the company out. As there were 2,122 shareholders, some of them MPs and other persons in high places, it reached a wide and influential public.

Howell's *Statement* was also important because P&O had been thoroughly grilled in a Select Committee. This was the doing of Robert Wigram Crawford, MP for the City of London and a Liberal. In February 1866, he moved for a Select Committee to be set up on East India Postal and Telegraph Contracts. He had lived in Bombay for fourteen years as a partner in Crawford, Remington & Co., and returned to London a few months before the commercial crash in 1847–48 to take up a partnership in Crawford, Colvin & Co., East India Merchant & Agents.[37] Thomas Matthias Weguelin, MP (Wolverhampton, Liberal), a director since 1858, represented P&O at the Select Committee; and because Anderson was in Egypt, Howell was called several times to give evidence in this 'very searching inquiry'. Robert Knight, editor in Bombay of the *Times of India*, spoke on behalf of the British India Steam Navigation Co., Ltd (BI), formed in 1856 as the Calcutta & Burmah Steam Navigation Co., but reconstituted and renamed in 1862 and working in Indian waters. Knight asserted that BI would work a contract for India and China better than P&O, and complained of P&O's inefficiency and the slowness of the mails, but his evidence was contrived and he had little knowledge of shipping. After criticizing almost everything about P&O, Knight was asked by Weguelin if he thought the French MI was better. Knight's response was 'most unquestionably not; I do not want to throw the slightest reflection upon the Peninsular & Oriental Co; I believe that they perform their contract service, and that they keep to time; but the contract itself is what I complain of, as being an improper contract, and I have no doubt that the Peninsular & Oriental Co would be delighted to enter into a new one'. Although there was criticism from other quarters, Howell came out with 'credit and approbation'.[38]

Crawford had moved for this Select Committee because the Liberal Government wanted, as we have seen, to reduce the growing expense of mail contracts. In 1860, mail contracts cost a total of nearly £1 million per annum, while the Post Office's revenue from postage was only one-third of that sum,[39] and Frederick Hill, assistant to the PMG, was anxious to make up the loss. Another reason for holding the Select Committee was the development of the Indian railways. A network of lines constructed to radiate from Bombay was almost finished and both Indian and British Governments had agreed to make Bombay the mail port for the whole country. In consequence, the Select Committee recommended the Government to set up 'an express service, entirely unconnected to the eastward of Suez with any other mail services' for a line to and from London and Bombay. Tenders should be either for 'the entire service to and from Bombay or for the sections to the east and west of Egypt separately'. It was also suggested that MI might be able to help P&O with the China line, but the wording of this recommendation was so obscure that it could be interpreted in many ways. Moreover, 25 per cent of the total value of British produce and manufactures came from or was sent to the East and merchants, bankers and others engaged in these vast operations called for more tonnage and greater speed. P&O's fifty-seven steamers had performed well under several contracts and no mail had ever been lost, but Howell agreed that their ships 'had not come up to their own expectations'. P&O's average speed east of Suez was 9.5 knots; under the new contract, vessels were to perform at 11 knots, but that meant more coal and more money. Joseph D'Aguilar Samuda, Liberal MP for Tower Hamlets and a London shipbuilder – he had built some of P&O's vessels – told the Committee that 44 tons of coal a day would be consumed at the slower speed and 60 tons at the faster. However, the Committee recoiled from assenting

> to the doctrine, that interests so important from every point of view, whether political, social, or commercial, as those which connect the United Kingdom with the largest and most valuable possessions of the Crown, should be prejudiced by an insufficient postal service . . . A question of profit or loss, within reasonable bounds, is a consideration entitled to little weight in the case of so important a postal service as that between England and India.[40]

The view expressed here by the Select Committee was not new. An earlier parliamentary Report[41] had stated that a mail contract was 'not a mere Post Office question, but frequently involves considerations of an imperial character affecting our political relations, our colonial empire, the efficiency of our army and navy, and the spread of our commerce'. And again, in 1865, Sir Charles Wood (now at the India Office) had insisted that the 'profit and loss' system should not be applied to India because increased postal communication meant 'growth in commerce, greater investment of English capital and more English settlement in that country . . . from all these sources came the wealth and prosperity of England'.[42]

However, by the time Crawford's Select Committee ended in July 1867, Russell's Liberal Government had been voted down to be replaced by Derby's minority Tory ministry with the Duke of Montrose at the Post Office, Disraeli as Chancellor of the Exchequer and George Ward Hunt Financial Secretary to the Treasury. The Tories had been out of government since the summer of 1859, so none of them had experience of the new regulations for mail contracts that came into force in 1861. Hunt was a genial man 'more than six feet four inches in stature, but did not look so tall from his proportionate breadth'.[43] In this rickety Government, he wanted to show the public that the Tories were not as prodigal as they were said to be. Crawford's colleague Hugh Culling Eardley Childers (MP for Pontefract, Hunt's predecessor as Financial Secretary and a member of the 1866 Select Committee) was particularly keen to see his policy of financial rigour carried out. According to P&O's director G.C. l'Estrange, it was well known that Hunt intended to follow the Liberal Party's recommendations for the new mail contract, a road 'most disastrous to our Company'.[44]

On 1 February 1867, notice of termination was served on P&O for the India and China lines: tenders would be sent out in June, and the new contract would start in February 1868. Hunt, having indeed invited 'all the world to tender', expected a fair competition. In June, Childers asked him whether he had made any overtures to the French Post Office and Hunt answered that he had sent out forms of tender and 'it was hoped that the 'Société Impériale [i.e. MI] might be induced to make an offer'.[45] Unknowingly, he thereby ignited a slow explosive. P&O's shareholders were outraged. A Dr Beattie said it was 'an unpatriotic and very questionable proceeding to solicit a foreign Company to compete with English shipowners to convey English mails to English colonies . . . Richard Cobden, with his earnest efforts for free trade, would not have contemplated such a thing.' It was a most mischievous proposition, said J. Jones, and if carried out it would 'make the English people play second or third fiddle to the French everywhere in the East'. If English commerce was to be handed over to French ships, 'why not invite the French to carry on the entire business of the English Post-office, on the ground that they might do it cheaper . . . perhaps at half price', but he hoped it would be many years yet before such 'liberal and unpatriotic' measures; and several other men 'entered their indignant protest against such a proposal'.[46] P&O sent a memorial to the Treasury 'with considerable surprise and alarm', praying that no contract be made with a 'powerful Foreign Government'; its enterprise and resources would seriously damage P&O, if not ruin it. To subsidise and employ MI would not only be 'unjust and highly detrimental' to the British company, but also 'impolitic' for 'important national interests': the French Government was increasing its commercial and political interests in the East. As for 'loss' and 'fiscal sacrifice' in postal communications, they were trifling when compared with the wealth and industry that P&O had created. Hunt was clearly checked by these arguments, for though he covered himself by saying that it was the duty of the Government to open a competition to the public without reference to nationality, to persons or companies 'inclined to submit offers for the whole or any portions of the services', he added that the Government was not bound to accept the lowest or indeed any tender, and would only look for the most advantageous arrangements.[47]

Parliament would not be in session on the 16 September deadline for the submission for tenders, so in July the Post Office asked the MDs if P&O would go on as before for another 6–12 months at a 'reasonable' price so that the new contract could be presented to the next session of Parliament. The MDs, however, were not in a mood to help the Post Office. They knew from an 'authentic source' that MI was about to start a line between China and Japan which would give the French 'the carrying trade of the East'. P&O would not make any tender for the remaining portion of the current contract 'except at a very considerably enhanced cost'. The cost worked out at £563,000 per annum.[48]

This appeared to be an exorbitant sum indeed. Crawford, Childers and many other Liberals came to the House on 1 August to see the explosive go off. The occasion was the Committee on Supply (Civil Service Estimates) for the following financial year, which of course included the new contract for India and China, and the most curious debate took place about P&O and the contract. Crawford declared that there was 'a question of grave national policy involved in our maintaining these great lines [P&O, Cunard and Royal Mail] of Packet services' and that the nation should protect them. He denied that he was speaking for P&O: 'I have not anything to do with that Company; I never had, and am not likely to have, anything to do with it.'[49] But there was nothing to stop him from talking to people in it: almost certainly, Crawford had been in touch with Weguelin or Anderson or Hadow, all of them Liberals, and he and his friends had come to knock Hunt off his perch. Crawford told the assembled members that P&O had to work its lines at the rate of 4*s* 6*d* per mile while MI had 20*s* per mile. Was that a fair competition? The 1866 Recommendation of Crawford's Select Committee suggested only that MI might be asked to alter some of its departures from Marseilles, not to replace P&O, and he protested against any action that would 'saddle this country with a contract either with the Messageries Impériales or any other foreign company'. Such a course would be 'contrary to public policy and unfair and unjust to the Peninsular and Oriental Company'. Moreover, it would be 'an act of political insanity for us to put such a weapon into the hands of any foreign Government whatever nor should we employ them in the conveyance of our Eastern mails'. The Tory Government's disposition was 'to follow the principle of economy' which gave foreign companies the power of competing with British steam companies. But, Crawford argued, 'You may carry the principle of economy too far. Such a course of proceeding would be Free Trade gone mad.' Crawford gave the Government 'proper warning . . . that if we find that a contract had been entered into with the Messageries Impériales, we shall then avail ourselves of the Resolution which the House recorded in July 1860, under which no contract is to take effect until it has . . . [been] approved by a direct Resolution of the House', knowing very well that if the contract was challenged, the Tories could be voted out.[50]

Several other members took up the cry. Childers had no special sympathy for P&O, he said, but it would be 'most inexpedient for this country to enter into a contract . . . with a foreign company'. He regretted that the Tories had not complied with the Liberals – a bit rich, given that Hunt had set out to mimic what he took to be Liberal policy – or if they had done so in letter, they had 'departed from them in their spirit'. He reminded Hunt that there could only be one company east of Suez. If it was to be P&O 'which has done its work remarkably well', no other company would be able 'to compete with it on anything like an equal footing'. Samuda picked on Hunt because 'without reference to nationality' Hunt had taken 'a most ruinous policy'. Moreover, the House should not forget the enormous advantage Britain had with P&O's 'magnificent fleet' – an undeserved compliment – nor that 'the quality of a tender [was a] more [important] consideration than actual price and in no case more so' than in P&O's. During a quarter of a century, P&O had spent something close to £3 million on vessels and the establishments to maintain them. If the Government were 'suddenly and violently to stop its operation as a mail company', the vessels would not fetch more that £1 million. Why waste that money? The subsidy paid to P&O should be seen as money given by the Post Office for the nation.[51]

Samuel Laing (MP for Wick, Secretary to the Treasury in 1859–60 and then Finance Minister for five years in India) was afraid that the Government did not 'fully appreciate the gravity of the issue involved'. By asking the French to tender, the Government might have to give 'important portions or . . . [the] whole of the service to that foreign Company'. The French Government would be pleased because it had established MI 'especially with a view to acquiring political influence in the East . . . [and] showing the French flag at as many points as possible'. With his experience in India, he could not think of 'a course of policy more disastrous to the security of our Indian Empire' than that which the current Government had proposed:

> Look at the political interests and prestige involved in the question. I am not one of those who attach an exaggerated importance to what is called 'prestige' . . . [But] when all the steamers that enter the ports of the East are seen to carry the French flag, then I say there is nothing so dangerous to the prestige of the English name . . . [We will see] that the French flag has taken the place of the English. There is nothing . . . that tends so surely to keep up the name and the influence of England in the East as the sight of those splendid steamers coming and going with the regularity of clock-work . . . And I say that to put up these contracts to tender when no real competition is possible, is simply a device for sheltering departments of the Government from responsibility, and is not conducive to the best and most economical result.

It was preposterous to look at the contract simply as an issue of profit and loss in the narrow way some Post Office officials (like Frederick Hill) did. His conclusion was that the Government should support P&O. You cannot afford to try experiments and run risks: 'your first object must be to deal with a company which, you are sure, has capital, power, experience and [is] able to do the work successfully'.[52]

Hunt was taken aback by these put-up tirades. As he had very little time to deal with the new contract, he thought he would be playing safe by following the 1866 Select Committee's Recommendation on MI and had used MI to give a signal that he would be setting up a proper competition. This mistake gave the Liberals a chance to make him look ridiculous. The Opposition was only too happy to show the House that the Tories were unable to run a government. Hunt defended himself as well as he could in the circumstances. He acknowledged that he had advertised very widely for tenders because 'the text book' (the Report of the 1860 Select Committee) commanded it. Having done so, 'were we to say, as is done in advertising for servants, that "no Irish need apply", that "no French need apply"? . . . We would not exclude French, or even Chinese or Japanese, if they choose to come forward.' But Hunt had to bow to the House: somehow 'an impression [had] got abroad that it was the desire [of the Government] to hand over the whole of the services to India and China' to MI if its tender was lower than P&O's, 'but', he assured the House, 'the Government never contemplated anything of the kind'. Montrose had to give a similar assurance to the Lords.[53]

The daily press and the journals had field-days in August: no doubt the Liberal editors were fed by the Liberal MPs, enjoying the opprobrium piled on Hunt and the Tories, and P&O tacked the 'Opinions of the Press' to the annual Report in December. However, Hunt still maintained that if P&O and MI were to convey mails in alternate fortnights, 'it would relieve both governments from a high subsidy . . . [and be] far more economical than the present'; he would arrange it 'if the House [does] not object'.[54]

No vote was taken in the Supply debate, and the deadline for tenders had still not expired. However, the Liberals had won the first round and reminded Hunt that the Tories were a minority ministry.

The turning point

In the two years before 1867, there had been two portentous changes in Britain's international position that called in question the country's status as a great power for the first time since 1815. The end of the American Civil War presaged the growth of a giant across the Atlantic, and in the following year the Prussian victory at Sadowa after the unprecedented and almost unbelievable course of the Seven Weeks' War proved that a new power was emerging on the continent of Europe. Britain had to face the fact that, in the age of armed peace now begun, it could claim no place among the great military powers. Its constitution stood in the way of a large conscript army, and what forces the country had were scattered all over the world and were glaringly deficient in organization and antiquated in style and equipment. Paradoxically, the most advanced industrial nation was the least able to wage a modern war. Unless Britain found other ways of maintaining itself as a great power, its international position would be irreparably damaged. The best course was to base its future unequivocally on its strength in trade and on its naval power. National greatness must therefore rest on imperial possessions.[55]

The change of government in 1866 gave Disraeli, the effective leader of the Tory ministry, a chance to bring this national need into the political arena and to act on it. In his re-election speech in 1866, he gave an incisive account of the position less than a fortnight after Sadowa:

> England has outgrown the continent of Europe . . . England is no longer a mere European Power; she is the metropolis of a great maritime empire, extending to the bounds of the farthest oceans. It is not that England has taken refuge from a state of apathy that she . . . declines to interfere in the affairs of . . . Europe . . . England is as ready and willing to interfere as in the old days . . . There is no Power, indeed, that interferes more than England. She interferes in Asia . . ., in Australia, in Africa, and in New Zealand.

Shortly afterwards he urged the Earl Derby, the Prime Minister, to bring this orientation – greatness through imperial power – into government policy to set at rest public anxiety about foreign affairs. 'Power and influence we [should] exercise in Asia', he wrote, 'consequently in Eastern Europe, consequently also in Western Europe', the focus on Egypt, India and the East being what necessity dictated. As Chancellor, he saw that 'essential economies' must be made in the Atlantic and on the west coast of Africa so that the Government had savings for new ships without the liability of additional taxation, for it was above all necessary to spend money on Britain's primary defence.[56]

The year 1866 was a bad one for many reasons and for many people, but in July 1867, with the Second Reform Bill all but passed after years of argument, Disraeli's vision of the 'metropolis of a great maritime empire' became a reality for the citizens of London. It began with the Sultan visiting London, followed shortly by another visit from his vassal Khedive Ismail, the Viceroy of Egypt. Both notables had been invited to Paris for the International Exhibition by Napoleon III. Derby was 'alarmed' to hear that the Sultan's reception had been 'of the most magnificent description', and that of the Viceroy much the same. The British Government saw political significance behind all the imperial pomp and show in Paris, so, not wanting Britain to be upstaged, persuaded a very reluctant Queen Victoria to entertain the foreign dignitaries. Then, once the holiday mood took hold, institutions and individuals came forward to help make the whole effort worthy of a great city, while government officers rushed about, seeing to processions, banquets, balls, fêtes, receptions, illuminations and ceremonial calls every day from the first state visitor's arrival on 6 July till the departure of the second one eighteen days later. Nothing on such a scale had ever been witnessed before. It was an 'uninterrupted succession of spectacles and entertainments' which even the poorest could stand and stare at as the colourful pageants went by several times a day. London was proud to show itself and the world that imperial pomp and ceremony came as easily to the English capital as it did to Paris. Heads were held high.[57] London was a metropolis; its focus was Egypt and the East.

Having become newly aware in July of the imperial mantle resting on their shoulders, MPs and others who read the newspapers woke up to find that their refurbished nation had not only a great empire but also a symbol to go with it – P&O's 'splendid steamers'[58] which called regularly at ports all over half the globe. And, fortuitously, those ships were about to give the world an example of their work. A tortuous dispute of several years with King Theodore, the ruler of Abyssinia, gave the Government an excuse for a convenient act of aggression: it could be safely undertaken because it would not provoke the Great Powers, and yet it would also show an efficient army and – though more a military exercise than a war – win a battle. The Abyssinian Expedition was officially announced in September, after the parliamentary session was ended. 12,000 troops, British and Indian, were transported to the Abyssinian coast. P&O hired vessels to the Indian Government and to the Admiralty for the purpose, and sold 70,000 tons of coal immediately, with more to come from the company's depots at Alexandria, Suez, Aden and Bombay. In addition, large supplies of water for the troops while they were in the arid terrain of Abyssinia were produced by P&O's powerful condenser at Aden.

To ensure the Expedition served its purposes, it was conducted in a blaze of publicity. The new Snider rifles were used by the British soldiers for the first time, and the Indians were equipped with Enfields, a much better weapon than the matchlocks and muskets of the enemy. Not one man on the British side was killed. An explosion of praise greeted the successful outcome. Disraeli declared that the Expedition had 'elevated the military [and moral] . . . character of England through the world'; the *Economist* believed the exploit added 'immensely to the strength of the nation'; and a commemorative medal was struck to mark the 'national exultation' over the re-establishment of Britain as a great power in the world. Afterwards, Select Committee inquiries held into the Expedition referred to P&O as the 'natural resource' for the 'appliances and facilities' that enabled the 'war' to go ahead as planned.[59] As in the Crimea and elsewhere, P&O demonstrated its 'great national value in times of emergency'.

Saved

We must now go back to the end of July 1867 to see what happened to P&O and the mail contract. Crawford's strong objection to foreign companies taking British mail was a balm for the MDs, but their offer of £563,000 per annum for an extension of 6 months was, in the Post Office's view, 'exorbitant'. The Duke of Montrose told the Treasury he could not go to Parliament with 'so large an addition' to P&O's current subsidy unless it was 'clearly shown, by public competition, [that] such an addition was absolutely necessary'. But where would another 'substantial company' with 'full means' and time to build for the service be found? P&O's current rate of payment was 4*s* 6*d* per nautical mile and it was demanding 10*s*. With a few extra calls, the subsidy would indeed be about £563,000, and this was 'already far from self-supporting'. But Montrose realized that if the excessive sum turned out to be the lowest subsidy 'for which responsible contractors' would undertake to perform the service, he could not object; the only question was whether the service could be modified.[60]

While P&O was basking in the praise that was by then being heaped on it in Parliament for its part in the Abyssinian Expedition, the MDs were determined that the tender should be the only one received at the Post Office on 16 September. They made a fuss about MI even though the French company showed no interest in competing with P&O. But the smaller BI was more problematical. Only just over ten years old,[61] this enterprising company held contracts from the Indian Government that gave it the monopoly of steam shipping along the coast from Karachi to Singapore. William Mackinnon, its chairman, was interested in the Bombay-Suez section of the service for he would be able to extend it to England once the Suez Canal was opened, and the Post Office thought that 'the service is of so moderate an extent that it is likely that [BI] may be willing to undertake it'. However, some months before September, Mackinnon and James Macalister Hall, a director, met Allan and other directors of P&O to make 'verbal proposals' for 'arrangements between the two companies' that would be 'advantageous to both parties'. There were then several meetings and exchanges of letters between them. BI wished to maintain and extend friendly relations with P&O but was concerned that the new contract, if P&O were to win it, might 'possibly lead to competition between the Companies for the traffic on the Coasting part' of P&O's lines. In response, P&O assured BI that there was no danger of competition: the two companies always had different freight rates – P&O's was higher than BI's – and if they carried on like that, their friendship would continue. To refrain from 'prejudicial measures towards each other', both parties agreed that they would not make a formal agreement. However, on 28 August, BI's directors discussed whether they should send in a tender themselves. They concluded that their vessels would not be able to compete on the Bombay–Suez line with P&O and MI. Those companies had large ships and carried passengers; BI was not familiar with that type of work and did not have the resources required to perform efficiently and adequately. In any case, if BI did win the Bombay–Suez line, P&O would oppose it by running steamers on BI's coastal lines from Calcutta to Burma 'where greater damage would be inflicted than could be made up for by any advantages on Bombay–Suez'; and even if BI tendered and failed, P&O's hostility 'might still be aroused, with similar retaliation'. So, after very careful consideration, BI's directors decided not to tender but to take P&O's friendly assurances 'in the spirit in which they [were] made' in Allan's letter. This decision gave P&O a clear run at the contract. It was as well that BI's directors did not know that P&O's board was just as frightened: Thomas Sutherland, in a private letter to P&O's superintendent at Bombay, said that 'our friends the British India Company are afraid that we will ruin them in the Coast', but 'we would rather keep on terms with them or they might otherwise give us a very great annoyance on the China [line]'.[62]

P&O's tender, the only serious one,[63] was sent in on 16 September 1867, proposing a subsidy of £500,000 per annum for a term of six years for all lines to India, China and Japan. Though this was lower than the original figure of £563,000, the price was still too high for the Post Office and the Treasury, and Frank Ives Scudamore, until recently receiver and accountant-general and now an assistant secretary to the Post Office, was chosen to negotiate with the MDs for a lower subsidy. However, during a private conversation with the MDs, Scudamore was given the chance to examine all the company's books and accounts.[64] After going through as much material as was necessary, Scudamore, 'well qualified for the business' and 'with his usual ability', found that £500,000 per annum was neither exorbitant nor unreasonable: 'no man of business . . . would have asked for less'. Concurring with the substance of the case the company had been making for years, P&O's longstanding rate of 4*s* 6*d* per mile was, Scudamore said, 'altogether inadequate to compensate for the extra expenditure caused by higher speed, as well as the diminution of the principal sources [of revenue] – their freight and passenger traffic – caused by the conditions of the contracts'. Moreover, the company had spent £500,000 on a 'superior class of vessels', but the first wave of the new compound engines with which they had been fitted had failed to come up to expectation, so P&O would have to invest in more new ships sooner than it had planned.

For all these reasons, the company had 'a prior claim to employment', whether temporary or permanent.[65] Scudamore reckoned that P&O would give way from £500,000 only if the Post Office offered a contract for 10 years. John Tilley, the secretary to the Post Office, agreed; he would even go to twenty years: 'We shall do well to recognize the fact that the Peninsular & Oriental Compy having established the route to India and China to the practical exclusion of all competitors the question is no longer whether or not we shall employ them for the conveyance of the Mails but simply what sum we are to pay them for their services.' 'Having come to the same conclusion [the company] will be indisposed to make any abatement in their terms', said Scudamore, but he observed that its directors 'were much alarmed at the possibility of the withdrawal of the . . . subsidy – and well they might be'. On the other hand, the permanent source of a subsidy would 'to say the least be very agreeable' to both the officers of the company and to the shareholders. So, 'by personal negotiation' with Anderson and the other MDs, Scudamore succeeded in reaching an agreement. P&O would work in partnership with the Government for 12 years, and would receive between £400,000 and £500,000 each year, depending on how much profit for dividends was made. If a dividend went over 8 per cent, P&O would give back to the Government one-quarter of the excess profit over 8 per cent; and if the dividends were lower than 6 per cent, the Government would make it up to that figure. P&O's vessels would run at the rate of 6*s* 1*d* per mile, at 10 knots in European waters and at 9.5 east of Suez. These terms were satisfactory to everyone – except Frederick Hill who adhered to 'pedantic theories' and could not see anything but 'profit and loss'.[66] In the real world, postal losses on P&O's services were 'the cost of keeping up communication with the East'.[67] Even Parliament would gain something: members, Scudamore said, would be so unwilling to 'be compelled . . . to vote annually so enormous a sum as half a million of money for one item of Post Office service' that the House would 'gladly sanction any plan by which [the] prospect' of having to declare such a sum more than once might be avoided.[68]

Scudamore was so confident about his arrangement of the contract that he believed the dividends would never be lower than 6 per cent. Thus there were only two questions left for the Post Office to consider: 'first what is the nature of the service that the Nation requires and second what is the proper price to pay for it'? The proper price had to cover the working expenses and a moderate dividend on capital, after taking account of the revenue from traffic. In his opinion, 'it is impossible to obtain good service on any other terms', and 'for the sake of keeping up such a communication with the East as the Nation requires they must set commercial principles at defiance, and, cost what it may, the Nation must either pay them what they lose thereby, or forego the communication'.[69]

The contract had yet to be approved in Parliament. Because the House had to authorize funds for the Abyssinian Expedition, MPs were recalled for an unusual November session. This was a lucky chance for P&O: if the contract could be approved in November, the problem of the temporary extension from February 1868 would be cleared away. P&O's director l'Estrange was able to play a small but significant part in the final act, underlining Anderson's wisdom in insisting, back in the 1840s, on the value to the company of political connections. Of Tory persuasion, he was a member of the Carlton Club, and he made use of other men in the Carlton:

> Our Brother Shareholders remonstrated with the Chancellor of the Exchequer [Disraeli] in & out of Parliament, and opposed him so effectually when the question of the Contract & subsidy were brought forward that he was forced, finding his own party against him, to come to terms with the Peninsular & Oriental Co. Mr Ward Hunt was then glad to receive Mr Allan who placed matters in a clear light, & converted the Chancellor of the Exchequer into a staunch supporter.[70]

The contract was approved by the Cabinet on 12 November. Derby wrote in his diary:

> Queen's Speach read and partly considered: also the Manchester Fenians; but our chief business was the renewing of the contract of P. and O. company, which we agreed to, at £400,000 a year for twelve years, and a guarantee of 6%: high terms, I thought, but nobody would compete with them, and they are masters of the market.[71]

Hunt, however, still had a hard time with the Liberals who, disappointed that they had not upset the Tory Government, rounded on him again. Crawford was indisposed and could not give his opinion, but Acton Smee Ayrton, recently elected MP for Tower Hamlets and 'universal critic of the House', observed that Scudamore 'displayed great ingenuity in discovering reasons why the Government should do everything the Company proposed'; and Childers, though he saw that were was no alternative but to accept the contract, assented 'with considerable reluctance'. Hunt, justifiably perplexed, argued that he wanted to 'promote economy'; what was wrong with that? In August he had heard much about 'the poor, trodden-down' company, 'perfectly helpless', so the House 'must pay whatever sum that Company might demand' and 'come to its rescue and preserve it from the ruin it was threatened with, owing to the policy of the Government'. Now the Government was blamed for placing itself 'altogether in P&O's hands and they must pay whatever the Company might demand'. But he voted with his party when the House divided: of the 68 MPs who voted, there were 55 in favour and 13 against. P&O was safe at last.[72]

On the next day, 30 November, *The Times* announced that though there would not be a dividend that year, the new contract was granted. Relief was palpable at 122 Leadenhall Street. When Anderson entered the boardroom on 6 December, just over a severe bout of bronchitis, he was loudly cheered. He had always worked towards a consolidation of the lines to India, China and Japan, and he believed that the company stood on 'a more solid basis than it had ever done during any part of its existence' now that it had the Government's guarantee. At a cost of 'no little amount of anxiety and arduous exertion', he lived to see all his targets achieved. At the beginning of 1867, P&O's survival was doubtful; by the end, its future was assured. For all his foibles and the autocratic style of management that handicapped the company in his last years, Anderson was a formidable fighter to the end. He died three months later, on 27 February 1868.[73]

Notes

1 For Anderson's early visits to Egypt, see P&O/1/102, 14.11.1851–24.2.1852; P&O/1/103, 11.1.1853, 7.6.1853, 24.1.1854–26.5.1854.

2 *Herapath*, 8.12.1855, pp. 1235–6; POST 51/31, Union Steam Ship Co. Ltd, 12.9.1857, 2.3.1863 and 19.10.1869; *Encyclopaedia Britannica* (1911 edn), p. 858.

3 POST 51/31, Union Steam Ship Co. Ltd, 12.9.1857, 2.3.1863 and 19.10.1869; *Encyclopaedia Britannica* (1911 edn), p. 858.

4 *Herapath*, 10.12.1859, pp. 1244–5.

5 P&O/1/105, 15.11.1859, 2.8.1861 and 26.6.1862.

6 *Ibid.*, 15.1.1861.

7 *Ibid.*, 15.1.1861, 18.1.1861 and 7.1.1862.

8 P&O/91/8, Kendall's letters to his mother, 1858–66 (Letters), fo. 151, 6.6.1861; fo. 177, 22.11.1861; fo. 195–6, 21.3.1862.

9 Anderson intended to give Olding a salary of £1,500 per annum and Bayley £1,100; when Ritchie arrived, he and Olding were given £1,400 each and Bayley £1,200: P&O/1/105, 18.1.1861 and 7.1.1862.

10 P&O/91/8, fo. 172, 21.10.1861; P&O/100/9, Sutherland's Typescript Diary, June 1914, a story from his career; P&O/1/105, 6.11.1860, 8.3.1861 and 28.4.1863.

11 P&O/1/105, 15.1.1861, 18.1.1861.

12 P&O/1/106, 3.10.1865, 31.10.1865.

13 *Herapath*, 8.12.1860, p. 1220.

14 *PP*, 1860, 16 (328), *SC on Packet & Telegraphic Contracts, First Report*, pp. xvi–xvii.

15 P&O/1/105, 13.7.1860, 17.7.1860. I have not found the 19 July letter in the Post Office Archive but much of it seems to have been said again in November and December.

16 P&O/1/104, 2.10.1857.

17 J.K. Fairbank and E.O. Reischauer, *China: Tradition and Transformation* (Boston, MA: Houghton Mifflin, 1978), pp. 288–306.
18 POST 29/105, China, 22.11.1860; *Herapath*, 8.12.1860, p. 1218.
19 *Ibid.*, 21.11.1860, 22.11.1860, 23.11.1860, 29.11.1860, 30.11.1860, 4.12.1860 and 6.12.1860.
20 *Ibid.*, 3.12.1860, 6.12.1860.
21 *Ibid.*, 4.12.1860, 6.12.1860, 11.12.1860, 24.12.1860 and 4.1.1861.
22 *Ibid.*, 17.5.1861 and 20.5.1861.
23 *Ibid.*, 13.6.1861.
24 *Ibid.*, 31.7.1861.
25 *Ibid.*, 16.11.1860.
26 *Ibid.*, 11.12.1860.
27 D.S. Landes, *Bankers and Pashas: International Finance and Economic Imperialism in Egypt* (London: Heinemann, 1958), pp. 156ff.
28 P&O/1/105, 31.10.1862, 28.11.1862.
29 JMA, Reel 59, p. 202, 22.4.1865; p. 204, 13.5.1865; p. 207, 14.6.1865.
30 *Herapath*, 10.12.1863, pp. 1397, 1408.
31 P&O/6/3, Report, 1.6.1865, p. 7, 5.12.1865, p. 9.
32 *Herapath*, 9.12.1865, pp. 1365–6.
33 *Ibid.*, 8.12.1866, pp. 1337–8; for Thornton and l'Estrange, see ch. 5 above, pp. 149, 162.
34 *Ibid.*, 8.6.1867, pp. 571–2.
35 *PD*, 3rd series, col. 698, 1.8.1867.
36 P&O/6/3, Correspondence Between the Directors . . . and the Post Master General, 15.2.1867, 23.2.1867, pp. 3–7, 15.
37 *PP*, 1867, 72 (3891), *SC on Growing Cotton in India*, qq. 917–9, 928; on Crawford, including his part in the Eastern Steam Navigation scheme in 1851, see above, p. 129, and Harcourt, 'Black Gold', pp. 24–5 and 30. Patrick Hadow's father was a partner in Colvin, Ainslie, Cowie & Co. in Bombay.
38 *PP*, 1866, 9 (425), *Report*, q. 4559, and generally, and qq. 462ff., 2332ff., 2358.
39 *PP*, 1860, 14 (328), *SC on Packet and Telegraphic Contracts, Report*, p. xv.
40 *PP*, 1866, 9 (428), *SC on East India Communications*, q. 2949, *Report*, pp. vii, viii, nos 21, 26–8.
41 That of the SC on Packet and Telegraphic Contracts: see above, this chapter, 'Postal payments and non-postal services'.
42 *PP*, 1860, 14 (328), *SC on Packet & Telegraphic Contracts, Report*, p. xvi, no. 1; *PP*, 1866, 9 (428), *SC on East India*, p. vii, no. 21.
43 Disraeli's description for the Queen in R. Blake, *Disraeli* (London: Eyre & Spottiswoode, 1966), p. 488, from *Letters of Queen Victoria*, 2 series, vol. 1, 509, 2.3.1868.
44 P&O/3/20, Memo by l'Estrange, 26.11.1873.
45 *PD*, 3rd series, vol. 187, cols 1493–4, 3.6.1867.
46 *Herapath*, 8.6.1867, p. 573.
47 P&O/6/3, Correspondence Between the Directors . . . and the PMG, Appendix A, 'Memorial of the Board of Directors of [P&O] to the Rt Hon. the Lords Commissioners of the Treasury on the Subject of the Postal Service to India and China', pp. 3–7, 27.6.1867, and Hunt's response, p. 8, 29.6.1867. (This memorial is also in P&O/30/15.)
48 *PP*, 1867–68, 41 (1), *Further Correspondence . . .*, no. 1, enclosure 1, 27.6.1867, no. 2, 29.6.1867.
49 *PD*, 3rd series, vol. 189, col. 671.
50 *Ibid.*, cols 672, 669, 673.
51 *Ibid.*, cols 685–7, 688–91.
52 *Ibid.*, cols 691, 692, 693, 694–5.
53 *Ibid.*, cols 679, 1563; HoL, 1201–2.
54 P&O/6/3, 'Opinions of the Press'; *PD*, 3rd series, vol. 189, col. 1563.

55 *Times*, 21.7.1866, pp. 9, 13; 20.8.1866, p. 8; see W.F. Moneypenny and G.E. Buckle, *The Life of Benjamin Disraeli, Earl of Beaconsfield* (London: John Murray, 1929), vol. 2, p. 201. For more on the domestic political context of the Abyssinian Expedition, see F. Harcourt, 'Disraeli's Imperialism, 1866–68: A Question of Timing', *Historical Journal*, 23:1 (1980); also Harcourt, 'Gladstone, Monarchism and the "New" Imperialism, 1868–74', *Journal of Imperial and Commonwealth History*, 14:1 (1985). That a new wave of imperialism was launched in the period 1866–68 has been questioned: see for example N. Rodgers, 'The Abyssinian Expedition of 1867–68: Disraeli's Imperialism or James Murray's War?', *Historical Journal*, 27:1 (1984). Though it is not possible to enter into the details of the controversy here, it may be worth underscoring the fact that, *pace* Rodgers, pressure on the Foreign Secretary Lord Stanley to mount an Expedition to Abyssinia came not only from his undersecretaries Hammond and Murray but also from Disraeli, who reassured the Queen that Stanley would 'ultimately be the Minister who will destroy and shatter to pieces the decaying theory . . . of non-interference' (Harcourt, 'Disraeli's Imperialism', p. 98); and that, far from the Cabinet agreeing 'automatically' to Stanley's request that hostilities be launched, Disraeli's cabinet ally Sir Stafford Northcote tried unsuccessfully to persuade it in this direction in April and May 1867: Harcourt, *ibid.*, p. 100.

56 Disraeli to Derby, 30.9.1866, Derby Papers, Queen's College, Oxford (by kind permission of Lord Blake), Box 146/2.

57 F. Harcourt, 'The Queen, the Sultan and the Viceroy: A Victorian State Occasion', *London Journal*, 5:1 (1979), pp. 35–56; Harcourt, 'Disraeli's Imperialism', p. 96.

58 See above, n. 53.

59 Harcourt, 'Disraeli's Imperialism', pp. 99–104; *PP*, 1868–9, 6 (380), *SC on the Abyssinian War*, q. 1242; *PP*, 1870, 5 (410), *SC on the Abyssinian Expedition*, qq. 3880, 3886.

60 *PP*, 1867–68, 41 (1), *Further Correspondence*, no. 3, 23.7.1867; no. 4, 20.8.1867.

61 See above p. 209.

62 National Maritime Museum, BI Archive, BIS/1/2 Minutes, 30.5.1867, 15.8.1867, 28.8.1867; P&O/12/1, fos 21–3, 17.4.1868.

63 The Società Italiana di Navigazione Adriatico Orientale, which had worked between Brindisi and Alexandria since 1863, tendered for this line for £15,000 per annum but the tender was not taken seriously: *PP*, 1867–68, 41 (1), *Further Correspondence*, no. 7, PMG to Treasury 1.11.1867, and enclosure 1 therein.

64 POST 34/128, no. 878.S, 3.10.1867.

65 *PP*, 1867–68, 41 (1), *Further Correspondence*, no. 7, PMG to Treasury, 1.11.1867, and enclosure 2 (P&O's Tender, 16.9.1867) and enclosure 3, Memorandum of Mr Scudamore, 26.10.1867, therein.

66 POST 34/128, minute no. 877.S, 2.11.1867.

67 *PP*, 1867–68, 41 (1), no. 7, enclosure 3, para. 18.

68 POST 34/128, minutes no. 882.S, [n.d.], 11.1867.

69 *PP*, 1867–68, 41 (1), no. 7, enclosure 3, paras 19, 20.

70 P&O/3/20, Memo by l'Estrange, 26.11.1873.

71 J. Vincent (ed.), *Disraeli, Derby and the Conservative Party: Journals and Memoirs of Edward Henry, Lord Stanley, 1849–1869* (Hassocks: Harvester Press, 1978), p. 322.

72 *PD*, 3rd series, vol. 190, 29.11.1867, cols 450–75.

73 *Herapath*, 7.12.1867, p. 1217.

AFTERWORD

Sarah Palmer

Freda Harcourt's account of the formative years of one of Britain's greatest shipping companies takes us beyond the limits of a conventional business history. As she amply demonstrates, the impossibility of separating P&O's fortunes from their political and economic context means that this wider environment is central. Government and empire are foreground as much as background. Here, as with P&O's struggles first to establish and then maintain a privileged position against competing interests, its history provides a route into a better understanding of the challenging conditions shaping mid-nineteenth-century British maritime and commercial imperial enterprise. In the end, of course, the particular response of P&O came down to the decisions of the MDs, where Harcourt provides insight into the inner workings of the company and the personalities at its core. In both its external imperial and internal managerial dimensions, *Flagships of Imperialism* also invites comparison with the now considerable number of scholarly studies of other British liner shipping companies in the nineteenth century.

P&O itself has been reasonably well-served by popular 'house' histories. A 1937 centennial study by Boyd Cable was succeeded in 1986 by David and Stephen Howarth's, *The Story of P&O*, with a second, revised edition published in 1994.[1] Rabson and O'Donoghue's 1988 World Ship Society publication *P&O: A Fleet History* provides details of the company's many distinguished vessels.[2] Neither of the company-sponsored general histories provide an in-depth narrative and, while the amply illustrated Howarth study is not entirely lacking a critical edge, the account they give is necessarily committed, as well as broad-brush. Harcourt is the first author to exploit fully P&O's extensive surviving business records in the National Maritime Museum, Greenwich, and to use these in conjunction with a range of other primary sources. By using these to focus on a relatively short period in the life of the company, she overturns much of the traditional version of its origins and motivations. The result is not simply a more detailed history: it is a new history.

P&O is unexceptional among steamship companies in the oceanic liner trades in the richness of its archive. As highly capitalized joint-stock companies managed by boards of directors (in an age when most firms were private family-based enterprises) the activities and decisions of such businesses were the subject of minutes and correspondence which were initially retained as a bureaucratic managerial resource, but subsequently often became valued as part of company heritage and identity. Second World War destruction and the lure of the rubbish bin to the tidy but unhistorically minded have taken their toll. Even so maritime historians are generally more fortunate than those with research interests in many other industries. In addition, the public prominence of shipping enterprises meant that many attracted local and national press attention, and where central government was also involved, as in the case of mail contracts, there is the opportunity to draw on parliamentary and departmental records.

Flagships of Imperialism is an addition to a string of shipping histories initially identified particularly with the 'Liverpool School' of business historians represented by Francis Hyde, John Harris and Sheila Marriner. These were the first scholars to take full advantage of the survival of internal maritime business records. Under Hyde's leadership and inspiration Cunard, Harrison's Charente and Holt's Ocean were among Liverpool-based companies subjected to scrutiny in the 1960s and 1970s. Peter Davies's studies of Elder Dempster and West African shipping maintained the Liverpudlian connection, but the pool of those researching in the field then widened to include, among others, Edwin Green, Michael Moss, Stephanie Jones and Malcolm Falkus.[3] While several of these histories benefited from the contemporary support and encouragement of the companies or families concerned, they succeeded in moving the genre well away from the uncritical style of the traditional 'house' history. Their scholarly credentials were based not only on sound research, but also on the managerial and financial orientation of the approach, interpretation and conclusions. As Peter Davies has noted, capital accumulation, decision-making and investment policies were central concerns for the Liverpool School of historians and their methodology owed much to a grasp of applied economic theory.[4]

The strength of these studies as works of economic history, however, created a problem for some commentators with interests in the growth and development of British maritime enterprise. Not all were satisfied to see these refracted through the narrow prism of the boardroom. Nor were they convinced that the evidence offered by voluminous company papers captured the variety of considerations, possibly social and political as much as economic, which underpinned decisions. From a slightly different perspective, those with a background in imperial history, among them Freda Harcourt, also judged that the history of the great shipping companies serving the empire could, and should, be used to illuminate wider issues of British politics, power and authority.

With the publication of Andrew Porter's *Victorian Shipping, Business and Imperial Policy: Donald Currie, the Castle Line and Southern Africa* (London, 1986), maritime business history took a new, arguably more ambitious, direction.[5] In contrast to some other shipping magnates Currie left few personal papers and scant records of his businesses survive. Yet Porter demonstrated that it was possible to uncover a great deal of information by following alternative routes, utilising official records and drawing on the archives of other enterprises. He argued, indeed, that there might be a positive advantage for scholarship in the limited survival of a company's records: 'companies with the most voluminous records are in danger of becoming subjects of the narrowest histories'.[6] The fact, however, that Currie's African undertakings, which also included railways, mining and real estate, were a subject of considerable interest to government made Porter's task more feasible than might otherwise have been the case. This provided an avenue into an appreciation of the interdependence of imperial ambitions and those of merchant shipping. Porter established that, in this region of the world at least, the business of shipping was also the business of empire.

J. Forbes Munro's more recent magisterial study, *Maritime Enterprise and Empire: Sir William Mackinnon and His Business Network*, relies on a similarly eclectic line of attack, though with Mackinnon's interests extending from Asia to the Middle East to East Africa and to Australia the scale of research endeavour is even greater.[7] Mackinnon's success was not, however, founded on government's need for regular oceanic communication between Britain and its overseas possessions and dependencies. His group of shipping companies, which included the British India Steam Shipping Company, linked together in a complex web of connection and investment, operated at the interstices of imperial maritime economy defined by the routes served by the great public mail contract companies, of which P&O was one. Much of Mackinnon's diverse commercial interest was directed towards short-sea shipping and provision of mercantile services within the imperial periphery. Mail contracts were important, but most were awarded not by the Admiralty or the Post Office but by local administrations, both British and foreign. In Mackinnon's enterprise network, London was just one centre among many where its business was done. Munro's research is, then, a reminder that 'shipping and Empire grew together, and supported each other, in a variety of different ways'.[8]

Despite contrasts between Donald Currie's affairs and those of Mackinnon and his group, both biographies testify to the significance of government in shaping the maritime business environment. This also stands, of course, for Freda Harcourt as a central *motif* of P&Os early years. Here was a company whose fortunes and fate were inextricably linked with the aspirations and concerns of Victorian governments. As she shows, its founding was in direct response to the business opportunity created by the decision to subsidize steam shipping from the public purse. In this P&O was not alone. On the Atlantic routes two other companies, Royal Mail, serving the Caribbean, and Cunard, serving Canada and the USA, were similarly conjured into existence at this time by the lure of postal contracts. But these were truly infant enterprises, whereas the directors of the fledgling P&O brought to their Indian initiative maturity and experience in owning and managing steamers, both with and without government support.

The background of P&O's founders is relevant here. By uncovering the part played by two very successful Irish shipowners and businessmen, Charles Wye Williams and Richard Bourne, Harcourt has redressed the emphasis of previous writers on the role of the shipbrokers Brodie McGhie Willcox and Arthur Anderson and provided a further explanation of the confidence and ambition which marked P&O's initial plans. Experience had taught Williams and Bourne the practical economics of operating a liner service, which differed from that applicable to cargo-seeking sailing vessels. Chief among requirements were sufficient vessels to work to a timetable, matched by a regular supply of profitable cargo and the determination to repel competitors. Given the state of steam technology in the 1840s, meeting these conditions could not compensate for the heavy capital and running costs of oceanic steamship voyages – hence the need for subsidy. But given the risks of providing the link with India, a sound track record in steam shipping gave the P&O promoters, backed by Irish capital, an advantage over the rival City bid.

Rather than being the brain-child of two men, underpinning the foundation of P&O was a business network.[9] Such networks featured much in nineteenth-century steam shipping, framing and interweaving the activities of owners, agents, brokers, merchants, bankers and shipbuilders. That later associated with Mackinnon was exceptional in its scale and scope, but P&O's entrepreneurs equally needed contacts and supporters to bring their plans to fruition. The same considerations applied once the company was established, as was demonstrated, for example, when its ambitions extended to securing the transport of opium. The directors took care to draw into its ambit men with the background and experience to assist in the promotion of its interests in the Far East and the Pacific. Faced with the 1851

Select Committee investigation, for example, it was able to provide a witness from Australia, who subsequently joined the board.

Harcourt's research reminds us that P&O's initial triumph in gaining the mail contract to serve the sea passage to the East did not guarantee its longer term success. Gaining and keeping of government contracts was no small challenge, even though the rivals for these subventions were not well placed to step in, however much discontent was expressed by the company's critics in Parliament. Good relations with ministers and officials were important and operated at informal as well as formal levels. Willcox and Anderson moved in elite metropolitan circles – they fit Cain and Hopkin's 'gentlemanly capitalist' model – and there were good reasons for their entry into Parliament.[10] Harcourt shows that government, concerned about P&O's monopoly status, was much constrained by the difficulty of replacing an established operator by an untried competitor. Already within just ten years of the company's foundation, a situation of mutual dependence had been created. P&O could not survive without state support, but equally the British Government relied on this great enterprise to support or further its ambitions. P&O provided the essential communication with the East, with its vessels carrying the mails, specie and employees that underpinned its interests. Always a means of 'power projection', visible evidence of the British presence, in emergency they were a military resource. Influential overseas economic interests also ensured that the domestic political dimensions of P&O's activities could not be disregarded either. The China 'second line' controversy in the early 1860s demonstrated Anderson's craftiness in exploiting government's weakness here.

Quite how important the subsidy was to P&O is clear.[11] Between 1846–47 and 1867–68 there were only four years when receipts exceeded outlays, in all cases by minute amounts. Dividends were frequently propped up from sources other than profits and fell in 1853, 1854, 1860 and 1866. In the crisis year of 1867 nothing at all was paid to the shareholders. Despite an impressive public profile, deliberately cultivated by its directors and exemplified by the hubris of the giant *Himalaya*, P&O was far from financially secure. The company was utterly reliant on mail contracts, which were under pressure first from Admiralty stringency then from Post Office reforming zeal, even though the perennial threats of transfer to other steamship lines did not materialise.

This is part of the context for the boardroom and shareholder disputes which Harcourt explores in some detail. Personalities, as ever, came into this. But the prime reason for such difficulties, besides shareholder concern about profits, was the conflict between the expectations created by P&O's character as a public joint-stock company with a board of directors and its management by the two dominant MDs, Willcox and Anderson, in more of the style of a traditional private partnership. There are parallels here with other liner companies in this period: Cunard, Burns and MacIver governed the British and North American Royal Mail Steam Packet Company, while the Royal Mail was the fiefdom of James Macqueen.[12]

Two aspects of the mail contract business perhaps encouraged such concentration on the strategic skills of so few individuals. The relatively routine character of liner operation meant that day-to-day management could be left to others and neglected, though not without impunity, by those at the top. Anderson's involvement here was the opposite of *hands on*, though we have seen that his absences from London and significant outside interests drew critical comment from the other directors and shareholders. At the same time, negotiations around seven different mail contracts required individual attention by those with status and authority. Only those men could represent the company view in private discussions, or defend its interests when confronted with hostile questioners at Westminster. However seldom P&O's MDs might be seen in its Leadenhall Street headquarters, their public *persona* was equalled by few other business leaders of the day.

P&O's financial dependence on the mail contracts and other national commissions should not be taken as evidence of failure. Providing a public service was, after all, the reason why the company existed. But the MDs' undoubted talents in bargaining with government were not matched by an equal ability to run the business efficiently and economically under the constraints such agreements imposed. The practical implications of taking on ever more commitments were also apparently not fully appreciated, as was shown by the problems of financing additional vessels following the award of the 1853 contract. An ageing management, intent on securing the contracts and maintaining the monopoly, failed to face up to the challenge of making these hard-won settlements pay. It was left to Anderson's talented and more practical successor Sir Thomas Sutherland, who became MD in 1872, to solve the problem by revolutionizing P&O's organisation, cutting expenditure and investing in new efficient vessels.[13]

Flagships of Imperialism stops logically short of this fresh, post-Suez Canal, phase of P&O's history. With the achievement of the new contract, followed closely by the death of Arthur Anderson, the old gave way to the new. By defining the relationship between government and company as a partnership, the twelve-year consolidated contract of 1867 finally established P&O's special status in imperial policy. This was an acknowledgment both of how far the company had come since its beginnings in the Mediterranean, and also of the link it had succeeded in forging between maritime enterprise and empire. P&O had indeed become, in Derby's words, 'the masters of the market' in the East, but this market for steamship services was one that it had done much to promote and develop. In the process, under Anderson's leadership, P&O had managed to create an identification in the public mind between itself and the national interest. Such a large and prominent enterprise could not be allowed to collapse. Thanks to Freda Harcourt's scholarship, we can now appreciate that P&O's first three decades were shaped as much by politics as by economics.

Notes

1 Boyd Cable, *A Hundred Year History of the Peninsular and Oriental Steam Navigation Company 1837–1937* (London: Nicholson & Watson, 1937); David Howarth and Stephen Howarth, *The Story of P&O: The Peninsular and Oriental Steam Navigation Company* (London: Weidenfeld & Nicolson, 1986); David Howarth and Stephen Howarth, with additional text by Stephen Rabson, *The Story of P&O: The Peninsular and Oriental Steam Navigation Company* (London: Weidenfeld & Nicolson, 1994).

2 Stephen Rabson and Kevin O'Donoghue, *P&O: A Fleet History* (Kendal: World Ship Society, 1988).

3 See Francis E. Hyde, with the assistance of J.R. Harris, *Blue Funnel: A History of Alfred Holt and Company of Liverpool from 1865 to 1914* (Liverpool: Liverpool University Press, 1957); Sheila Marriner and Francis E. Hyde, *The Senior, John Samuel Swire 1825–98: Management in Far Eastern Shipping Trades* (Liverpool: Liverpool University Press, 1967); Francis E. Hyde, *Shipping Enterprise and Management 1830–1939: Harrisons of Liverpool* (Liverpool: Liverpool University Press, 1967), and *Cunard and the North Atlantic 1840–1973: A History of Shipping and Financial Management* (London: Macmillan, 1975); Peter N. Davies, *Sir Alfred Jones: Shipping Entrepreneur Par Excellence* (London: Europa, 1978), and *The Trade Makers: Elder Dempster in West Africa, 1852–1972, 1973–1989*, 2nd edn (St John's Newfoundland: International Maritime Economic History Association, 2000); Edwin Green and Michael Moss, *A Business of National Importance: The Royal Mail Shipping Group, 1902–1937* (London: Methuen, 1982); Stephanie Jones, *Two Centuries of Change in International Trading: The Origins and Growth of the Inchcape Group* (London: Macmillan, 1986), and *Trade and Shipping: Lord Inchcape 1852–1932* (Manchester: Manchester University Press, 1989); Malcolm Falkus, *The Blue Funnel Legend: A History of the Ocean Steamship Company 1865–1973* (Basingstoke: Macmillan, 1990).

4 Peter N. Davies, 'The Liverpool School of Maritime History', unpublished paper given at the 'Developing the Maritime World' colloquium, University of Leicester, April 2005.

5 A. Porter, *Victorian Shipping, Business and Imperial Policy: Donald Currie, the Castle Line and Southern Africa* (London: Royal Historical Society, 1986).

6 *Ibid.*, p. 7.

7 J. Forbes Munro, *Maritime Enterprise and Empire: Sir William Mackinnon and His Business Network, 1823–1893* (Woodbridge, Suffolk: Boydell Press, 2003).

8 *Ibid.*, p. 498.

9 See Gordon H. Boyce, *Information, Mediation and Institutional Development: The Rise of Large-Scale Enterprise in British Shipping 1870–1919* (Manchester: Manchester University Press, 1995), p. 67.

10 P.J. Cain and A.G. Hopkins, *British Imperialism: Innovation and Expansion, 1688–1914* (London: Longman, 1993).

11 See table 7.1.

12 See Hyde, *Cunard and the North Atlantic*; Stuart Nicol, *Macqueen's Legacy: A History of the Royal Mail Line* (Stroud: Tempus Publishing, 2001).

13 Jones, *Trade and Shipping: Lord Inchcape*, p. 67.

BIBLIOGRAPHY

Unpublished sources

Footnote references to unpublished sources, whatever their location, are by the archive catalogue references given below.

Public records

Records held at the National Archives (formerly the Public Record Office), London

Records of the Admiralty, Naval Forces, Royal Marines, Coastguard and related bodies: ADM 2 Admiralty: Out Letters (Packet Services)

Records of the Office of the Commissioners of Bankrupts, the Successor Bankruptcy Courts and the Court for the Relief of Insolvent Debtors: B 11 Court of Bankruptcy: Gaolers' Returns and Miscellanea

Records of the Admiralty and Board of Trade: BT 1 General In-Letters and Files; BT 41 Companies' Legislation Office: Files of Joint Stock Companies registered under the 1844 and 1856 Acts; BT 107 General Registry and Record Office of Seamen: Transcripts and Transactions, series 1

Records of the Colonial Office, Commonwealth, and Foreign and Commonwealth Office: CO 201 Colonial Office and Predecessors: New South Wales Original Correspondence

Records created and inherited by the Foreign Office: FO 7 General Correspondence before 1906, Austro-Hungarian Empire; FO 97 Supplement to General Correspondence before 1906; FO 120 General Correspondence with Austria; FO 590 Consulate: Trieste, Austro-Hungarian Empire: Letter Books – Entry Book of Out-letters

Records of the Prerogative Court of Canterbury: PROB 11 Prerogative Court of Canterbury and Related Probate Jurisdictions: Will Registers 1384–1858

Records created and inherited by HM Treasury: T1 Treasury Papers

Records held at the Royal Mail Archive, London

Records created and used by the British Post Office: POST 29 Packet Minutes: Documents; POST 34 Packet Minutes: Volumes; POST 36 Irish Minutes; POST 51 Overseas Mail Contracts

Records held at the National Maritime Museum, London

Records of Coastlines Ltd: CST 38 Contracts and Agreements

Records of the Peninsular and Oriental Steam Navigation Company: P&O 1 Board Minutes and Agenda; P&O 2 Committee Minutes; P&O 3 Board Papers; P&O 6 Reports to Shareholders; P&O 15 General Correspondence: Peninsula and Levant; P&O 20 General Letters; P&O 30 Papers relating to

Royal Charters and Mail Contracts; P&O 51 Legal Matters: Agreements; P&O 65 Ships: Individual Ships; P&O 91 Miscellaneous; (ex-catalogue) MS 92/031: Deed of Settlement

Records of the British India Steam Navigation Company Ltd: BIS 1 Minutes

Records held at the Glasgow University Archive, Glasgow

GD 319 Scotts's Shipbuilding and Engineering Company Ltd

Private papers

Derby Papers (Queen's College, Oxford)

Jardine–Matheson Archive (University of Cambridge)

Other unpublished works

Neal, F., 'Liverpool Shipping, 1815–1835', MA thesis, University of Liverpool, 1962

Official sources

Acts of Parliament

9 Geo. 4, c. lxvi: 'An Act for regulating and enabling the City of Dublin Steam Packet Company to sue and be sued, and thereby to encourage the Use of vessels propelled by Steam in the Trade of Ireland', *Local and Personal Acts 1828*, vol. 2, pp. 1461–90.

3, 4 Will. 4, c. cxv: 'An Act to amend an Act, passed in the Ninth Year of the Reign of His Late Majesty, for regulating and enabling the City of Dublin Steam Packet Company to sue and be sued, *Local and Personal Acts 1833*, vol. 3, pp. 2593–618.

6, 7, Will. 4, c. c: 'An Act to authorize the City of Dublin Steam Packet Company to apply a Portion of certain Monies already subscribed in fulfilment of their Contracts for building Six additional Steam Vessels, and to legalize such Subscription', *Local and Personal Acts 1836*, vol. 4, pp. 3841–5.

23, 24 Vict., c. xcviii: 'An Act for incorporating "The City of Dublin Steam Packet Company"; and for authorizing them to raise additional Capital; and for other purposes', *Local and Personal Acts 1860*, vol. 2, pp. 1343–50.

Parliamentary Papers

1828, (volume) 11, (paper no.) (501), *Post Office Steam Packets, Steam Communication*

1829, 12 (353), *Nineteenth Report of Commissioners of Revenue Enquiry, Part II – Ireland*

1830, 7 (667), *Select Committee on the State of the Poor in Ireland*

1830, 14 (647), *Twenty-Second Report of the Commissioners of Revenue*
1831–32, 12 (735–11), *Select Committee on the Affairs of the East India Company*
1831–32, 17 (645), *Select Committee on Turnpike Roads*
1831–32, 17 (716), *Select Committee on Post Communication with Ireland*
1833, 6 (690), *Select Committee on Manufactures, Commerce and Shipping*
1834, 7 (667), *Select Committee on the State of the Poor in Ireland*
1834, 14 (478), *Select Committee on Steam Navigation to India*
1836, 28 (–), *Sixth Report of Commissioners to Inquire into the Management of the Post Office Department*
1837, 6 (539), *Steam Communication with India*
1837, 20 (484), *Select Committee on Turnpike Roads, Ireland*
1839, 47 (273), *Report on Steam Vessel Accidents*
1840, 7 (353), *Select Committee on the Petition of the East India Company*
1840, 7 (359), *Select Committee on Trade with China*
1843, 51 (358), *Mail Coach Contract (Ireland)*
1847, 36 (117), *Copies of the Contracts*
1849, 12 (571), *Contract Packets*
1850, 53 (693), *Correspondence Regarding the Establishment of Steam Communication with India*
1851, 21 (372), *Steam Communication*
1851, 21 (605), *Second Report, Select Committee on Steam Communication with India*
1851 (10–II) (187–II), *Select Committee on Steam Communication to India*
1852, 49 (249), *Mail Services, India and Australia*
1854–55, 20 (–), *First Report of the Postmaster-General on the Post Office*
1857, 43 (2221), *Opium Trade in China, 1841–56*
1860, 14 (328), *Select Committee on Packet and Telegraphic Contracts*
1860, 18 (450), *Select Committee on Transport Services*
1866, 9 (428), *Select Committee on East Indian Communications*
1867–68, 41 (1), *Further Correspondence Relating to the Conveyance of Mails to India and China*
1894, 61 (C. 7397), *Royal Commission*
1895, 42 (C. 7723), *Royal Commission*
1914–16, 49 (Cd. 7766), *Review of the Trade in India in 1913–1914*

Hansard, Parliamentary Debates, 3rd series, 1830–91, 356 vols

Newspapers and periodicals

Newspapers

Dublin Almanac and General Register of Ireland
Hampshire Advertiser
Illustrated London News
Morning Advertiser

New York Herald
The Times

Periodicals

Annual Register
Dublin Mercantile Advertiser
Herapath's Commercial & Railway Journal
Shetland Journal
Shipping Gazette
Shipping and Mercantile Gazette
Economist

Other published works

Anderson, A., *Steam communication with India, a letter to the Directors of the projected East Indian Steam Navigation Company, containing a practical exposition of the prospects of that proposed undertaking, and of the real state of the question of steam communication with India* (London: Smith, Elder & Co., 1840).

Anderson, A., *Communications with India, China, &c.: observations on the practicability and utility of opening a communication between the Red Sea and the Mediterranean, by a ship canal, through the Isthmus of Suez* (London: Smith, Elder & Co., 1843).

Anderson, A., *Communications with India, China &c. via Egypt: The Political Position of Their Transit through Egypt* (not printed for sale, 1843).

Bagwell, P., 'The Post Office Steam Packets, 1821–36, and the Development of Shipping on the Irish Sea', *Maritime History*, 1 (1971).

Berridge, V. and Edwards, G., *Opium and the People: Opiate Use in Nineteenth-Century England* (New Haven, CT: Yale University Press, 1987).

Blake, R., *Disraeli* (London: Eyre & Spottiswoode, 1966).

Boase, F., *Modern English Biography*, 2nd impression (London: Frank Cass, 1965).

Bourne, K., *Palmerston: The Early Years 1784–1841* (London: Allen Lane, 1982).

Broeze, F., *Mr Brooks and the Australian Trade: Imperial Business in the Nineteenth Century* (Carlton, Victoria: Melbourne University Press, 1993).

Bruijn, J.R. and Mörzer Bruyns, W.F.J. (eds), *Anglo-Dutch Mercantile Marine Relations 1700–1850: Ten Papers* (Amsterdam: Rijksmuseum 'Nederlands Scheepvaartmuseum'–Rijksuniversiteit Leiden, 1991).

Cable, B., *A Hundred Year History of the P&O: Peninsular and Oriental Steam Navigation Company, 1837–1936* (London: Nicholson & Watson, 1937).

Coates, W.H., *The Old 'Country Trade' of the East Indies* (London: Imray, Laurie, Norrie & Wilson, 1911).

Cullen, L.M., *An Economic History of Ireland since 1660* (London: Batsford, 1972).

De Quincy, T., *Confessions of an English Opium Eater*, 2nd edn (London: Taylor & Hessey, 1823).

Divine, D., *These Splendid Ships: The Story of the Peninsular Line* (London: F. Muller, 1960).

Encyclopaedia Britannica (Cambridge: Cambridge University Press, 1911).

Fairbank, J.K., *Trade and Diplomacy in the China Coast: The Opening of the Treaty Ports 1842–1854* (Cambridge, MA: Harvard University Press, 1953).

Fairbank, J.K. and Reischauer, E.O., *China: Tradition and Transformation* (Boston, MA: Houghton Mifflin, 1978).

GEC, *The Complete Peerage* (London: St Catherine's Press, 1949), vol. 11.

Grant, H.K., *Samuel Cunard, Pioneer of the Atlantic Steamship* (London: Abelard–Schuman, 1967).

Greenberg, M., *British Trade and the Opening of China 1800–42* (Cambridge: Cambridge University Press, 1951).

Hall, W.H., *Sailors' Homes, Destitute Sailors' Asylums, and Asylums for Aged Seamen, Their Origin and Progress* (?London, 1852).

Hall, W.H., *Our National Defences* (London, 1876).

Harcourt, F., 'The Queen, the Sultan and the Viceroy: A Victorian State Occasion', *London Journal*, 5:1 (1979).

Harcourt, F., 'Disraeli's Imperialism, 1866–68: A Question of Timing', *Historical Journal*, 23:1 (1980).

Harcourt, F., 'The P&O Company: Flagships of Imperialism', in S. Palmer and G. Williams (eds), *Charted and Uncharted Waters: Proceedings of a Conference on the Study of British Maritime History* (London: National Maritime Museum, 1981).

Harcourt, F., 'Gladstone, Monarchism and the "New" Imperialism, 1868–74', *Journal of Imperial and Commonwealth History* 14:1 (1985).

Harcourt, F., 'British Oceanic Mail Contracts in the Age of Steam, 1838–1914', *Journal of Transport History*, 3rd series, 9:1 (1988).

Harcourt, F., 'Ownership and Finance 1820–1850: The Case of Ireland', in R. Bruijn and W.F.J. Mörzer Bruyns (eds), *Anglo-Dutch Mercantile Marine Relations 1700–1850: Ten Papers* (Amsterdam: Rijksmuseum 'Nederlands Scheepvaartmuseum'–Rijksuniversiteit Leiden, 1991).

Harcourt, F., 'Charles Wye Williams and Irish Steam Shipping', *Journal of Transport History*, 3rd series, 13:2 (1992).

Harcourt, F., 'Black Gold: P&O and the Opium Trade, 1847–1914', *International Journal of Maritime History*, 6:1 (1994).

Harcourt, F., 'P&O and Orient: A Cool Partnership, 1886–1914', *The Great Circle*, 17:2 (1995).

Harcourt, F., entries for 'Cunard, Sir Samuel', 'Waghorn, Thomas' and 'Williams, Charles Wye', in H.C.J. Matthew and B. Harrison (eds), *Oxford Dictionary of National Biography* (Oxford: Oxford University Press, 2004).

Harcourt, F., 'The High Road to India: P&O and the Origins of the Suez Canal' (forthcoming).

Hoskins, H.L., *British Routes to India* (New York: Longmans, Green & Co., 1928).

Hyde, F.E., *Cunard and the North Atlantic 1840–1973: A History of Shipping and Financial Management* (London: Macmillan, 1975).

Inglis, H.D., *Ireland in 1834: A Journey Through Ireland* (London, 1835), vol. 2.

Keswick, M. (ed.), *The Thistle and the Jade: A Celebration of 150 Years of Jardine, Matheson & Co.* (London: Octopus, 1982).

King, F.H.H., *The History of the Hong Kong and Shanghai Banking Corporation* (Cambridge: Cambridge University Press, 1987), vol. 1.

Landes, D.S., *Bankers and Pashas: International Finance and Economic Imperialism in Egypt* (London: Heinemann, 1958).

Lindsay, W.S., *History of Merchant Shipping and Ancient Commerce* (London: S. Low, 1876), vol. 4.

Liu, Kwang-Ching, *Anglo American Steamship Rivalry in China 1862–74* (Cambridge, MA: Harvard University Press, 1962).

Low, C.R., *History of the Indian Navy (1613–1863)* (London, 1877), vol. 1.

Lubbock, B., *The Opium Clippers* (Glasgow: Brown, Son and Ferguson, 1933).

Maber, J.M., *North Star to Southern Cross* (Prescot, Lancashire: Stephenson, 1967).

Matheson, J., *The Present Position and Prospects of the British Trade with China; Together with an Outline of Some Leading Occurrences in its Past History* (London, 1836).

Matthew, H.C.J. and Harrison, B. (eds), *Oxford Dictionary of National Biography* (Oxford, Oxford University Press, 2004).

Moneypenny, W.F. and Buckle, G.E., *The Life of Benjamin Disraeli, Earl of Beaconsfield* (London: John Murray, 1929).

Napier, C., 'Fixed Asset Accounting in the Shipping Industry: P&O 1840–1914', *Accounting, Business and Financial History*, 1:1 (1990).

Nicolson, J., *Arthur Anderson: A Founder of the P&O Company* (Paisley: A. Gardner, 1914).

O'Byrne, W.R., *A Naval Biographical Dictionary* (London, 1849).

Palmer, S., '"The Most Indefatigable Activity": The General Steam Navigation Company 1824–50', *Journal of Transport History*, 3rd series, 3:2 (1982).

Palmer, S., *Politics, Shipping and the Repeal of the Navigation Laws* (Manchester: Manchester University Press, 1990).

Petree, J.F., 'Charles Wye Williams, A Pioneer of Steam Navigation', *Liverpool Nautical Research Society: Transactions*, 10 (1961–71).

Petree, J.F., 'Charles Wye Williams (1779–1866), a Pioneer in Steam Navigation and Fuel Efficiency', *Transactions of the Newcomen Society*, 39 (1966–67).

Porter, A.N., *Victorian Shipping, Business and Imperial Policy: Donald Currie, the Castle Line and Southern Africa* (Woodbridge: Boydell Press, 1986).

Preble, G.H., *A Chronological History of the Origin and Development of Steam Navigation* (Philadelphia, PA: L.R. Hamersley, 1883).

Rabson, S. and O'Donoghue, K., *P&O: A Fleet History* (Kendal: World Ship Society, 1988).

Roberts, P.E., *History of British India under the Company and the Crown* (Oxford: Oxford University Press, 1958).

Robinson, H., *Carrying British Mail Overseas* (London: Allen & Unwin, 1964).

Rodgers, N., 'The Abyssinian Expedition of 1867–68: Disraeli's Imperialism or James Murray's War?', *Historical Journal*, 27:1 (1984).

Stenton, M. (ed.), *Who's Who of British MPs: A Biographical History of the House of Commons* (Sussex: Humanities Press, 1976).

Taylor, A.J.P., *The Italian Problem in European Diplomacy 1847–1849* (Manchester: Manchester University Press, 1934).

Thorner, D., *Investment in Empire: British Railways and Steam Shipping Enterprise in India, 1825–1849* (Philadelphia: University of Pennsylvania Press, 1950).

Vincent, J. (ed.), *Disraeli, Derby and the Conservative Party: Journals and Memoirs of Edward Henry, Lord Stanley, 1849–1869* (Hassocks: Harvester Press, 1978).

Walker III, W.O., *Opium and Foreign Policy: The Anglo-American Search for Order in Asia, 1912–1954* (Chapel Hill and London: University of North Carolina Press, 1991).

Watt, G., *Papaver Somniferum: Opium* (Calcutta, 1891).

Webster, C.K., *The Foreign Policy of Palmerston 1830–1841: Britain, the Liberal Movement and the Eastern Question* (London: Bell, 1951), vol. 2.

Williams, C.W., *Observations on the Inland Navigation of Ireland* (London, 1833).

Williams, C.W., *Reasons in Favor of the City of Dublin Steam Company's Bill for an Increase of Capital* (London, 1836).

Williams, C.W., *On the Steam-Generating Power of Marine Locomotive Boilers* (London, 1862).

Wilson, J.H., *Facts Connected with the Origin and Progress of Steam Communication between India and England* (London: W.S. Johnson, 1850).

Wright, S.F., *China's Struggle for Tariff Autonomy 1843–1938* (Shanghai: Kelly & Walsh, 1938).

INDEX